CORY, CORY, HALLELUJAH!

THE HISTORY OF CORY BAND

1884 - 2009

COMPILED AND EDITED
DR ROBERT B. CHILDS

THIS BOOK IS DEDICATED TO ALL PAST AND
PRESENT CONDUCTORS, MEMBERS AND
COMMITTEE OF

CORY BAND

First published in the United Kingdom in 2010
by
Prima Vista Musikk Ltd

www.primavistamusikk.com

CORY CORY HALLELUJAH 125 YEARS
The History of Cory Band
Compiled and Edited
Dr Robert B. Childs

ISBN 978-0-9566990-0-8

Design and Typeset by GK Graphic Design vof
Printed and bound in Great Britain by
CPI Antony Rowe, Chippenham, Wiltshire

Contents

Foreword

Preface And Acknowledgements

Appendices

Foreword

Before I congratulate Robert (Bob) Childs and the Cory Band on a superb book, I want to say to the readers how proud I am to be writing this foreword. Next year (2011), my family and I will have achieved "one hundred years continuous membership in the Cory Band" and I feel humbled that Bob has dedicated a full chapter about the Trotman family within this book.

Since helping my uncle Haydn (also known as Dai Trotman) produce the Band's Centenary Booklet in 1984, I realised there was very little literature written about the colourful history and splendid achievements of the Cory Band.

John Trotman

Helping Bob research this book has been a wonderful and rejuvenating experience for me. In my mind I've had so much pleasure reacquainting myself with many of my old friends and the great conductors of the past, including; J.G.Dobbing, Redvers (Reg) Little, Tom Powell, Walter Hargreaves, Arthur Kenney and Denzil Stephens. In more recent times I've revelled in the unprecedented success of Cory under Bob's fruitful direction.

Through reading this book I've also relived the trials and tribulations of the past, from the dramatic sudden death of T.J. (Tom) Powell whilst conducting a 'live' BBC Broadcast, to vandals burning the Bandroom down in 1990. The emotional roller-coaster ride has certainly had its ups and downs!

The obvious competitive highlights that shine through this book are: Kenney's first National win in 1974, the National Hat-Trick and European success in the 1980s and the wonderful resurgence of the Band since 2000. Especially winning the British 'Open' Championship for the first time under Bob and being ranked No.1 in the World for the past three years, during the period the Band won the prestigious Hat trick of European Championships.

In the wider world of brass music, the realisation that my family and the Cory Band were involved in an early broadcasting experiment personally supervised by Marconi and that my father Tom, was the featured soloist in the very first broadcast by the Band in the 1920's fills me with immense pride as does my life's association with Wales' finest band and one of the world leaders in contemporary brass band achievements.

Congratulations to those players past and present who have lived and breathed the Cory ethic. 'Good Luck' with this book"

John Trotman
(Life Member, Cory Band)

Preface and Acknowledgements

This absorbing book traces the proud history of the legendary Cory Band from the pioneering days of the fledgling Ton Temperance Band, through one hundred and twenty five (125) years of progress to their current status as world leaders in the brass band movement.

Initially formed to ease the perils of social deprivation that accompanied the development of coal mining in the Rhondda Valleys, the Band responded in fine style to the challenges of competitive music making that is often regarded as the life blood of brass bands throughout the world. However, success on the contest platform is much more than collecting trophies and titles; it provides demonstrable and irrefutable evidence that the standard of music making is being constantly refreshed and improved. An essential ingredient for lasting success!

Recognising and grasping elements of opportunism are also vital if success is to be nurtured to become long lasting. So it was fortuitous that the Band were able to engage a professional Conductor during their formative years due to the active interest shown by a leading member of the influential and philanthropic Cory family. Hence an early name change to the Cory Band – a name that throughout most of its history has been revered in Wales and for the past decade throughout the world – a band that on contest day must be listened to!

For more than half a century, I have been privileged to enjoy listening to this superb Band performing under the baton of a succession of high profile professional conductors. Of course, I did not have the opportunity to listen at first hand to the redoubtable Mr Dobbing, but I well recall my father's tales of this strict disciplinarian with an inherent ability to make quality music!

The pages of this book recounts in graphic detail the splendid achievements of the Band until 1990, when the Band room was virtually completely destroyed by fire. The decade that followed was indeed a low point in the history of the Band. Attempts to respond to the immense challenge of recovering from this disaster seemed to be constantly rebuffed, so it was obvious that if the "Phoenix was to be raised from the ashes" a drastic change of direction was urgently needed.

This wind of change was indeed both dramatic and severe, with long standing playing member – Austin Davies taking the lead as newly installed Chairperson, together with another long serving player – John Southcombe, in the role of Business Manager, both supported by a small but forward thinking committee. Sponsorship was sought and awarded by two extremely successful local businessmen – Bernard Jones OBE and the late Gerald Coleman, both of whom had previous personal links with brass bands. Historically, professional conductors had been lured from England and Scotland to hone their talents in Wales. At the Millennium, an accomplished leading professional brass musician who was working in England, but who had originated from Wales, Dr Robert (Bob) Childs, was persuaded to return to his Welsh roots. New management, forward planning, sponsorship and musical direction were now all firmly in place. The deed was done!

Consequently, the past decade has not only clearly demonstrated immediate and lasting success on the contest platform, but has seen the introduction and consolidation of highly influential commissioning policies using notable composers to extend the contemporary repertoire of brass bands; raising the profile of brass bands generally by participation in inclusive public performances with major professional orchestras and artists.

The book highlights the virtual one hundred years of close linkage of the multi-talented Trotman family dynasty with the Cory Band, representing so much that is good about a continuing enjoyment of a brass band and quality music making. Unlocking and sharing the treasured memories of octogenarian John Trotman, the sole surviving member of the Trotman's still actively serving the Cory Band has been an unforgettable and thoroughly stimulating experience.

It has been my privilege to write this Preface. My admiration for the dedication and pursuit of excellence of those associated with the Cory Band over so many years remains undiminished and has allowed me access to an enthusiastic enjoyment of this famous Band and its fine reputation for quality music making!

Many people have willingly assisted in the preparation of this book. In particular, John Trotman, who kindly agreed to write the Foreword and who with his illustrious family, is the focus of attention in Chapter 3.

Together with his brother-in-law the late Ron Pryce, a former long-serving secretary of Cory Band, John has been a major contributor to the contents of this book. His collection of photographs, private memoirs and phenomenal memory of the activities and timeline of the Band has been invaluable. The former long serving bass player – Graham Sheppard, supported by several past members and notably Ceri Lewis, readily provided information on the history and development of the Junior Band. Special thanks are due to former principal percussionist Clayton McCann, who readily provided access to and use of his comprehensive library of personal memoirs; also to former long serving players – John Prosser, Gwyn Thomas and Jeff Thomas, (a past chairperson) for their readiness to contribute to several of the Chapters.

Denzil Stephens for preparing Chapter 8 and describing his period of tenure with the Band; also to Bram Gay and Dr Roy Newsome for their colourful recollections of the Band's tour of America in the late 1970's.

Chapter 11 would not have been possible without the continuing support of Bernard Jones OBE and the widow and close family of the late Gerald Coleman. The significance of the financial support proffered by these two local philanthropic entrepreneurs who had the sounds of brass bands firmly implanted in their minds during their formative years is inestimable. John Southcombe's research and contribution to this Chapter also merits sincere and special acknowledgement.

The contributions of current senior members of the Band - Lisa Fitzgerald-Lombard, Chris Thomas, Chris Turner, Phil Harris and Fraser Bish are greatly appreciated, with Lisa capturing to the full, the emotive trauma experienced in preparing for major contest performances and awaiting the results, as recorded in the Coda to the Book – A Remarkable Tale to Tell!! Thanks also to Joanne and David Childs for compiling the many varied statistics and lists included in the appendices.

The permission to publish the detail of Dr Robert (Bob) Childs' presentation to the Band's Chairperson – Austin Davies and his supporting committee prior to his appointment as MD is warmly acknowledged.

Cory band are extremely grateful to Gerard Klaucke of GK Graphic Design, for designing all of their 125th Anniversary logos and programmes and, of course, his patient and tireless work in designing this Book. His contribution is much appreciated.

The Cory Band is inherently grateful to Ida Birch – The Cory Society archivist and co-ordinator for Devon, Cornwall and South Wales – for her informative contribution on the relevant history of the Cory Family and permission to publish historical photographs.

Cory Band acknowledges and thanks Ian Clowes, Gerard Klaucke, John Stirzacker and Steve Jack for permission to use their contemporary photographs of the Band.

Cory Band readily acknowledges the use of historic photographs, published by courtesy of Cardiff Libraries and Information Services.

The copyright of V&A Images – Victoria and Albert Museum, London is fully acknowledged in this publication.

- Cory Band acknowledges Brass Band World magazine for giving permission to reproduce extracts
- Cory Band would like to acknowledge the help from Iwan Fox and 4BarsRest for providing and granting permission to use extracts from their website.
- Cory Band would like to acknowledge the help of the British Bandsman and its editor, Kenneth Crookston, for providing and granting permission to use extracts from the magazine.
- Cory Band also acknowledges the following newspapers for permission to reproduce photographs and text extracts – Rhondda Leader, South Wales Echo, Western Mail, South Wales Argus, The Daily Mountain Eagle Newspaper, Jasper, Alabama (USA).
- Cory Band would like to thank their Musical Director, Dr. Robert Childs for having the vision and expertise to compile and edit such a concise record of the Band's history.

To others not specifically mentioned who have in any way at all assisted in the preparation of this worthy book, please accept the sincere thanks of the Cory Band for your advice and readiness to contribute.

C Brian Buckley
Swansea
July 2010

Robert Childs would also like to sincerely thank C. Brian Buckley for writing Chapter Three, The Trotman Family, and for his expert advice and thorough proof reading throughout the preparation of this book.

Brian Buckley

Chapter 1
How It All Began (The Formative Years)

Until the South Wales valleys were converted into hives of intense industrial activity, with coal mining and iron-making furnaces reigning supreme, the valleys were very sparsely populated. Prior to this historical period of rapid industrialisation, the scenic splendour of the Rhondda Valleys had been favourably compared to that of parts of the Wye Valley, with several writers commenting upon the natural beauty of the wild, picturesque mountains, liberally laced with dramatic cliffs, the valley walls being clothed with lichens and evergreen shrubs.

In 1851, fewer than 1,000 people lived in the Rhondda Valleys, yet during the next fifty years, the numbers of inhabitants increased dramatically to 114,000. Most of this huge population shift was made up of English speaking men (and their families) from the border areas of England, appearing with the Irish as immigrant workers and diluting the everyday use of the Welsh language. In 1911, it was estimated that the continued rapid upsurge in the development of coal mining and linked industrial progress had increased the population to a staggering 153,000. Not surprisingly, the emergence of groups of people seeking outlets for communal hobbies was encouraged and supported by the mine-owners and ironmasters leading to the prolific formation of choirs and brass bands to help counter the discomfort, grime and smoke filled environment in what had previously been a tranquil rural area.

Located several valleys to the east of the Rhondda Valleys, the Blaina Band is believed to be one of the oldest brass bands in the United Kingdom. Several books describing the development of the brass band movement, cite Brown's Ironworks in Blaina as the main sponsor of the Blaina Band, known to have been established in 1832. Almost midway between the Blaina and the Rhondda Valleys lies Merthyr Tydfil, Wales' largest town during this period, due to the development of Crawshay's Cyfarthfa Ironworks. Robert Thompson Crawshay founded his 'Cyfarthfa Brass Band' in 1838, the Band gaining third place at the prestigious Crystal Palace competition in 1860. As iron-making and the ironmasters were the catalysts for forming and supporting the early emergence of brass bands in South Wales, so was the textile industry similarly associated with the formation of brass bands in the North of England. Meltham Mills Band, founded in the 1840's, closely followed by the Black Dyke Mills Band founded in 1855, are two such famous names connected with the Yorkshire textile industry. As these industries developed and became more mechanised, their dependence on the use of steam as an empirical source of energy intensified; coal being the fuel needed to produce steam.

The quality of coal mined in the South Wales valleys was of a very high standard, with the coal abstracted from mines in the Rhondda Valley becoming famous for its suitability in generating steam for both industry and shipping. Transportation of coal downhill to the coastal docks of Cardiff and Barry was relatively straightforward, with South Wales producing a third of the world's coal exports in 1913. At its productive peak, the coal industry employed over forty thousand (40,000) men in the myriad of mines located in the Rhondda Valleys. Not surprisingly, several families soon became both rich and famous as a result of the rapid growth and marketing of the coal industry in the South Wales valleys and coastal areas, with the Cory family being one of the most prominent and philanthropic dynasties of this period. Although the family, (Richard, his wife Sarah and eight children) moved from Bideford in North Devon to Cardiff in 1838, it was not until 1859 that the two elder brothers – John and Richard formed a company called 'Cory Brothers'. This followed the retirement of their father from the ongoing family business of ships brokers, agents and provision merchants, based at Cardiff Docks. Rapidly acquiring several collieries in the Rhondda and neighbouring valleys, within a short space of time 'Cory Bros.' were responsible for mining, marketing and exporting in excess of four million tons of coal annually.

Richard Cory senior, was the first person in Cardiff to sign the pledge of the Temperance Movement. This led to the naming of a major public building in Cardiff, in his honour. The Cory Memorial Temperance Hall, was much used for concerts and brass band contests. Sadly, this architecturally attractive building was demolished in the 1980's – a victim of redevelopment! Not surprisingly, the Cory family have always been generous benefactors, giving unstinted assistance to charities and evangelical movements in the areas that provided them with the beneficial source of their wealth.

John Cory developed a close and meaningful friendship with founder Salvationist William Booth, donating monies to the fledgling Salvation Army movement, also naming one of the Company's ships – "The William Booth" to mark this special bond. William Booth also displayed reciprocal friendship, clearly epitomised when he named his daughter, 'Evangeline Cory Booth'. In the Journal "Friends of the Army" (Volume XIII, 1907), John Cory is afforded three full pages highlighting his work and assistance in support of these developing Missionary activities. The article begins by stating "Among the faithful and distinguished friends of the Salvation Army, who have stood by it in all weathers, few deserve to hold a higher place than Mr. John Cory". Upon their deaths, both Cory brothers, Richard and John, had full obituaries published in the Salvation Army magazine 'The War Cry'.

Alongside the prosperity and wealth generated by the industrialisation of the Rhondda Valleys, the evils of over-indulgence and alcohol abuse loomed large. This was counteracted by the work of the 'Temperance Movement' and William Booth's 'Salvation Army', both of which inspired the formation of brass bands to help reject drunkenness, and to encourage all to respect and abide by the values of responsible living and family life. One such band was formed in the village of Ton Pentre, Rhondda, in 1884. This was 'The Ton Temperance Band', the first incarnation of the 'Cory Band'. It was also around this time that local rivals 'The Parc and Dare Band' were called *Cwmparc Drum and Fife Temperance Band'*. In the late 1880's, brass bands were forming on a weekly basis. In 1889, the editor of the 'Brass Band News' stated that "there were over 40,000 brass bands in the United Kingdom and that they were increasing rapidly!"

Very little is known about the 'Ton Temperance Band' and its conductor Mr. John Treharne. There is only one surviving photograph of the Band. It was taken outside Ystrad railway station. The actual date the Band was formed is not known, however records show that initially, rehearsals took place in a draughty shed behind the Blacksmith's shop in Gelli. The Band later moved to a large building in Ton Pentre. The 'Ton Temperance Band' was a competitive band and although records show that they did not realise any premier honours at major competitions in South Wales, they were listed as prizewinners at several local competitions.

In 1895, the 'Ton Temperance Band' was invited to play at the official opening of Gelli Colliery Library in Ystrad. Sir Clifford Cory, the highly influential son of John Cory performed the ceremony. He was so impressed by the standard of the Band's performance that he offered to provide financial assistance and provide suitable employment to enable the Band to engage a first class conductor. The 'Ton Temperance Band' changed its name to reflect the generous financial assistance from Sir Clifford Cory and his family business, 'Cory Brothers'. Consequently, from 1895, the Band became known as 'Cory Workmen's Band'.

Subsequent photographic evidence shows several variations on this name.

These include:
Cory Workmen's Band
Cory's Workmen's Band
Cory's Prize Band
Cory Workmen Silver Band
Cory Workmen-
Silver Prize Band
The Cory Band
Cory Band.

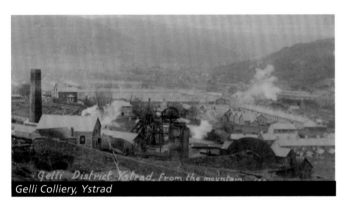
Gelli Colliery, Ystrad

Pentre Colliery, the bandroom

Ystrad and Gelli Library

Chapter 2
Ton Temperance Band – The Early Years

Mr John Treharne was the first conductor of the Band known today as the Cory Band. He was the conductor of the Ton Temperance Band from 1884 to 1895. Over this period, Mr Treharne developed his band, but despite taking them to a small number of contests in the South Wales and Monmouthshire area, the fledgling Ton Temperance Band rarely featured in the prizes.

Ton Temperance Band, conductor John Treharne, 1884 Ystrad Station

The programme for a South Wales and Monmouthshire Brass Band Association Contest held on the 16th April 1949 included a cautionary tale of an occurrence which took place fifty years earlier in 1899. The story cites a contest in South Wales where the test piece was *Mercandante*. As was customary at that time, medals were awarded to one or more of the 'best' soloists in the contest. On this occasion a medal was awarded for the best G Trombone (Bass Trombone) player. At this point in the story the writer digresses describing in detail how the euphonium medal was closely fought for by Ferndale's Gus Foxhall, Cory's John Bailey and Tonyrefail's Herbert Scott, with the medal going to John Bailey. Now back on track, the writer continues the story of the infamous G Trombone medal. When the adjudicator gave his award, he stated that almost every G Trombonist that day had "overblown" his part. He awarded the medal to the Cory Band whose G Trombonist did not do so. However, as Cory's G Trombone player had broken his leg in a colliery accident the day before the contest, the Band had to play at the contest without him! The medal was duly presented to Charlie 'G' as he was affectionately called. Charlie wore his medal with pride for many years often boasting that he won it lying flat on his back with a broken leg.

Following a performance at the ceremonial opening of Gelli Colliery library in 1895, sponsorship from Sir Clifford Cory was secured and the Band was able to afford a salaried conductor. The Ton Temperance Band became known as the Cory Workmen's Band and the services of Mr E Ambler were engaged. Mr Ambler had one thing in common with the Band's current conductor, Dr Robert (Bob) Childs, in as much as he also gave up playing the euphonium with the famous Black Dyke Mills Band, to live in Wales and conduct the Cory Band. This is the only similarity one can draw between the two conductors, as Mr Ambler's tenure was extremely brief. He was succeeded the following year by John Bailey, another celebrated euphonium player from the Black Dyke Mills Band.

John Bailey, conductor

Cory Workmen's Band 1911 (inset Sir Clifford Cory)

Cory's Prize Band, conductor J.G. Dobbing

Under Bailey's guidance, the Cory Workmen's Band started to cultivate their reputation locally in South Wales, achieving a number of Second Class contest victories. Bailey was also an accomplished composer and wrote the Band's signature march 'The Singer'.

Following Bailey's death in 1912, J. G. Dobbing of Birkenhead was the next professional conductor to be employed by the Band. He was provided with a job at Gelli Colliery that allowed him plenty of time to study the scores of music the Band were rehearsing and also to arrange music especially for the Cory Workmen's Band. Allocated the sole use of a small shed near the entrance of the colliery, his job was to paint the tare (weight) on the side of new and recently repaired coal wagons so that when they were filled with coal and re-weighed, the amount of coal in each wagon could be calculated to ensure that customers

J.G. Dobbing, conductor

Cory's Prize Band, c. 1920

would be correctly charged for the amount of coal delivered to them. Apparently, many weeks could pass by without him having any wagons to paint!

During Dobbing's 27 years as conductor between 1912 and 1939, (thereby making him the longest serving conductor in the Cory Band's 125 year history), he soon secured First Class (now Championship Section) status and in so doing amassed many contest prizes. Successes gained under his baton were as follows:-

> **79 First,**
> **36 Second,**
> **19 Third and**
> **5 Fourth prizes.**

Numerous trophies were won, together with 36 Gold Medals. Many premier honours, including: Welsh National Eisteddfod Winners at Treorchy, 1928; at Liverpool, both the Open and Welsh Sections in 1929; and then at Neath, were also gained. A much coveted 2nd prize was won by the Band at the Spring Festival, Belle Vue, Manchester in 1930.

CORY WORKMEN SILVER BAND, PENTRE, 1923.

When Robert Jones, a non-playing member of the Band and Blacksmith at Pentre Colliery died in 1925, a letter of condolence was sent to his daughter, Mrs Clare, dated 22nd February 1925. The letter reveals several interesting facts about the Band at that time. It confirms that the Band added the word 'Silver' to its name; previously they were known as, 'Cory Workmen's Band'. Many brass bands did this after purchasing new silver plated instruments. Prior to silver plating, band instruments were sold in raw polished brass. It was also confirmed that the Conductor, J G Dobbing lived at 60 Bronllwyn Road, Pentre. This address is in close proximity to the current bandroom. The President of the Band was Mr T Williams MBE, JP, who worked as Supervisor for Cory Brothers. The Secretary was Mr John Carter and the Financial Secretary was W Margery. It was also interesting to note that the Band prominently advertised that they are available for Engagements at Parties and Demonstrations and that they wear "Full Dress Uniform". The letterhead also records in detail, along with adjudicator's comments, some of their first prizes in 1922, including:-

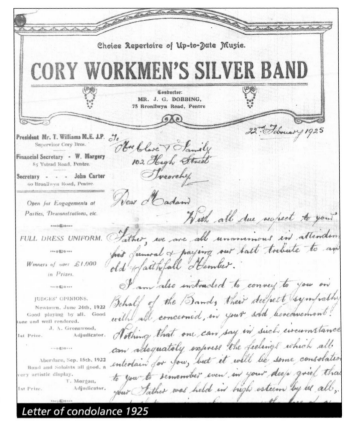

Letter of condolance 1925

Newtown, 24th June,
Aberdare, 15th September and
Cardiff, 30th September.

The adjudicator in the latter (Mr H Scott) commenting that, 'I have never heard a better performance!'

In Cardiff on 19th July 1923, the Cory Workmen's Band also took part in what is believed to have been the first radio broadcast of a Brass Band. By the mid 1950's Cory Band had notched up an impressive two hundred and fifty (250) BBC Broadcasts. Mr Dobbing had conducted the Cory Band in many of these. Several newspaper reports from 1923 to 1924 gave a valuable insight into the type of concert programmes he compiled. All featured a vocal soloist with the Band. Morgan Morgan (baritone), Gwladys Partridge (soprano), Miss Isabel Davies (soprano), Mr Archie Gay (tenor) and Mr Erbin Thomas (tenor) appeared frequently. Also included in the programmes were arrangements by Mr Dobbing. W J Davies (euphonium) is featured playing *Annie Laurie, a Gypsies Warning* and *Old Folks at Home*. Tom Trotman is also featured as a euphonium soloist playing Hartmann's Air and Variations

Sen Sucht. Cornet duets were also popular favourites, usually performed by A. Trotman and J. Carter. Aaron Trotman also performed a range of solos in a concert programme in 1924, playing William Rimmer's virtuoso Air and Variations, *Jenny Jones*. Most of Dobbing's programmes also featured difficult overtures including Rossini's ever popular *William Tell*.

In April 1940, Dobbing was succeeded by Redvers Little. Redvers who was popularly known as Reg, started his banding career in 1915 with Dalton Town Band, progressively developing his experience with the famous Gwaun Cae Gurwen, Creswell Colliery and Barrow Shipyard Bands. He formed a Junior Band at Swanwick Collieries in 1935, subsequently attending eleven contests, winning nine of them. Reg continued his winning ways, when he was appointed to conduct Cory Workmen's Silver Band, by winning a host of local contests, most notably the Welsh Regional Championships in 1941, 1943 and 1945.

Cory Workmen's Band 1942, conductor Reg Little

However, competitive success outside the Principality still remained elusive, although the Cory Band were invited to play at many prestigious concerts. Mr Little and the players took their banding very seriously. John Trotman recalls a lighter moment during a Hyde Park concert in London in 1942, (one of a week long twice daily concert series) "The Bandroom was underneath the Bandstand and we all lined up in order to take the stage. I was playing flugel horn that day and as I walked to my seat I noticed a contraceptive sheath hanging above the Conductor's stand. When Reg Little took the stage he took one look at it and turned to Stan Williams the Principal Cornet player and asked him to remove it. Stan looked at Reg, and then looked at the sheath replying, "Remove it yourself!" Using his baton, Reg threw the offending object out of the rear of the Bandstand. The audience and band were doubled up in laughter and it was the most prolonged and enthusiastic applause we received all week!"

Cory Brothers' provided Reg Little with a day job working on the House Coal weigh bridge. At that time, every male colliery employee was allowed one ton of coal each month. The coal was distributed to their homes by horse and cart and Reg's job was to check that each cart load was carrying the appropriate amount of coal. Reg Little resigned from the Band and Gelli Colliery in 1946 to move to North Wales as Musical Director of Rhyl Urban District Council with responsibility for the Rhyl Silver Band. He lived in Bettws Private House, Kimmel Bay. Interestingly, when Cory's new conductor, Walter B Hargreaves was appointed, he was given Reg's job in charge of House Coal, also moving into the Gelli Colliery house that was once the home of his predecessor, Redvers (Reg) Little.

Chapter 3

THE TROTMAN FAMILY
The Talented Backbone of the Band

The truly amazing and influential link between the highly musically talented Trotman family dynasty and the world famous Cory Band began in 1911, almost 100 years ago. Such pairings in other spheres of life are commonplace. In food, it is bacon and egg; in sport, bat and ball; but in the brass band musical heartland of Wales, centred upon Pentre in the Rhondda Fawr valley, it must be caviar and champagne. Yes! This pairing aptly describes the irrevocable intertwining of the immense influence of successive generations of the Trotman family on the management and musical achievements of the famous Cory Band during this virtual 100 year span.

Aaron Trotman (senior)

The story of this truly remarkable family association began in 1911, when Aaron (senior), the paternal grandfather of John, the sole remaining family link with the Band – went along with his son, Aaron (junior), to join the Cory Band. Aaron (senior), a BB^b Bass player and a strong disciplinarian, remained with the Band until 1932, taking part in many prestigious events, notably an early experimental broadcast between two venues a short distance apart from each other, under the supervision of the celebrated pioneer of wireless transmission – Guglielmo Marconi. This was circa 1920. In 1916, another son – Thomas William (Tom) became a member of the Band and remained so until his death in 1980. Tom soon became the Band's Principal Euphonium and enjoyed the distinction of playing a solo in the Band's first official broadcast in July 1923. Tom, who worked in the local coal mine, occupied the Principal Euphonium chair until the 1939/45 war years, eventually progressing, initially to E^b Bass and subsequently to his father's chair on BB^b Bass, helping to sustain the wonderful bass sound that has traditionally been the bedrock of the Cory Band's fine tonal quality. For several years the Trotman brothers – Aaron (junior) and Tom were firmly ensconced in the Principal Cornet and Euphonium chairs until Aaron decided that his future lay within the music profession, becoming Principal Trumpet of the BBC Welsh Orchestra under the baton of their Principal Conductor at that time, the distinguished Welsh composer/conductor and Rhondda born Mansel Thomas OBE.

Aaron (Ron) retained his association with the Band throughout his professional career, eventually conducting the Band at intervals in the 1950's and early 1960's. He also influenced the introduction of females into the Cory Band in the 1950's. Aaron taught at the then, Cardiff Castle College of Music – this was at the time when the college activities were actually carried out within the confines of the castle. One of his students was a girl named Pat Davies and she played with the Band from time to time. He was an uncompromising teacher, always setting stretching goals for his students. Those who worked hard to improve their playing standards were respected by him, but he certainly did "not suffer fools gladly." Interestingly, the Band's current prestigious Musical Director Dr. Robert (Bob) Childs, is Director of Brass Band Studies at the Royal Welsh College of Music and Drama (RWCMD), now situated in Bute Park immediately to the rear of Cardiff Castle. Several of the contemporary principal players in the Cory Band are currently Senior Tutors on the Brass Band Pathway at the RWCMD.

By contrast, Tom remained a coal miner, relishing his membership of the Cory Band. The ever present dangers of coal mining reared their ugly head when Tom severely injured his right hand in an underground accident, just days before the Band were to play twice daily for a week in the Bandstand at Hyde Park, London. His disappointment at being unable to appear with the Band was mollified by the opportunity to listen to the fine playing of his eleventh hour replacement - the renowned euphonium soloist - Harry Cheshire.

A memorable achievement for Tom and one that was forever etched on his mind was the occasion when, as bandmaster, he prepared and conducted the Cory Band to second place in a championship contest just after the end of the Second World War. He always felt proud that he had amply repaid the confidence placed in him, during the period in the late 1940's when he was responsible for maintaining musical standards. This was during the period that the Band were in the process of changing their Professional Conductor from Reg Little to the inimitable Walter B. Hargreaves.

The Trotman family backstage at the Royal Albert Hall, 1956. from left to right: Tom, John, Haydn (Dai), Jeff, Steve, Norman, Aaron jr. (inset Aaron sr. , BBb Bass)

A younger brother, Steve, joined the Band in 1925, initially as a cornet player, eventually occupying the Solo Horn chair for 25 years, until he retired from playing in 1973. Steve was thrilled to have been asked to join the Foden's Band when he was a member of Harry Mortimer's 'All Star' Brass, but was unable to accept the offer owing to family circumstances at that time. Nevertheless, he remained well satisfied with the standards of performance constantly maintained by the Band in their broadcasting, contest and concert engagements throughout his career. Steve was a vice president of the Band at the time of his death in 1983.

John Trotman age 3

John Trotman age 11 in Cory Band uniform

During the 1930s, yet another brother, Haydn Charles affectionately known as "Dai" joined the Band, initially as a cornet player, receiving daily tuition from his older brothers, obviously a strict and thorough regime. He was given set pieces to perform on Sunday afternoons in front of the entire family. If expectations fell short there was trouble for him. Despite this strictness, he always spoke of his gratitude to his family who encouraged him to migrate to trombone and then onwards to London to study with Sidney Langston – the trombone supremo at that time. Joining the Band of the Irish Guards, his talents were quickly recognised by the major London orchestras. His freelancing activities were hectic and long recording sessions with the Philharmonia and the London Symphony Orchestra sometimes led to him being late on parade, with the inevitable consequences of abuse from an irate Sergeant Major. Eventually he was lured into accepting the Bass Trombone chair of the orchestra of the Royal Opera House, Covent Garden – a position he filled with distinction for seventeen years before returning to Wales, to help form the orchestra of the Welsh National Opera. "Dai" Trotman subsequently succumbed to the pull of the

From left to right; John Trotman, Stan Williams and Don Tanner, each wearing a National Band of Wales sash

Metropolis so that he migrated once again to London, to manage the BBC Concert Orchestra from 1974 to 1982. In this role he was very much an 'iron fist in a velvet glove' disciplinarian, being particularly meticulous about punctuality and strict about the wearing of black socks with dinner jackets and evening dress attire. To those musicians who thought that navy blue socks were near enough, he quickly disabused them of their folly in short basic Anglo Saxon phrases. Throughout his successful professional career as player and administrator, he retained his strong links with the Cory Band holding the position of President of the Band until his death in 1986. What an exhilarating time to be President – with the Band completing their hat trick of wins at the Royal Albert Hall (RAH) National Championships from 1982 to 1984 under the baton of the enigmatic Arthur Kenney (The Major!).

The 1930s saw an influx of Trotmans into the Cory Band, initially "Dai" and finally John, the son of Tom Trotman, who joined as a cornet player in 1937, four years after his cousin - Tommy Roberts (a gifted baritone player), who played with the Band until 1969. John has now been actively involved with the Cory Band for a staggering 73 years! Successively moving from cornet to flugel then to 1st tenor horn where he supported his uncle Steve for several years, ultimately being "promoted" to the Bass Section, thereby following in the footsteps of his father Tom and grandfather Aaron, who started this proud dynasty in 1911.

The fourth generation of this gifted family – the two great grandsons of the first Aaron (senior) - became playing members of the Band in the early 1970s. Huw Jones enjoyed a seven year span of playing in the Band initially on baritone, before transferring to euphonium. Huw remains indebted to the inspiration of his teacher during those early years – his Grandfather Tom, who was a strong motivator, instilling much enthusiasm in Huw in his formative years despite Tom's strongly disciplined approach to the daily practice routine. Huw left the Band to study in London under the guidance of the much revered Tuba Soloist John Fletcher,. Huw's successful studies led to his appointment as Principal Tuba with the BBC Concert Orchestra. Now based in Tring, Herts, he combines a busy teaching practice in Hertfordshire schools with freelance playing. Ian Jones played 2nd Cornet with the Band from 1973 until his untimely death in 1980.

There were two further musical members of the Trotman family – Jeffrey, who was a 2nd cornet player with the Cory Band in the late 1950s; whereas Norman, son of Aaron (junior) went in his early teens to study cornet at Kneller Hall. Norman's stature and reputation as a teacher is warmly and most readily recalled by his contemporaries in the music service of the British Army. Under his strict guidance, many of his students progressed to principal positions in regimental bands and subsequently to appointments in leading British and Continental orchestras. Several recall his inherent ability to successfully link the teaching of harmony and performance in an exemplary manner. Norman had the distinction of being a member of the select team of Trumpeters that played at the coronation of Queen Elizabeth II.

Retiring from army musical life, he was appointed Head of Brass at Bromley Education Authority, where he continued to inspire and motivate students and tutors alike. Norman's capacity for talent spotting was second to none.

Now, in 2010, John is the sole remaining member of the Trotman family who is still closely involved with the Cory Band. Until his enforced early retirement from playing in 1981 due to ill health, a member of the Trotman family had played in every concert and contest since 1911 – an incredible 72 years of active involvement. This achievement prompted the publication of an article in the South Wales Echo in 1983 under the caption – "What? No Trotmans!" The article was accompanied by a photograph of the Cory Band taken in 1916 showing Aaron (Senior) sitting behind his BB^b Bass; Tom standing proudly upright with his euphonium and Aaron (Junior) clutching his cornet and kneeling alongside the bass drum. The autocratic figure of the Conductor J. G. Dobbing, in

John Trotman celebrating 70 years with Cory Band, 2007

civilian attire and complete with bowler hat stands proudly in the centre of the photograph. John remains a Trustee and Librarian of the Band. Chatting with John at his home in Pleasant View, Pentre, he readily recalls his first contest with the Cory Band. This was a Semi-National Eisteddfod contest held at Treorchy, just a few miles away from the Cory bandroom and in the homeland of their great rivals of the 1930's and 1940's, the Parc and Dare Band. The test piece was *Haydn's Works*, comprising a selection of music taken from Haydn's symphonies, oratorios and songs. John gave a vivid description of the attention given to the back row cornets by the famous and redoubtable task master – J.G. Dobbing, to properly establish the rhythmic pattern of the excerpt from the *Clock Symphony*. Mr. Dobbing was a fearsome disciplinarian, but a highly successful Conductor of the Cory Band from the early 1900s to 1937. At John's first contest, the victors were the then well known Gwaun-Cae-Gurwen (GCG) Band from South West Wales, conducted by another supremely talented musician, Dan Lloyd. Cory were runners up, beating Parc and Dare their local rivals into third place – so honour was well and truly satisfied! The 1930's were the years of the industrial depression, so it is worth recalling the very different conditions under which bands performed at this contest. These were certainly not ideal! The venue was a "building" normally used for the repair of the wooden coal wagons that transported coal from local collieries to Cardiff Docks. The stage was constructed of railway sleepers and the thick wooden planks needed to repair the base and sides of these wagons. Indeed, performance conditions were far removed from today's prestigious venues such as the Royal Albert Hall, London; Symphony Hall, Birmingham; Brangwyn Hall, Swansea and St David's Hall, Cardiff. There remains however, a commonality of purpose between players and conductors of yesteryear and those involved in the contemporary band scheme – that is the ambition to constantly perform at a level that will achieve and maintain lasting success.

As the sole surviving member of this well known, highly accomplished and well respected brass dynasty, still linked with the famous Cory Band, John also has the distinction and privilege of being the positive link with the conducting skills of the much admired Mr. Dobbing with one of today's leading conductors – Dr. Robert (Bob) Childs who has joined a most distinguished line of accomplished conductors that include:-

Walter B. Hargreaves – the wee Professor;
T. J. Powell,
John Harrison,
Bram Gay,
Harry Mortimer CBE,
Rex Mortimer,
Geoffrey Brand,
Elgar Howarth,
Major Arthur Kenney,
Sq Leader Denzil Stephens,
Reg Little,
George Thompson and
Eric Bravington.

A veritable Who's Who of conducting greats in the world of brass bands. Whilst John's father Tom had the privilege of playing a solo in the Cory Band's first broadcast, John starkly recalled the traumatic shock of playing 1st Horn in a live broadcast when their conductor – the well respected T. J. (Tom) Powell suddenly collapsed and died. This was in a studio near Cathays Park, Cardiff in 1965. The Band's Principal Cornet – Stanley Williams leapt to his feet and continued conducting the Band until the broadcast ended; an unwanted and intensely emotional experience.

John also enjoyed playing, together with his Dad - Tom and Uncle Steve in the National Brass Band of Wales, a representative band of some forty of the best players in Wales that was selected to play in the evening concerts of the Annual Royal National Eisteddfod of Wales during the 1950's and 1960's. The Associate Musical Director of this band was T. J. Powell, affectionately known as the Welsh 'Sousa' March King.

In 1983, after John had retired from the rigours of Bass playing, he was asked to play in the percussion section for the Band's winning performance of Ballet for Band (Horowitz) – an opportunity he firmly grasped with both hands! He said it was a new experience to stand throughout the entire performance on the stage of the Royal Albert Hall, having sat through all his previous appearances at the National Championship held at this venue. He was also pleased to be part of the percussion team that played at Cory's Centenary Concert in St. David's Hall in 1984, again under the inspired baton of Major Arthur H. Kenney. This team received an unusual tribute when a letter from an 'avid concert goer' appeared in the letters column of the Western Mail, informing readers that – "although unfamiliar with brass band concerts she had been greatly impressed by the standard of performance and presentation achieved by the Band. Particularly so, when her enjoyment of the entire concert had been enhanced by the beaming faces and obvious proficiency of the percussion and timpani team", who on that special occasion was John; Clayton McCann; Alan O'Leary and a youthful Richard Buckley (now principal percussionist with the Orquestra Sinfonica Portuguesa based in Lisbon, Portugal).

In keeping with his family traditions, John, who still lives a short ten minute walk from the Cory Band HQ, has enjoyed playing at the highest level throughout his banding career. His first registration card contains date stamps from only the most prestigious of contest venues – what an achievement! He confirmed that the high point of his membership of the Cory Band was their success at winning the 'British Open' contest in 2000. John had waited for that success for 50 years since playing in the Band that had been runners up at this contest in 1950. The thrill of this success was paramount, despite earlier accolades of winning the National Championship title on four occasions (including a hat trick) together with the European Championship in 1980 and more recently, in 2008, 2009 and 2010

Not content to sit on his personal and family laurels, John remains an extremely busy and efficient librarian to the current Band. In his role as Chairperson of the Cory Junior Band, John is constantly seeking funding to aid their development.

John has followed in his father Tom's footsteps as a member of the Executive Committee of the South East Wales Brass Band Association, serving as Chairperson of the South East/West Wales Brass Band Association's Test Piece Committee. Yes, John remains an ever-present and hard working official at all local competitions! He is a constant, friendly and familiar figure to all contemporary band-folk. He is also a superb example of the manner by which the Trotman family contributed so effectively for nigh on a century to the exceptionally high standards achieved and maintained by the Cory Band. It is however, equally clear that complacency with playing standards have no place whatsoever in the Cory Band's long standing ethos, obviously, a culture that was readily embraced by this immensely talented, family dynasty.

If there was a Trotman family motto, it is likely to have read - 'Dedication, Discipline, Loyalty and the Pursuit of Excellence!'

Chapter 4

Walter Hargreaves – The "Wee Professor"

One of the most celebrated conductors during the Cory Band's 125 year history, Walter B Hargreaves (1907-98), was born in Glasgow and began playing the cornet at an early age. Having attended the Royal Scottish Academy of Music, Glasgow, Hargreaves began his career as a professional trumpet player with the Scottish Symphony Orchestra before returning to the brass band realm in 1944 as conductor of the City of Edinburgh Brass Band.

The legendary cornet player, conductor and broadcaster, Harry Mortimer CBE, recommended Walter Hargreaves for the post of conductor of the Cory Band. In his book 'Harry Mortimer on Brass,' he remembers auditioning the City of Edinburgh Band for BBC broadcasting work. He said "The Band itself were not of a very high standard, but it was clear they had an outstanding conductor – a small man of flair, who also played the cornet very well, but was a stranger to me. Appreciating his talent, I enquired what he was doing conducting a band of this calibre, to which he replied in a broad Scottish accent, 'Can you find me a better job?' I was able to tell him that I could, and forthwith recommended him to the Cory Band". Harry Mortimer's father, Fred affectionately referred to Walter Hargreaves as 'Taffy McTavish after Walter's successful sojourn in Wales.

CORY WORKMEN'S SILVER BAND
(*Director of Music*: WALTER B. HARGREAVES, L.T.C.L., B.B.C.M.)
Runners-up "Daily Herald" National Championship of Great Britain, Royal Albert Hall, London—October 16, 1948

The appointment of Walter B Hargreaves in 1946 proved to be the catalyst to place the Cory name firmly on the National platform of contesting success. Despite his diminutive stature, the charismatic Hargreaves commanded a huge amount of respect from his players and drew a unique sound from his Band. His efforts came quickly to fruition in 1948 at the National Championships held in the Royal Albert Hall, London. Playing the test piece *On the Cornish Coast*, (Henry Geehl) the Cory Workmen's Band were rewarded with second place on only their third (and Hargreaves' first) appearance at the competition. Cory had previously competed at the National Championships in 1925 and 1945 but had been unplaced.

This was a significant achievement not only for the Cory Workmen's Band, but for the whole of the rapidly developing Welsh brass band scene since, at the time, second prize was the highest position ever achieved by a band from the Principality (their close neighbours and rivals the Parc and Dare Band had achieved third place at this contest in 1945). This was followed by sixth place at the National Finals in 1949 on Ireland's *Comedy Overture*. Incidentally, some 25 years later under the baton of Major Arthur Kenney, the Cory name would also become the only Welsh band to lift the National Championships trophy and take the coveted trophy from the hitherto firm grip of English Bands for the very first time in the history of the contest.

It was under the charismatic leadership of Hargreaves that Cory also enjoyed, what was at that time, their most successful spell at the British "Open" Championships. In 1950, on his first ever appearance with the Band in this contest held at Belle Vue, Manchester, Hargreaves led the Band to another superb second prize-winning performance of Eric Ball's *Resurgam*; the highest placing ever achieved by a Welsh band at this historically prestigious contest. The magnitude of this achievement is highlighted by the fact that it would be another fifty years before a non-English band would surpass second prize, when Dr Robert (Bob) Childs and the Buy As You View (Cory) Band secured the famous "Open" Shield in 2000 – a truly historic date for a momentously historic and prestigious occasion.

In his remaining two years with the Cory Workmen's Band, Hargreaves won most of the domestic contests he entered, including first prize playing Beethoven's 5th *Symphony* in an open air contest at Duffryn Park, Blaina in 1948. First prize playing *Morning Rhapsody* on the tiered stage of the Great Central Hall, Newport in 1949 and first prize playing *Resurgam* at the Workmen's Hall, Ferndale in 1951. Also, in 1951, they gained first prize playing *Festival Overture* by Henry Geehl at the Great Central Hall Newport, with Walter programming this work for a subsequent BBC, 'Listen To The Band' programme.

During the 1950's, bands were able to purchase 12inch black disc recordings of works they had performed for the BBC (as part of their broadcast programme). The receipt document received from the BBC confirms that the Cory Band ordered 50 recordings from Times Recording Studio at a cost of 9 shillings and 6 pence each. John Trotman recalls the Band selling the recordings to Band and committee members for £1 per disc!

Walter Hargreaves and Cory Band performed consistently well in the two foremost national competitions in the brass band calendar. In 1951 and 1952 they finished fourth and eighth respectively at the British 'Open' Championship, and attained a respectable sixth place at the 1956 National Championships. Cory had at last, become a national force representing Wales

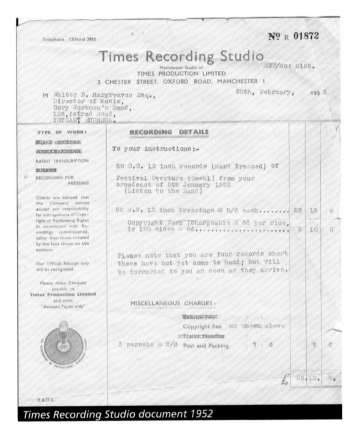

Times Recording Studio document 1952

with distinction, competing at a level of performance unachieved previously and unheard of in their increasingly illustrious history.

However, it was not solely this unprecedented contesting success that earned Walter Hargreaves his distinguished reputation. More celebrated was his ability to draw the best from his players, but above all, it was his enthusiasm, professionalism and dynamism which endeared Hargreaves to the players who performed under his direction. Bram Gay described him as a "creative conductor with a nearly infallible instinct for the right thing in music; the right turn of phrase, the right balance, and above all perfect intonation." John Trotman endorses Bram's words, adding, "Hargreaves could spend thirty minutes tuning one chord, he wouldn't let it go until it was right. He certainly didn't take any prisoners in band practice. He would insist that you play your part on your own, he was likened to a dog, a terrier with a rabbit, keeping on and on until you got it right." Many of the receipts for mutes and music were sent directly to Walter Hargreaves' home address. This would suggest a strong controlling arm on most things to do with the Band; he was obviously a very strong character who got exactly what he wanted. (See receipts from Besson).

By contrast, John Trotman also commented on the compassionate side of the man, saying, "Walter Hargreaves was the only professional conductor I can remember that showed any active interest in the Cory Junior Band. He attended

Besson receipt 1951

Besson letter 1952

most of their weekly rehearsals and occasionally conducted them at concerts. Walter's way was quite different with the youngsters than it was with the Senior Band. He gave them a lot of confidence and nurtured their talents. Not surprisingly, quite a few members of the Junior Band progressed into the Senior Band to occupy solo positions.

Walter Hargreaves didn't concentrate exclusively on contest results; he was also passionate about developing the Band's concert repertoire. Records show that during a full week of concerts for London County Council at the Embankment Gardens, the Band would play two full programmes a day at 12.30pm and 8.00pm respectively. Each programme required twelve items including; marches, selections, overtures, waltzes, tone poems, solos, duets, intermezzos, paraphrases, suites and a signature tune. Frank Wright was the Music Director for London Parks and he would frequently listen to the Band to check the quality of the performance. During the week, the Bank played in excess of eighty concert items without any repetition (apart from the National Anthem UK and their signature march).

Unlike the sponsored Bands in the North of England and the Midlands who would have paid leave of absence from their work, to fulfil these week long engagements, Cory players had to take annual leave or unpaid leave and pay for their own lodgings in London!

John Trotman recalls an amusing occurrence when the Band once did a week of engagements in London under the baton of the wee Professor "Every Band has a comedian, and ours was the euphonium player William Davies, Will had two nick-names, Will-Knocky-Davies (because of the way he knocked his final domino on the table during a pub game) and Will-Prisoner-Davies (because he was a prisoner of war during World War 2). One morning when we were leaving our over-night accommodation to walk to the Embankment Gardens, Knocky had us all marching, military style and he was shouting the commands from the front. Our uniforms were similar to those of the Guards Bands and were often mistaken for soldiers instead of bandsmen. As we marched down the pavement to Knocky's instruction, a real Army Officer stepped to one side and saluted us all.... We must have looked smart!"

One of the most prestigious concerts undertaken by Walter's Cory Band was a concert promoted by the National Brass Band Club. The concert was part of the Festival of Britain celebrations and was financially assisted by The Arts Council of Great Britain. The venue was the Royal Albert Hall and the event took place on Saturday 12th May 1951. The concert which was also broadcast, featured the first performance of *The Rainbow (A Tale of Dunkirk)* by Christopher Hassall, (better known for his lyrics to operettas by Ivor Novello) and set to music by Dr. Thomas Wood. The work included thirteen choirs and six brass bands with the well known orchestral conductor Sir Adrian Boult wielding the baton. In addition to performing *The Rainbow*, the massed bands of Black Dyke, Munn and Feltons, Fairey Aviation, Cory Workmen's Silver, Morris Motors and Scottish C.W.S. were conducted by Harry Mortimer CBE and Dr. Denis Wright. This concert was repeated on 11th November 1951 at the Polikoff Factory Canteen, Rhondda. The famous Australian arranger Frank Wright then London based, was the guest conductor, with New Zealand's Ken Smith the guest cornet soloist. On this occasion, the voices were those of the famous Treorchy Male Voice Choir. In addition to performing *The Rainbow,* the Band also played: *March Old Comrades,* (Teike) *Solemn Melody*, (Walford Davies) with Ken Smith playing *Haydn's Trumpet Concerto*. The first half of the concert closed with a performance of *Eric Ball's Resurgam*. The final performance in this series of three concerts was given in the Brangwyn Hall, Swansea. As in the second concert, the Treorchy Male Voice Choir, were on stage together with the massed bands of Cory, Parc and Dare, and Gwaun Cae Gurwen, under the masterful direction of maestro Harry Mortimer CBE.

It's interesting to note that the Band's Income and Expenditure account for the month of March 1952, includes music hire fees and printing costs for the second Rainbow Concert, together with a significant fee for a broadcasting session with the BBC. The document is in free-hand, written by the Band Treasurer Mr. T. George Harding.

Rainbow programme 1951

Rainbow programme 1952

Income	£	s	p
Bright and Early Broadcast	34	0	0
Concert Fee Ton Pentre Conservative Club	10	0	0
Expenditure			
T. Evans Printer second Rainbow Concert	11	2	0
Stainer and Bell Fees for Rainbow Concert	6	7	8
W.B. Hargreaves monthly tuition to March 7th	10	0	0
Entry fee Daily Herald (National Championships)	3	0	0
Entry fee Abertridwr (Local Contest)	0	10	6
Starkey Bus Broadcast	5	0	0
Telephone Charges February	1	4	9

During the time that Walter Hargreaves conducted the Cory Band he lived in the Rhondda at 126, Ystrad Road, Ystrad, Glamorgan. This house was owned by the National Coal Board (NCB), the Band paying a rent of £1.1 shilling and 3 pence a week directly to them. It would appear that the Band inadvertently carried on paying Walter's rent for a short time after he left the Band, as confirmed by a letter and returned cheque from N.C.B. - Llwyncelyn Office, Porth dated 31st October 1952.

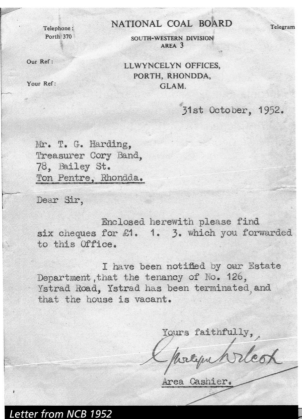

Letter from NCB 1952

Mr. Hargreaves left Cory in 1952 to take up the appointment of Professor of Cornet at the Royal Marines School of Music at Deal, Kent. It was here that the Scot acquired his unofficial title, the 'Wee Professor'. Briefly returning to Cory's in 1961, he conducted the Band to victory at the Annual Welsh Regional Championships on G. Vinter's *Salute to Youth* also being awarded the third prize in 1962 at these Championships, playing Haydn John's arrangement of Wagner's *Rienzi* overture. In 1961 he was presented with the 'Baton of Honour' at the prestigious 'Spotlight on Service Ceremony', held in the Royal Albert Hall, London following in the eminent footsteps of such brass band luminaries as Dr. Dennis Wright, Eric Ball and Frank Wright.

As a consequence of his success with Cory Workmen's Band, Hargreaves' conducting career flourished. He became the most sought after Brass Band conductor of the 1960s, conducting Brighouse & Rastrick, Fairey Aviation, Stanshawe (Bristol) and the Ever Ready Band as well as free-lancing with many other

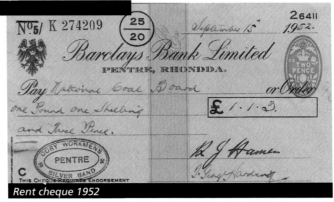

Rent cheque 1952

bands often achieving major competitive successes. One such success in Wales in the mid 1960's was the reward for his skilful direction of the Mozartian style 'Festival Music' by Eric Ball, when he ensured a high profile victory for local rivals – the Tredegar Band at the Royal National Eisteddfod of Wales. He directed the inaugural course of the Northern Ireland Youth Brass Band in 1964 and in addition to his busy conducting activities, also accepted many invitations to adjudicate and transcribe music from the orchestral concert repertoire for Brass Bands. Two of Walter's most famous arrangements for bands which are still regularly played by many of the top bands today, are Camille Saint-Saens' - *French Military March* and Mikhail Glinka's *Overture to Ruslan and Ludmilla*.

Cory Band, Ninian Park Foorball ground, 1947

Cory Band, Caerphilly, 1953

He retired from competitive conducting circa 1985, leaving many contest and concert goers with fond memories of him as one of the most well known and beloved characters in the history of the Brass Band movement. His departure from the movement signified the end of an era. Walter B. Hargreaves died on 24th June 1998 aged 91.

His time with the Cory Workmens' Band during 1946-52 was the period when the 'Wee Professor' showed the Banding World his talents as a motivator and a musician. Cory had for many years been one of the most successful bands in Wales. Walter Hargreaves' tireless work, talent and determination, coupled with the dedication and ability of his players both elevated and consolidated the Band's position and reputation from being just the best in Wales to one of the best in the World.

Other notable Musical Directors who continued to deliver Walter Hargreaves' high expectations for the Cory Band were: L. Wainwright, Stan Brown, Aaron Trotman, T.J. Powell, John Harrison, Gerald Gentry, Bram Gay, Sq Leader Denzil Stephens, Major Arthur Kenney, Brian Howard, Nigel Seaman, Malcolm Brownbill and, the current M.D. Dr. Robert Childs, who consistently delivers performances of the highest quality.

Aaron Trotman conducted the Band for two years, being at the helm when Cory were included in the 1958 Guinness Book of Records for being involved in the fastest production of a music recording. The Band recorded 'God Bless the Prince of Wales' on the Black Mountain label. They recorded the song on a Saturday and by the following Monday morning the record was on sale at retail outlets!

T.J. (Tom) Powell (1897-1965) was born in Tredegar and played with the local Salvation Army Band before joining the Royal Marines.

Cory Workmen's Band, conductor Aaron Trotman c. 1957

Returning to civilian life in 1920, T.J. conducted the Melingriffith Works Band in Cardiff for many years, achieving considerable success at local contests and concerts. He became the leading Brass Band conductor in Wales during the middle and late 1950's being appointed Musical Director of Cory's in 1959. He conducted the Band to their 1961 Welsh Annual Regional Championship win, but because of T.J.'s failing health, Walter Hargreaves returned to conduct the winning performance the following year. T.J. Powell was widely and affectionately known as the 'Welsh March King.' Amongst his considerable compositions are several well known and well used contest marches together with quite challenging test pieces. Tom Powell was a leading adjudicator officiating at both of the major contests in the UK; the September "Open" Championships and the National Championship Finals. He died of a heart attack whilst conducting the Cory Band in the Cardiff BBC studio, when the Band were actually taking part in the BBC's 1965 Challenging Brass competition. The Band's performance continued uninterrupted with Principal Cornet Stan Williams taking over the conducting duties whilst 'T.J.' was taken from the studio. It was at the end of the broadcast, that the Band became aware that 'T.J.' had actually died during the transmission and for those involved, a never to be forgotten tragic experience of the cliché – "the show must go on".

Cory Workmen's Band, conductor T.J. Powell c. 1960

The Band eventually secured the services of the experienced Mr. John Harrison of Halifax, who was very successful in leading the Band to several annual Welsh Championship successes.

Cory Workmen's Band, conductor T.J. Powell c. 1960

Cory Workmen's Band, conductor John Harrison c. 1965

Chapter 5
Cory Junior Band

The Cory Junior Band was founded in 1934, when Tommy Armstrong, the Solo Baritone of the Cory Band (Senior) responded to the challenge of encouraging and nurturing young players to become future members of the Senior Band. Existing members of the Senior Band responded swiftly. Their young children, sons and daughters were encouraged to join and take advantage of the free tuition offered to them by Tommy Armstrong. At that time, the opportunity to learn was only available from resources within the Band, since there was little opportunity for the youngsters to obtain instruments from other sources. It was many years later that the local education authorities started funding the provision of instruments and instrumental tuition. In the early 1940's, Tommy Armstrong was joined by another Cory Band stalwart – Tom Trotman, as the urgency to provide 'home grown' players for the Senior Band intensified. When Tommy Armstrong retired from teaching the youngsters, Tom Trotman's role became more meaningful, as did the task ahead – that of fully realising the obvious, that there was likely to be a lack of players of sufficient ability and calibre to fill future vacancies in the Cory Band. There was a clear need to ensure the establishment of a nursery of talented and properly trained young players to serve the needs of the Cory Band well into the future, following the end of the Second World War in the mid 1940's.

Fortuitously, the appointment of the late and great Walter B. Hargreaves as the professional Musical Director of the Cory Band coincided with this prophetic realisation. Walter Hargreaves was quick to recognise the benefits of the system already in place, so it was due to his vision and leadership that the Junior Band really flourished. Several players who eventually became household names in the brass band world were initially developed in the Cory Junior Band, before gaining promotion to the Cory Band itself and thence to much wider recognition by brass band enthusiasts throughout the United Kingdom. A typical example of this development pathway was Gwyn Davies, who returned to the Band after completing his National Service, but who was eventually appointed as the Principal Cornet of Morris Motors Band (Oxford). The Eb Soprano Cornet legend – Emlyn Bryant, was lured from the Cory Band to add style and class to several leading bands in the North of England and the Midlands.   His brother, Arthur, a noted trombonist left to build local bands in Devon, whereas James Hargreaves, the talented son of the enigmatic Walter, progressed to become Head of Music for the Canadian Armed Forces. Whilst National Service was also a significant contributor to the development of players who received their early tuition in the Junior Band, many of these never returned to the Rhondda Valleys, preferring to respond to the challenge of playing with the industrially sponsored famous name bands in the North of England. This was the period when players were also offered employment by the sponsors of these leading bands.

Nevertheless, Walter Hargreaves masterminded a system designed to both develop local players whilst also encouraging them to stay local and loyal to the Cory Band. He encouraged a local lower section band – Glenrhondda Band – later to become the Treherbert Band, to take on the role of a bridge organisation, where players could gain experience in contesting

Cory Junior Band, conductor W. B. Hargreaves, Pentre Park 1952

and concert work at a more advanced level than was available to the Cory Junior Band at that time. It was accepted that the Band would fulfil this "nursery" role, feeding players to the Senior Cory Band as required. To aid this process, Will Davies, (well known throughout South Wales as "Will Ruth"), the Cory Band's former euphonium player who was for many years their left handed BBb Bass player of 'On the Cornish Coast' fame , due to the accidental loss of several fingers on his right hand. He was appointed Conductor of Glenrhondda Band, in succession to the former Parc and Dare star euphonium soloist – Fred Prior. The flow of players between these bands then began in earnest. Whilst many players trod this pathway, others not surprisingly, were enticed to join one of the many local bands in the area, (who were quick to spot the benefits of this system), prior to moving to play with the Cory Band when the opportunity presented itself. However, there were a few who stayed many years with this feeder or nursery band. Walter Hargreaves, supported by Tom Trotman, had indeed provided a solid foundation to nurture and develop future players. Not surprisingly, it was often quoted that "you can take a person out of Cory's, but you can never take Cory's out of the person". A truism indeed and vouched by many folk both internal and external to the Cory organisation!

Of course, many players that were taught the basics in the Cory Junior Band, but who never played in the Senior Band have confirmed the accuracy of the above quote, none more so than the late Gerald Coleman, who became a truly major influence on the Cory Band's fortunes in later years. During this period, others such as Dennis Summers, Cyril John, Alan Smith and Stuart Lewis were privileged to complete this much sought after "circle of attachment" to Cory. When Walter Hargreaves left the Cory organisation in 1952, the Junior Band was at its zenith. He was succeeded in his leadership of the Junior Band by Don Hendy – a back row cornet player in the Senior Band, who later led the neighbouring Markham Colliery Band with distinction. At this time, payment for brass band tutors commenced via Government Youth Schemes, whereas prior to this, tuition had been given without financial help to either the tutors or the players.

Throughout the 1950's a veritable stream of players flowed from the Junior to the Senior Band – Percussionist Alan O'Leary was percussionist in the 'Hat Trick' Cory Band of the 1980s, whereas Ralph Morgan and Huw Williams were members of the Band that won their first National Finals title in 1974 and the European Champions title in 1980. During the 1970's, Huw Williams was the first brass band tuba soloist to play 'live' on TV (Granada Contest 1971). He was also the first brass band tuba soloist to perform Edward Gregson's Tuba Concerto, under the baton of the composer, during a live broadcast from St. John's Church, Smith Square, London in 1976.

Former Junior Band players who certainly made a lengthy, successful transition to the Senior Band were Ceri Lewis, Alan Goodridge and Haydn Lawthorn. Alan Jacobs returned from National Service to return to Cory's only to leave once again to become Principal Cornet of the Band of the Irish Guards. Billy Jenkins, probably one of the Senior Band's youngest players at twelve years of age, left to take up a career in the Forces.

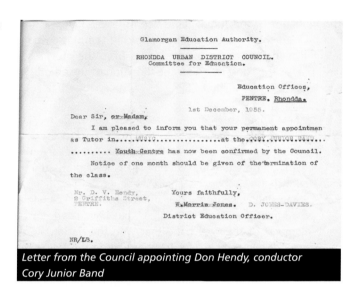

Letter from the Council appointing Don Hendy, conductor Cory Junior Band

Cory Junior Band, conductor Don Hendy, 1955

The first female to have played with the Cory Band was Joan Powell, a stylish cornet player from Newbridge, but only one female from the Junior Band – Pat Davies – was promoted to the Senior Band. This was during the late 1950s. Members of the Junior Band were extremely successful when auditioning for the National Youth Brass Band of Great Britain. In 1956, seven of the thirteen strong contingent from Welsh bands were from the Junior Band. During the 1960's, contests for Junior and Youth Bands came into popularity. Local industrialists such as T.C. Jones Ltd. (of the 600 Group of Companies) based at Treorchy, sponsored annual competitions, some of which were held at the Cory Band Hall on Pentre Hill. The stage of this hall was later converted into a music library. The Rhondda Eisteddfod was initially held in Tonypandy. Major rivals at this time were the Treorchy Youth Band under the direction of the illustrious Ieuan Morgan MBE (the euphonium soloist and later the successful conductor of near neighbours – Parc and Dare Band). Under the direction of Don Tanner, the Senior Band's Principal Trombone, the Junior Band and their players won a proliferation of prizes at these events.

Silverware was always on display, with the trombone quartet of Wyndham Williams, Paul Williams, Mike Chinnock and Graham Sheppard being prolific prize winners.

The highlight of the Junior Bands' contest calendar was the Parc and Dare Contest, held in nearby Treorchy. The Band participated in the massed bands' evening concert – the Bands selected being the three prize winners from the previous year. The Band were excited to have played the concert, under the direction of the adjudicator – the brass band maestro, par excellence - Harry Mortimer CBE.

Don Tanner's wife was an invaluable leader and instigator of support to the young competitors, acting as their accompanist and in initiating the first Ladies' Committee from the mothers of the members of the Junior Band. During Don Tanner's sixteen year span of responsibility (1959-1975), many of these talented young players were promoted to the Senior Band – Gwyn Thomas, Paul Hedditch, Roy Roberts, Graham Sheppard, Jeffrey Sheppard, Graham Lewis, Huw Jones, Ian Jones, Keith Williams, Greg Jones and Huw Watkins are names that are readily recalled, (with unreserved apologies for those names that have been missed from the list). Six such players were members of the Cory band that won the National Championships four times, the first, in 1974 and the incredible 'Hat Trick' of wins in the 1980's. Tales can be told from each era of Solo contests where the Junior Band members were involved. One such story involves Senior band member Ian Jones (Grandson of Tom Trotman), who was accompanying Angela Guy, an extremely talented tenor horn player at the finals of the Butlin's Youth Solo Contest held in Cardiff. Waiting for the adjudicators to reach their verdict, the announcer asked if there was a volunteer to entertain the audience until the verdict was ready to be announced. Ian raised his hand, walked to the stage, sat at the piano and proceeded to play a few items culminating in an impersonation of the Les Dawson rendering of the Scott Joplin rag – The Entertainer, with the audience and competitors collapsing in stitches of laughter. This recollection is a fitting tribute to the memory of Ian Jones who sadly died whilst still a young man. Ian was sadly missed by all associated with the Junior and Senior Bands.

Cory Junior Band, conductor Don Tanner, 1966

The Junior Band appeared at many concerts, always supported by a soloist from the Senior Band. In the early days it was invariably Stan Williams who thrilled the young players with his spellbinding performances of *Post Horn Gallop*. Some years later it was Jim Davies's turn to bring both sparkle and tears to the eyes of the youngsters with his utterly compelling cornet playing.

At this time, residential courses had started to be organised by the Glamorgan Education Authority. Most of the Junior Band won places at those much sought after courses. Later the work of the Junior Band was supplemented by Saturday morning rehearsals held under the auspices of the local authority.

The Senior Band was always fully supportive and encouraged the Junior Band members to attend local contests during the year, with the Ladies' Committee financing a coach and purchasing tickets for the Junior Band members to attend the Annual Welsh Regional Championship Contests at Swansea.

Cory Junior Band, conductor Don Tanner, 1970

During the 1980's, the age profile of the Senior Band became much younger than hitherto, so the flow from the Junior Band virtually ceased, with only Philip Privett being promoted to the Senior Band.

Many highly promising young players were unfortunate to emerge at a time when there were no vacancies to be filled in the Senior Band. Angela Guy, Lynda and Julie Singleton, John Fletcher, Leighton Stevens, Wayne Eldridge and John Lewis joined other local bands, but Dave Singleton and Andrew Howells eventually gained places in the Senior Band. Graham Sheppard and Gareth Key worked tirelessly to maintain the standard of the Junior Band, but eventually support for the Band dwindled, due largely to the many other interests that emerged to pressurise the time of young people.

Cory Junior Band, conductor Graham Sheppard, 1979

It was not until 1999, that the Senior Band decided to re-activate and revive the fortunes of the Junior Band. Former Junior Band members and Senior Band stalwart and local businessman – Ceri Lewis responded positively to the challenge, the Junior Band now having its own management team. Ceri has been supported by the indefatigable John Trotman, son of Tom, an early pioneer of both the Senior and Junior Bands.

In 2010, the Band is supported by many former Senior Band players. Rehearsals are held twice weekly and of course, the Junior Band has its own website – http://www.coryjuniorband.co.uk. The Band are always seeking information from former members and their families. To realise that the Cory Junior Band is still surviving after its tentative formation seventy six (76) years ago is an incredible achievement, but to have also had resounding success in developing so many players who were promoted to the Senior Band is also a remarkable feat.

Might the success of the future reflect the diligence and patience of the tutors of the past!

Cory Junior Band, Christmas Concert 2005

Chapter 6
"Major" changes in musical direction!

All great wines have a year that history deems an exceptional vintage. There is no doubt that in the history of the Cory Band, 1970 was special. Although the year didn't yield a significant accumulation of silverware, it was the year that new and fruitful vines were planted. History has confirmed that difficult decisions made then were meaningful, providing significant success for the next fifteen years. John Harrison's tenure as Musical Director had ended earlier in the year, his replacement was Albert Meek, who had conducted the Band at the British 'Open' Championships in Manchester, where the Band were placed eleventh. Cory hadn't qualified for the National Championship Finals of Great Britain in October, so the last important contest of that year for the Band was the National Mineworker's (CISWO) Championship Finals held at Blackpool in November. Albert Meek was unavailable, giving the Band Manager, Gwyn Dackins the task of finding a suitable replacement. Mr. Dackins noted that a recently retired Musical Director of the Band of the Welsh Guards had visited the Principality to conduct a local band, so after consulting the Band committee, he made a telephone call that changed the destiny of the Cory Band forever, initiating a relationship that grew and prospered like no other in the previous history of the Band.

Major Horatio Arthur Kenney, 1974

Telephoning Major Kenney, who was in Scotland on a family visit, Gwyn Dackins established the Major's availability to conduct the Band at the National Mineworker's (CISWO) Championships in mid November 1970, then asked if he was familiar with the score of the test piece – *Sinfonietta* by Eric Leidzen. The reply was swift and sure. "Of course, I know it very well."

Major Kenney and Cory Band c. 1970

That was in September 1970 Graham Sheppard, the long serving BBb bass player with the Band remembers the sequence of events in detail. Just two weeks prior to the contest, the entire Band was apprehensive as they awaited the arrival of the Major to start his first rehearsal. He arrived and with the minimum of fuss worked his way steadily through the four movement test piece, his eyes being riveted to the score. As the players subsequently learned, this was so uncharacteristic of him because he conducted most of his contest performances from memory. It was sometime later that the Band realised that he had been sight-reading the score, which at the time, had been completely unknown to him! Graham recalls that even when sight-reading, the Major's interpretive musical nuances and phrasing were immediately intuitive and remained constant even to the contest performances. Such was the outstanding musicianship of the man chosen to change the fortunes of the Band in such a radical and convincing manner.

Indeed his musical pedigree was most impressive. Major Horatio Arthur Kenney was born in 1919 at Iver, Buckinghamshire, and was educated at Wells Cathedral School where he was a chorister from 1925 to 1934. He enlisted into the Somerset Light Infantry as a band boy on 15th June 1934 playing the trombone, and served as an infantryman during the war, the Band having disbanded. He transferred to the King's Own Yorkshire Light Infantry in April 1945. He entered Kneller Hall as a student in 1945 and at the end of the course in 1947 was awarded the Worshipful Company of Musician's Medal for the most outstanding student in his class. He also gained the Director's Prize for Conducting and the Commandant's Prize for composing the best march. On 22nd September 1949, he was appointed Bandmaster of 1st Battalion the Oxfordshire and Buckinghamshire Light Infantry. He was commissioned as a Lieutenant on 6th April 1960, as Director of Music of the Royal Artillery (Plymouth) Band, transferring to the 'Alamein'

Major H.A. Kenney

Staff Band on 23rd April 1961. On 22nd May 1962 he was appointed Director of Music, to the Band of the Welsh Guards. He was promoted to Captain on 10th August 1962 and Major on 10th June 1968. In July 1969, this Band played a prominent part in the celebrations connected with the Investiture of Prince Charles as Prince of Wales. This was one of the last of Major Kenney's official engagements, for he resigned his commission in October of that year in order to devote more time to his burgeoning interests in civilian music. Mr. Dackins had indeed secured an

Major Kenney meets the Queen Mother

eminent and influential musician. Major Kenney's impact was immediate. The Band took first prize after only two weeks rehearsal!

Brass banding has an uncanny knack of bringing players down to earth with a bump. After the euphoria of winning at Blackpool, the very next contest in the locality was at the village of Upper Cwmtwrch in the Swansea Valley. The Band was placed second and left licking their painful wounds. The very first Granada Band of the Year contest was held in 1971 in the King's Hall, Belle Vue Gardens, Manchester, the traditional venue for the British 'Open' Championships. Initially, Cory were not included in the 'top ten' line-up of bands taking part in this event. However, both Black Dyke and G.U.S. (Footwear) - Bands' both withdrew from the contest. The latter had withdrawn well in advance of the contest, but Black Dyke withdrew just two weeks before the event took place, resulting in the Cory Band being invited to the event as an 'eleventh hour' replacement. Ron Massey, reporting for the British Bandsman magazine said, "Arthur Kenney had everything ready for the programme and they went on stage and won it. That was the beginning of the rise of the mighty Cory Band."

Major Kenney in the 1970's

Major Kenney conducting Cory 1971

The programme the Major had chosen was:

> *Trumpets Wild* (Walters), *Polly Wolly Doodling* (arr. F. Bryce), , *Moonriver* (Mancini), *Relaxation* from *Salute to Youth*, (Vinter), *Bombastic Bombardon* (Siebert, played by Huw Williams) and *March Paraphrase: Men of Harlech* (E. German),.

In April that year, Cory Band qualified for the Finals of the B.B.C. Band of the Year competition, playing against fellow finalists Ransome Hoffman Pollard (R.H.P.) Band from the East Midlands. The music for this programme was a little more substantial, the final piece being Gilbert Vinter's James Cook *"Circumnavigator"*. A return to Blackpool later in the year to attend the National Mineworkers (C.I.S.W.O.) Championship contest resulted in the Band being awarded first prize for the second successive year playing G. Vinter's *Entertainments*.

In 1972 the signing of Jim Davies as the Band's new Principal Cornet was a significant event for the Band. Jim had joined Cory from the Mid Rhondda Band just in time to play at the British 'Open' Championship, where the test piece was Jack Beaver's *Sovereign Heritage*. The Band were placed a creditable third. Jim Davies remained with the Band until the mid 1980's, leading the Band with considerable distinction and aplomb, carving a reputation for himself as one of the finest cornet players of his generation. Having secured a podium position in 1972 at the British 'Open' Championship, the Band were again brought down to earth with a bump at the next local contest held at Ebbw Vale, where the Band were not amongst the prize winners. Graham Sheppard described the inconsistent results, but not the quality of the performances as, "a highly emotional roller coaster ride." After the disappointment of Ebbw Vale, another creditable fifth place was achieved at the National Championship Finals held at the Royal Albert Hall, London, playing Eric Ball's *Kensington Concerto*. This result put the Band in buoyant mood for their assault on a hat-trick of wins at the National Mineworker's (CISWO) - Championship Finals held at Blackpool. The Band were not disappointed, winning the contest playing the test piece *Judges of the Secret Court* – Berlioz. This gave them the hat-trick they all so badly wanted and deservedly so.

1973 was uneventful and disappointing in terms of contest results. Cory only managed tenth (10th) place at the British 'Open' Championship contest and eleventh at the National Championship Finals in London in October. Earlier in the year at the Annual Welsh Regional Championships, the Band were adjudged runners-up, by adjudicator Major James Howe of the Scots Guards, to a convincing four point winning margin performance by newcomers to the Championship Section – Rogerstone, conducted by C. Brian Buckley.

Jeff Thomas, (flugel horn soloist from 1969 – 2000) remembers the British 'Open' Championship performance of Cesar Frank's - *Accursed Huntsman* as being absolutely superb. "The work begins with the horns playing a hunting call fanfare with Cory using special mutes to produce a pure and unique sound, mimicking the original orchestral timbre of French Horns. It was both atmospheric and magical." The bitter disappointment of the result was even harder to bear, when Elgar Howarth, the celebrated conductor of the Grimethorpe Colliery Band turned to both Jeff and Gwyn Thomas (no relation) and said "It's yours today." Unfortunately, the adjudicators held a different opinion, placing Grimethorpe Colliery in second place with Black Dyke the winners.

The following year (1974) also started inauspiciously, with the Band failing to obtain a placing at the local Ebbw Vale Contest on 9th March being beaten by near neighbours, the Lewis Merthyr Band by five points! Nevertheless just three weeks later, Cory Band won the Annual Welsh Regional Championship contest in fine style. The test-piece was Gilbert Vinter's *Variations on a Ninth* and with Arthur Kenney casting his magical spell, the Band won by seven clear points, being awarded 192 points from adjudicator Walter B. Hargreaves. Tredegar were in second place with Mid-Rhondda third. Cory had again booked their place in the National Championships to be held at the Royal Albert Hall, in the Autumn. Later that year, they also improved their British 'Open' Championship contest form of recent years by gaining fifth place playing Gilbert Vinters *James Cook Circumnavigator*. A few weeks later they made history by winning the National Finals of Great Britain *playing* the test piece - Malcolm Arnold's *Fantasy for Brass Band.* Cory Band played a magnificent performance that gave the Band first prize for the very first time at this most prestigious contest and also for

Cory Band autographs 1974

the very first time in the contest's history, the title of National Champion Band went outside the boundaries of England. The adjudicators were Eric Bravington, Joseph Horovitz and Ernest Tomlinson. They awarded Cory first prize with 192 points, Grimethorpe Colliery were second with 190 points and Black Dyke third with 189 points. A clear winning margin! Jeff Thomas clearly recalls being taken aside by the Major the night before the contest who said, "Jeff, if you play the way I know you can play, you can make a name for yourself in the brass band world". Jeff played superbly, as did all the Cory soloists: It wasn't until after the contest that Jeff learned that the Major had said the same thing to all the players. John Prosser (Eb Bass), although not playing with Cory at that time can remember the 1974 win quite clearly. "I was still playing for my town band at Blaina and can remember listening to the results on the radio late on Saturday evening. I heard "Cory awarded first prize and I started jumping up and down and cheering (by myself) - How daft was that?"

Graham Sheppard succinctly summed up what the Major had brought to the Band. "Even though Cory were not competing on a level playing field with their heavily sponsored English rivals, the Major gave his players self-belief and absolute confidence in both his and their own ability to succeed. He was a great conductor and a truly effective motivator!"

After winning the National Championship in 1974, several of the players vividly remember that celebrations couldn't start straight away because the Cory Band was involved in the evening Gala Concert. The massed bands at the Royal Albert Hall, London on that occasion were Black Dyke, Brighouse and Rastrick, City of Coventry and Cory. Maurice Murphy was the guest cornet soloist playing the first performance of the *Cornet Concerto* by Ernest Tomlinson. The newly formed James Shepherd Versatile Brass also took part. The guest conductor was Sir Charles Groves

Frontpage British Bandsman 1974

Cory Band National, Champions 1974

and the compere, the B.B.C. presenter par excellence John Dunn. Graham Sheppard remembers it was a great experience, but he was pleased when the concert ended, so that he and the rest of the Band could celebrate their historic win in traditional style after arriving back at their London hotel.

There was unprecedented local press coverage of Cory's win. The Western Mail daily newspaper featured a full page spread of the Band's significant achievement. As far as they were concerned it was a double win for Wales, because during the same weekend, Tredegar Junior Band had won the youth section at the same venue with fresh faced seventeen year old 'Bob' Childs playing solo euphonium with them. Nevertheless, the main focus was obviously on Cory Band. The Secretary of the South Wales Brass Band Association, Mr. Tom Jones was overjoyed, commenting, "This is the best ever result achieved by a Welsh band and it is not only an honour for Cory, but for the whole of Wales. This is comparable to winning the World Championship because British bands have the reputation of being the best in the World." Mr Gwyn Dackins, Vice President and the long serving Treasurer of Cory Band said the result was, "the greatest!" He added, "We have been trying to lift this title since the Band gained Championship status in 1924. We were close in 1948 gaining second place and third place three years ago but at last we've won it." What a triumph!

Even with the euphoria of winning the National Championships at London, the year was not over, as the National Mineworkers (C.I.S.W.O.) Final in Blackpool was the final competitive event in the Band's 1974 calendar. Gilbert Vinter's - *Spectrum* had been chosen as the test piece. The Band were runners up, so after the contest it was honours even between Cory and the winners of the contest, their close rivals, the Grimethorpe Colliery Band. What a wonderful way to end a year which broke the mould of English domination forever.

Outside the Royal Albert Hall 1974

After the 1974 National Championship win, the Cory Band's engagement diary became very full and they were guest artists at many concerts and charitable events. A typical example was at the Festival Theatre in Paignton on 19th April 1975. The concert was organised by the South West Brass Band Association in aid of charity. The compere for the evening was Mr. Phillip Hunt and Cory's programme included Arthur Kenney's *Big C March,* Elgar's *Cockaigne,* Vinter's *John O Gaunt* and of course the winning test piece Malcolm Arnold's *Fantasy for Brass Band.* Featured soloists were Jim Davies (cornet), Don Tanner (trombone) and Huw Williams (bass) who played the 1st movement of Vaughan Williams's *Concerto for Tuba.* Other solo contributions were given by trombonists Terry Lambert, Gareth Key and Norman John in a bright rhythmic number called *Half Cut in ¾* and a cornet quartet called the *Four Caballeros* played by Paul Hedditch, Stewart Lewis, Stanley Williams and Alun Jones. The concert closed with Walters' *Hootenanny* as the ever popular grand finale.

The prize money for winning the 1974 National Championship was £500. In addition to this, the winning band were invited to record a Long Playing Record on the Decca label. The recording took place in November 1974 at Swansea's Brangwyn Hall. The centre piece of the recording was Malcolm Arnold's *Fantasy for Brass Band* Opus 114. Other items included on the recording were:
  Cotswold Lullaby (Hughes), *Carambina* (Mozart, arr Siebert),
  Allegro Preciso, (E Hughes) *Waltz with a Beat* (Hanmer),
  Hootenanny, (Walters) Marriage of Figaro (Mozart),
  Believe Me If all Those Endearing Young Charms (arr Langford),
  Slavonic Dance No. 3 (Dvorak) and *Latin Americanna* (Walters),

Peter Wilson then the long serving Editor of the British Bandsman magazine wrote the sleeve notes and his opening statement reads, "Saturday, 5th October, 1974 will go down in brass band history as the day the National Championship title was captured from the English for the first time since the competition began in 1900." He described the day and all its drama, "From the early hours of that autumn morning the great gathering of dedicated brass band enthusiasts, packed into every available corner of London's Royal Albert Hall, had been engrossed in what was to become one of the most intriguing contests in memory. All the essential ingredients for a 'cliff-hanger' were present: an exciting test-piece, written specially for the occasion by Malcolm Arnold – surely one of the most extrovert of composers. A dramatic 'draw' (that nerve-wracking traditional procedure to determine the order of play, which never fails to produce waves of excitement or gloom, depending on one's allegiance, at the very start of the day), had placed illustrious names like Cory, Grimethorpe, Black Dyke Mills and G.U.S. (Footwear) in a tight cluster right at the climax of the contest: and a distinguished panel of adjudicators, hidden from view in their eyrie-like enclosure in the grand tier level of the auditorium.

Would Brighouse and Rastrick (the defending Champion Band) hold on to the title, just as they did in 1969 after having won the previous year, or would the challenge of oft-times champions like Black Dyke Mills and G.U.S. (Footwear) or the panache of Grimethorpe Colliery – a band which had recently made national news by its unexpected flirtation with avant-garde composers-prove too strong? These were the questions being discussed in the corridors, bars and boxes, as animated supporters hurriedly swapped notes between performances.

But as the day wore on, the name of Cory Band was on everyone's lips. Playing from the number fifteen spot in a field of nineteen bands, this valiant group of musicians from Ton Pentre, deep in the heart of the Rhondda Valley, had responded to the magnificence of the occasion to deliver the performance of their lives; one which, by virtue of the confirmation of the adjudicators later in the day, has now become immortal.

The shriek of delight which greeted the announcement that Cory Band had taken the title (and with it a £500 cash prize and the contract to record for Decca) might have been heard throughout the Rhondda. Its echoes certainly reached the hearts of Welshmen everywhere, and resound to this day in the Bandrooms and homes of the Valley and beyond. At last England's stranglehold on the brass band world's most sought-after prize had been broken; a new name inscribed on the Trophy, bringing with it fresh hope to many bands for whom the ultimate prize has proved elusive. The contest scene had been given an injection of vitality and encouragement, and bandsmen everywhere applauded. The title 'Champion Band of Great Britain' sits comfortably on the shoulders of Cory Band.'

Names of the players who played in the winning champion band of 1974 are listed in Appendix C

By stark contrast the 1975 contest season was memorable, but for the wrong reasons. Elgar Howarth's *Fireworks* had been chosen as the test for the British 'Open' Championship and again the Major produced a performance of great stature and musical intellect that was awarded fourth place. However, the only recall the players have about the performance was the bass drum falling noisily out of its cradle and bouncing on the floor. After rolling through the Band it finally came to rest near the front row of the audience. What a traumatic experience! Dr Roy Newsome was one of the adjudicators that day and he clearly remembers the disturbance during the performance. "Elgar Howarth's *Fireworks* required about half a train-load of percussion instruments. I was seated behind the famous red velvet curtains, along with co-adjudicators Bill Relton and 'Gary' Howarth himself. One performance was going extremely well when something untoward happened. We knew not what, but for a few bars the performance rocked badly, and what might have developed into a winning performance ended up in fourth place. As adjudicators, we'd no idea what had happened, or, for that matter, which band was playing. It turned out that it was Cory, playing under Major Kenney, and that the bass drum had fallen from its cradle and created havoc amongst the bass end – or so we were told. That was rotten luck!

Un vie de Matelot by Robert Farnon was chosen as the test-piece for the National Championship Finals in the Royal Albert Hall, London, but unfortunately for the Band they had also been invited to play in the massed bands' Gala Concert held in the evening. Under normal circumstances this would have been a great honour, but the invitation seriously prejudiced the contest preparations. Graham Sheppard explains, "Gareth Wood had been commissioned to write the main work for the Gala Concert, it was called *Tombstone Arizona,* the Major had a tendency to love or hate music, and he immediately fell in love with *Tombstone Arizona,* consequently, Cory were the only Band in the Gala Concert to play the work properly. However the time and meticulous preparation allotted to rehearsing *Tombstone Arizona* clearly had a detrimental effect on the preparation of the contest piece" In addition to learning Gareth Wood's new work, Cory Band also accompanied Don Lusher in the World Premiere of Gordon Langford's *Rhapsody for Trombone*. Other major items on the same programme were: *Trojan March* – Berlioz, *Symphonic Prelude Prometheus Unbound* – Bantok, *Prelude to Hansel and Gretel* – Humperdinck and the first performance of Robert Farnon's *Colditz March* arranged by Gordon Langford. Cory were placed a disappointing tenth on Robert Farnon's *Un vie de Matelot*.

Although remembered primarily for his success as a magnificent conductor, Major Kenney was also a very talented composer. Marches such as *The Big "C"* and *St. Julians* are still being performed today. His arrangements of Berlioz's *March to the Scaffold* and the theme from the film *Rocky* all possess the hallmark of a thoughtful and learned musician of the highest order. Arguably, his best solo composition is *Concertino for Tenor Horn*. This was first performed in 1975 by John Bowen (principal horn) at the National Museum of Wales' Reardon Smith Theatre, Cardiff. John Bowen was in good company that evening because he shared the soloists' podium with Harold Nash, the long serving Principal Trombone of the Covent Garden Opera House Orchestra and Trevor Groom, the famous Principal Euphonium of the G.U.S. Footwear Band, Kettering. John was due to record *Concertino* for the BBC Bandstand programme a few weeks later at Llandaff Studios, Cardiff. However, John resigned from the Band just prior to the recording. With very short notice, the renowned horn soloist Gordon Higginbottom stepped in and performed the work in admirable style.

Through circumstances beyond Major Kenney's control, his tenure as Musical Director of Cory Band ended in 1975. Jeff Thomas has fond memories of the Major and praises his fantastic musicianship and his musical memory as well as his ability to pinpoint with amazing accuracy any musical problems within the Band. He recalls a lighter moment during a performance. "During the early days with the Major there was a very loud player in the tenor horn section. During a concert one evening, the Major was trying to gain the player's attention. He raised his eyebrows and on several occasions lifted his left hand pushing his palm downwards in a musical gesture indicating to play softer. Unfortunately non-verbal communication was not getting through and finally, at the end of his tether, the Major said (at a dynamic level that the entire Band and most of the audience could hear), "Shut up!" In those days, the Cory Band were not sponsored, so finances were a scarce resource. Funding the purchase of instruments, replacing uniforms and raising money to attend contests at home and abroad was a constant challenge. The Ladies' Committee worked extremely hard and supported the Band by organising a wide range of fund raising events. The Band tried to minimize costs wherever they could. Jeff Thomas remembers Mrs Barbara Kenney contributing to money saving ideas. "She took it upon herself to make a full set of red velvet stage bow ties. To state that they were quite large was a gross understatement. The players felt they had arm rests under their chins, the bows impeding breathing, especially when playing solos!"

Jeff Thomas had always been a stand-up soloist in the Band and the many solos he played are mentioned elsewhere in this book. However, Jeff used to be reluctant to play solos under the baton of Major Kenney because of his tendency to hum along with the tune. Jeff said "Whenever I played a solo, I was always aware of the Major humming along with me, it was so disconcerting, I had to get as far away as possible." Vocal contributions were not solely assigned to the conductor, Graham Sheppard remembers a rehearsal where although only after-beats should have been played, the Major could hear something else disturbing the rhythmic pattern of the music. Through a process of elimination, the Major whittled the problem down to the trombones then discovering it was the 2nd trombonist and local miners union lodge official - Ivor England producing loud grunts obviously mimicking bass notes to aid his afterbeats.

Major Kenney and Cory Band in the 1980's

The Major was respected by all the players in the Band and they would have followed him to the end of the earth if asked to do so, his small stature meant that he always conducted the Band on a small circular podium and the players knew that this piece of equipment had priority. When loading the coach before travelling to concerts or contests more than one player would ask, "Has the Major's rostrum been loaded". One act of supreme dedication from the players was epitomised when the Band was appearing in Manchester and the Major discovered he had forgotten his stage trousers. He took great pride in his appearance and was always the height of sartorial elegance. John Bowen, the Band's principal horn player offered to drive the Major back to Newport, in South Wales to fetch them, the Major accepting John's generous and timely offer to maintain his immaculate sense of presence.

Occupying the podium as Musical Director of Cory Band from 1970-1975, Major H Arthur Kenney's crowning glory during this period was his elegant direction of the performance that enabled Cory to win the 1974 National Championships of Great Britain for the very first time in their history. However, in 1982, the "Major" returned to the Band for a further seven years as Musical Director. During this period, Cory consolidated their supremacy at the National Championships, winning the prestigious title of National Champions on three consecutive occasions.

Chapter 9 -"The Thrills and Spills of the Glorious Hat-Trick Years", recounts this feat in graphic detail.

Chapter 7

Cory Conquers America

One of the highlights of Cory's Band's illustrious history was its tour of America in 1976. Local newspaper, The Rhondda Leader, broke the news that Cory Band had accepted an invitation to embark on a concert tour of the United States. They cited the trip as the first time the prize-winning band, the pride of the Rhondda Valleys, had played outside Great Britain since their formation in 1884. For many of the players it would be the first time for them to fly in an aeroplane.

Ron Pryce of Pleasant View, Pentre and secretary of the Band at the time said, "We first received the invitation to go to America in February 1975 and it was confirmed in September the same year. I think we were invited because we won the UK National Championships in 1974. The British Council contributed towards the cost of the tour, but the Band still needed to buy uniforms at a cost of £50 each." Two different programmes of music were prepared for their individual concerts, with a third programme being prepared for a joint concert with the Grimethorpe Colliery Band that was being performed in Philadelphia.

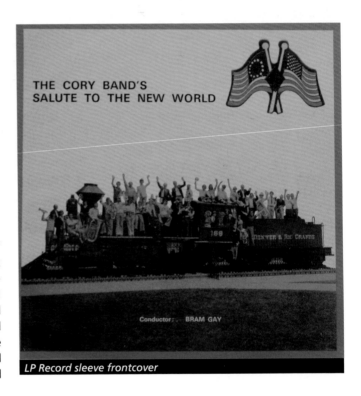

THE CORY BAND'S
SALUTE TO THE NEW WORLD

Conductor: BRAM GAY

LP Record sleeve frontcover

Cory flew to Washington on 26th June 1976. Their first concert was in front of two thousand distinguished guests in the foyer of the Kennedy Centre, before the audience were shown a Bicentennial film compiled by the American Revolutionary Bicentennial Administration. Jet lag was as tiring then as it is today, with John Trotman readily recalling that he suffered more than most. "I can only vaguely remember the concert; I nodded off during one or two of the slow quiet items." The following day the Band flew to St. Louis where they played two concerts; an afternoon concert on the riverfront and an evening concert in the Crest Mall. The Band commenced their programme with the Welsh National Anthem, the musicians being surprised that a substantial number of the audience knew the words. Commenting on this quite surreal experience, several of the Band said, "It was like being at a Wales International Rugby match at Cardiff Arms Park, except that we were half-way round the World." Both the St. Louis concerts and several others during the tour were sponsored by Peabody Coal Company. The following day, Cory were guests of honour at a brunch hosted by the Missouri Athletic Club. They were busy during the afternoon and the evening performing at concerts. Bram Gay conducted the Cory Band on the first leg of the tour with Dr. Roy Newsome conducting the Band on the final leg. Grimethorpe Colliery Band, conducted by Elgar Howarth also took part in the celebrations and it was planned that both Bands would combine together to present a joint concert in Philadelphia. Grimethorpe's tour was for three weeks, with Cory's tour lasting for just two weeks.

On the 30th June, Cory Band flew to Denver for several concerts, the first of which was held in the City Centre Opera House. The next day the Band played fanfares to open the National Coal Association's Annual Convention in the afternoon. This was followed by an evening concert that was part of the Convention's programme of cultural events. The Denver leg of the tour was jointly sponsored by Colorado Council of the Arts, the

Bram Gay conducts Cory in USA

National Coal Association and the Pittsburgh and Medway Coal Company. Conductor for this stage of the tour, Bram Gay, remembers that the tour was a great adventure, if not always musically satisfying. He recalls one concert in Colorado Springs where the Band was scheduled to play in an ice arena. "When we arrived it wasn't an ice rink but a roller skating arena. The noise from everyone skating made the concert impossible. We treated it as a rehearsal, but like true professionals in show business the show went on."

Nevertheless, Bram Gay recognised some compensation by having a magnificent Band photograph taken, "We stood, sat on, or climbed over the first locomotive that had ever crossed the Rockies. The poor thing had then blown up. As it had been found impossible to move it, they moved the rail station instead, leaving the train marooned in a field which had become part of a park."

On 3rd July, the Band flew from Denver to New York giving a concert in Greenwich Village. Whilst the Band was in New York, they also gave a concert in Trinity Church, Wall Street. Prior to Cory embarking on their U.S. tour they had been programming a superb arrangement of *Miller Magic* by Denzil Stephens. Several of the players wanted to feature this in their New York concert programme. Bram Gay had been advised by Elgar Howarth not to play it because the American audiences knew it so well and in the latter's words, "It would be like taking coal to Newcastle!" Nevertheless, at the end of a very successful concert in New York, the Band received a standing ovation from the crowd, so needed a suitable encore. Bram decided to perform *Miller Magic*, it was received with equal enthusiasm, another standing ovation ensuing. Bram Gay remembers that after the concert, a man walked towards him and began analysing Cory's performance, stating that he had been to a live Glenn Miller concert. Bram reflected on Elgar's Howarth's earlier advice and thought the man was going to criticise the performance. He was most pleasantly surprised when the man said excitedly. "*Miller Magic* was great! I'm sure Glenn Miller would have been proud of that performance."

Cory Band in America

From New York the Band flew to Philadelphia to give a joint concert with Grimethorpe Colliery Band in the Museum of Art. This was also where Cory met Dr. Roy Newsome who took over the conducting duties from Bram Gay. Bram's 'day-job' was at the Royal Opera House, Covent Garden, and whilst he directed the Band during the first week of its tour, it seems that this centre of operatic excellence couldn't survive without him for two whole weeks! Roy Newsome remembers the phone call he had from Bram Gay inviting him to join the tour, "One evening early in 1976, he rang to ask if I'd like to go to America to conduct the Cory Band during the second half of their American tour in connection with the Bicentennial Celebrations – the 200th anniversary of we 'Brits' being kicked out of America following the infamous Boston Tea-Party. It took me about a tenth of a second to decide that I'd accept the job, and plans were put in hand for me to join the Band in Philadelphia for the second leg of the tour. Both the Cory and Grimethorpe Colliery Bands had been invited as representatives of the British mining

A welcome 'American style' to Cory Band

community, to give a series of concerts under the auspices of the American mining unions. Roy's first day with the Band was unusual to say the least. "The Bands, both of whom had been touring separately, came together on the Monday of the second week for a joint concert in Philadelphia, conducted by Elgar Howarth. This was to be a quite serious affair, as the British Council were heavily involved in funding the tour. It was a scorchingly hot day and I went with the two bands to a school just outside the city centre where Howarth grilled them for almost two hours. We then went along to the steps in front of the main City Library, only to be told that chairs couldn't be provided for the Bands due to a strike by some municipal workers, consequently the concert had been cancelled. This wasn't funny! The players were now bathed in perspiration and not at all pleased that they'd had this heavy rehearsal for nothing. When Howarth found out that the tour organiser had known about the cancellation but just forgot to mention it, the atmosphere really intensified!

Jeff Thomas has his personal suspicions as to why they did the rehearsal, "The flugel horn player from Grimethorpe was my idol, his name was Malcolm Holmes (Tadge). During the rehearsal every time there was a flugel horn solo, Tadge sat with his instrument on his knee with Mr. Howarth asking me to play the solo. When both bands returned home from America, I received a phone call asking me to join Grimethorpe Colliery Band. I'm convinced that the rehearsal was my audition. I often wonder what might have been had I accepted their offer, but I have no regrets." John Trotman and Ron Pryce were both disappointed that the concert was cancelled, but every cloud has a silver lining and the cancellation meant that they were able to visit Ron's uncle Arthur who lived in Philadelphia!

From left to right; Roy Roberts (euph), Gwyn Thomas (sop), George Davies (euph)

Elgar Howarth had arranged several pieces for Grimethorpe Band for this tour and a quite modern setting of *The Bells of Aberdovey* for the Cory Band. He had also arranged a special piece for the Philadelphia concert called *Hunt the Hare*. It represented both the Cory and Grimethorpe Bands in as much as it was bi-tonal and combined a Welsh and English folk song.

Alabama's present to the Band

Roy Newsome said that after the problems in Philadelphia, the rest of the tour went to plan, "We travelled southwards about 250 miles each day, the temperature becoming hotter and hotter. Fortunately, the Greyhound Coach we travelled on and all the concert halls were air-conditioned. The following four days saw the Band performing concerts in Indiana, Charleston, Knoxville, Birmingham and Jasper before returning to Wales on 12th July. The final two concerts of the tour were in Alabama. On Friday in Birmingham, with the Saturday concert in nearby Jasper. By now the players were all pretty well exhausted, having travelled thousands of miles and given many concerts. On our arrival in Jasper, we were given a luscious lunch provided by the English Society and then, as we were all supposed to be connected with the coal mining industry, we had to sit on the floor and watch a film about open cast coal mining – not exactly ideal entertainment for an early Saturday afternoon. That wasn't all. We were then taken on a tour of the city. The Welsh humour was never far away though. One of the ladies in charge asked a cornet player if everyone was on the coach. 'Yes', came the prompt reply. The lady was quite impressed and asked how he knew; 'You just count the eyes and divide by two' came the answer."

The tour party comprised of thirty seven people this number included some of the Band members' wives. The Cory Band frequently featured vocal soloists on concerts so they had invited mezzo-soprano-Miss Elaine Hewitt as a guest soloist to accompany them on the tour. John Trotman remembers, "like many of the top bands of the time there were no women in the Cory Band, so women weren't allowed on the Band coach. This rule

A police escort after the coach broke down!

applied to the American Tour as well. Consequently, Ron Pryce and I hired two cars and we chauffeured the ladies throughout the whole tour, driving several thousand miles! Having a car available was fortuitous when the coach transporting the Band to Jasper failed to operate. A policeman borrowed my hire car to fetch a mechanic to fix the coach. Once the fault was repaired, Ron and myself had a police motorcycle escort to our next hotel.

This is the repertoire of programme music played by the Band during this historic tour:
The Star Spangled Banner – Sousa,
Pavane – John Bull, arranged Howarth,
Prometheus Unbound – Bantock,
Sinfonietta – Horovitz,
The Severn Suite – Elgar,
Spectrum – Vinter,
Suite Gothique – Boellman,
Fantasy for Brass Arnold,
Moorside Suite – Holst,
Fugue from Fireworks – Howarth,
The Liberty Bell – Sousa,
Overture to Iolanthe – Sullivan,
Stephen Foster Fantasy – arranged Hanmer,
The Last Spring – Grieg,

Second Slavonic Rhapsody – Friedmann,
Pel Mel – Howarth
Grand March from Tannhauser – Wagner,
Men of Harlech – German.
David of the White Rock – Welsh Traditional,
Miller Magic – arranged Stephens,

The Band also prepared another full programme for the cancelled Philadelphia concert and solos were performed by players in the Band. A representative selection of Welsh songs were sung by Elaine Hewitt.

The Cory Band had many glowing reviews of their concerts during the tour of which the following article is typical. Written by Jo Ziegler it featured in the Daily Mountain Eagle Newspaper, Jasper, Alabama on Monday 12th July 1976.

THE CORY BAND - It came, it saw, it conquered.
The British came to Jasper Saturday in the form of Cory Brass Band which appeared in concert at Municipal Auditorium at 7:30 p.m. They came, they saw and they conquered us in the nicest way possible! The concert climaxed a day of international friendship and warmth which will long be remembered here. In addition to being made up of thoroughly charming individuals, the Cory Brass Band is an aggregation of vastly talented musicians. With their rare musicianship, showmanship and jovial personalities, they captured and held our imaginations, our ears and our hearts. We responded with a volley of thunderous applause after each selection, along with three standing ovations. The Band moved with ease from John Phillip Sousa's rousing marches to the incomparable velvety Glenn Miller sound, a nostalgically beautiful Stephen. Foster Fantasy and Friedman's Second Slavonic Rhapsody. Among other selections were lilting Welsh melodies with Elaine Hewitt as soloist.

After the concert, Jasper Mayor Jack Moore Brown presented each band member with a certificate of honorary citizenship. An American Flag, an Alabama flag and a Bicentennial banner were presented to the group by Bicentennial chairman Clarence Farley. Tom Petzal, British Bicentennial Commission executive said, "We're absolutely shattered by the honours bestowed upon us. The hospitality which you have so graciously shown us has made us determined that the British are coming back!" Following the concert, The Drummond Company served as hosts at a reception for Cory Band members and members of their families who accompanied them. The reception provided an opportunity for townspeople to meet the Welshmen personally, and their sparkling personalities with ready wit and humour added still another dimension to the impact which the group made upon this community.

Progression of planned activities went as follows: Lunch at The Drummond Company after the Band's arrival from Birmingham by chartered bus; bus tour of downtown Jasper where visitors saw such points of interest as Walker College, Walker High School, new Carl Elliott Regional library, Walker County Courthouse and new annex under construction, First Methodist Church with its native marble construction, renovation of downtown Jasper after the tornado, and other local facilities; bus tour of area mining operations; dinner at the Holiday Inn after a cooling swim in the pool; concert at 7:30 p.m., at the Auditorium with over 900 in attendance; and reception at Drummond Coal Company. Earlier in the day, the weary visitors had arrived by bus from Birmingham where they had presented a concert on Friday night. In fact, they made 14 appearances during a 12-day period prior to their Jasper visit, playing concerts as far west as Colorado and in the East at New York, Philadelphia, Washington, D.C., and West Virginia.

After being served a light lunch at The Drummond Company, they were guests for a bus tour of mining operations in the Carbon Hill area. Only a few of the Welshman had seen open mining operations, and they were particularly interested in the vastness of our territory and in the amounts of coal which are obtained locally. Frank Cobb of Cobb Mining Company pointed out the productive reclamations which have been accomplished where strip mining has been completed, and he outlined the benefits which are derived. For example, according to Cobb, Southern pine for timber purposes grows 30 percent faster on soil which has been aerated in the reclamation process. During the afternoon trip, the conversation inevitably turned to the differences between Welsh cookery and Southern cuisine. Never having seen grits, the four wives who accompanied their husbands on the trip asked about a "white sauce" which they'd been served at each breakfast in the South. We asked about the most common foods in their homeland; and they listed kidney pie, rabbit, lamb and beef, and ever-present British fish and chips and lava bread which is made from seaweed. Religious faiths represented among the group included Church of England, Methodist, Baptist, Roman Catholic and Salvation Army.... which, in Wales, is considered as a denomination rather than an organization as it is in the States. Even though the Welshmen did not complain about the intense heat, they were obviously unaccustomed to the temperatures which prevail in the South at this time of the year. One of the Welsh ladies, though, came prepared with a small battery-operated fan which she used and shared when the group stepped off the air-conditioned bus.

At the reception, which was the Cory Band's last social event before their Sunday departure for Wales, each member was presented with a coal sculpture, a copy of the poster which announced the Jasper concert and a Chamber of Commerce booklet which pictures and describes points of interest in the Walker County area.

The tour, a Bicentennial gift to the United States from its mother country, was sponsored locally by The Drummond Company, Brilliant Coal Company, Alabama By-Products and Alabama Surface Mining Reclamation Council with the cooperation of Jasper Bicentennial Commission and Jasper Area Chamber of Commerce. Before the festive day ended, each visitor expressed the determination to return next June, if possible, when present plans call for another "people-to-people" project to be undertaken between Great Britain and the United States. Again and again, the visitors expressed profound appreciation for the many kindnesses which were extended to them; and they voiced the opinion that, since Southern hospitality has been demonstrated to them as a fact, they are looking forward to a return visit with us.

Two hundred years ago, the British came and saw and went home under unfortunate conditions in the aftermath of war. In this Bicentennial year of 1976, the British came and saw and liked us so much that they want to come back. After Saturday's delightful encounter, we go on record with the statement that they cannot possibly be so eager to return as we are to have them back again with us!

Chapter 8

Denzil Stephens' High Flying European Success!

When Major Arthur Kenney left the Band, Bram Gay accepted the mantle of Musical Director. He reflects on his time with the Band with bitter sweet memories. "I was invited to conduct Cory by the famous bass trombonist Haydn Trotman, the Band's President who was well known to us at Covent Garden (Opera Orchestra). He was known to the entire "London profession" as Dai. Obviously, the Band management were relying upon my affection for the Band and for the Rhondda Valleys to compensate for the hard fact that the Cory Band were in dire financial straits, simply relying on bingo sessions and weekly totes for funds. They could find no conducting fees at all and even struggled to find the railway fare to bring me from London to Pentre. I do not know how many truly amateur conductors remain in the Championship section, but in the financial sense, if hardly in the musical one, that is what I was for two years.

In a way the job was a poisoned chalice. Everyone expected great things from Cory following the win in 1974 at the National Championships, but there had been very many changes of personnel in the intervening period.

Although I had no musical difficulties with the work in hand, I was short of the technical expertise of the previous occupant. Arthur Kenney was a truly great musician and ought to be remembered as one of the most accomplished conductors the Band world has ever had. I think my occasional ineptitude with the stick must have been a source of worry to the players in the Band.

I was also much too pressed for time to do the job the justice it deserved. The Band rehearsed three times a week. There were two weeknight practices, which involved two train journeys to Cardiff and two overnight sleepers back to attend my office the next day. The third rehearsal on Sunday meant a three hundred mile drive there and back to my home.

The Band was blessed with fine 'corner' men led by cornet supremo - Jim Davies. First-rate talent existed, from Eb soprano cornet to basses. Unfortunately some seats were filled more with enthusiasm than with talent. The enthusiasm was wonderful; I rarely saw an empty chair, which enabled me to live by Fred Mortimer's dictum that if the rehearsal wasn't full I should go home immediately.

Contesting for me was a matter of beating the Tredegar Band at the Regionals, but I never did. John Childs was too hot a proposition for me during my two years tenure with the Band. Oddly, we always did better than most at the National Championships, collecting respectable places with *Connotations* (Gregson) and *The Wayfarer* (Eric Ball)."

Bram also cites the historic American tour as another contributor to the Band's declining contest results. "Unfortunately after the tour we lost even more players. It is a fact of life that when a band after many years of struggle reaches the height of its ambition as Cory had with Arthur, valuable old soldiers tend to retire satisfied with their achievements. The tour naturally added to that factor. The losses certainly didn't help me in my quest to win contests!" Bram Gay resigned his position as Musical Director in 1978. That same year Sq. Leader Denzil Stephens resigned from the RAF Music Services, initially moving to South Elmsall in Yorkshire to conduct the famous Carlton Main Frickley Colliery Band.

Cory Band 1979, conductor Denzil Stephens

After achieving significant success in a relatively short space of time, Denzil left 'Frickley' because their Band committee decided to engage another conductor for the National Championships at the Royal Albert Hall London later that same year. However, the 'brass band jungle drums' transmitted this hot news very quickly, and Cory Band's secretary, Ron Pryce, telephoned him to see if he was interested in conducting them. Agreeing to be Cory Band's new MD, Denzil wondered if it might turn out to be a repeat of the experience he had just had with the 'Frickley' Band.

Cory Band had not won the Welsh Regional Championship contest for a few years, and were anxious to improve upon their record. Denzil wasn't sure whether or not the Band consisted solely of mine workers (like 'Frickley' Band), because he'd read somewhere that they were called the Cory Workmen's Band, so he was a little surprised to find sat around the stand a Band of players from many different walks of life. He responded to the task in hand, rehearsing the Band very intensely and getting the sections to play various parts of the music, to check sound and balance, listening to all individuals, not just the soloists, but back row players too! It didn't take him long to realise that the Band consisted of players of varying ability, talent, age and experience.

Denzil Stephens

The committee wanted to know what he thought of the Band, and he told them it would require a lot of work to raise them to the highest standard. In fact, he told them it might take twelve to eighteen months before they could be considered serious contenders to win the Welsh Regional Championships. Denzil didn't believe in sacking players. He was prepared to train and improve the Band as a team using the players available to him, provided they were all prepared to work hard at rehearsal, and practice their parts diligently at home.

Denzil strongly believed in making maximum use of the two hours rehearsal time. He tried not to waste time talking, except to explain points of technique, or to sing parts to players. He rehearsed the Band for two hours without a break, probably because as a player himself, he used to get frustrated at the time wasted between playing pieces, sections of pieces and the largely unnecessary tea break in mid rehearsal.

Several of the Cory Band players commented that Denzil was a hard task master. Hard or not, the Band improved in both tone and ensemble. They began playing together as a team and soon became used to his style of conducting.

At that time Cory Band's concert programmes were quite traditional, Denzil recollects "Concerts consisted of standard marches, overtures, waltzes, solos etc. I started to introduce some of my own arrangements, and because I found the Band's reading ability to be rather poor, I kept changing the programmes as often as I dared to improve their sight-reading. This paid dividends over time, and it meant that instead of the players using all their concentration on reading their parts, they could relax and learn to play the music with feeling and understanding. I had experienced so many bands that played their music mechanistically with machine like qualities often playing with a hard sound, so I vowed to try to encourage the Cory Band to play music with a good sound, and to make the notes mean something, depending on the style of music being performed.

BBC Wales produced mini entertainment contests with knock-out rounds, and Denzil persuaded the Cory Band to enter them. He designed the short programmes based on the experience he had gained at the RAF College, Cranwell, ten years earlier.

Under such strong effective leadership, the Cory Band sailed through the opening rounds of the BBC Radio Wales competitions with ease, and they were BBC Radio Wales Champions on several occasions.

By now, the Band had got used to Denzil compiling adventurous concert programmes, not always without question, but it was obvious the players had great confidence in him, respecting his musicianship.

All this was effective preparation for the Granada Band of the Year Entertainment Contests, in which the Band did very well against Britain's finest bands.

One of the early Granada events took place at the former Belle Vue venue, Manchester, with the competing bands playing in the centre of the arena. Denzil readily recalls asking the Cory Band to play the Sousa March - *Semper Fidelis,* with two snare drums playing the middle drum section, the entire band being required to stand up and systematically turn in 90 degree segments so that the Band faced all the sections of the audience in turn. This was the emergence of more effective presentation at such events with Denzil trying to do something different with the Cory Band. He often featured his own new arrangements of music by Glen Miller, Dmitri Shostakovitch, Leonard Bernstein and other composers.

Denzil Stephens' output of compositions and arrangements was prolific. He created a new repertoire for Cory, much of his music being performed exclusively by them.

Ron Pryce and Denzil Stephens

There were other contests such as the Yeovil Entertainment event where the Band collected a hat trick of wins. Pontins' Brass Band Festival brought yet more successes, and several traditional contests such as the local Welsh Brass Band Association contests, where the Band became almost unbeatable.

Graham Sheppard was the Band's BB^b bass player at the time and recalled that the prolific success enjoyed by the Band wasn't always appreciated by their rivals. "We were sometimes called pot-hunters by other bands we beat, quite regularly, but it didn't bother us. We were a close-knit bunch of lads, not big headed in any way. We worked hard at improving our playing and there was always a great atmosphere in the Band. Rehearsals were intensive but enjoyable and we knew we had to work our socks off to match and then win against the best bands in England. There were no stars inside the Band, just plenty of good honest blokes who enjoyed each other's company and appreciated each other's talents."

Nevertheless, there was one notable exception to Graham's statement, namely Principal Cornet - Jim Davies, who was a star player! He remembers the time well. "I came to the Band in 1972 and over the years we had a fantastic camaraderie as well as excellent financial

Harry Mortimer CBE conducts Cory   *Cory wins Pontins, 1979*

support from our hardworking Ladies' Committee who organised events and raised money for the Band. Denzil Stephens came to the Band and immediately made an impact. He was just what the Band needed at the time, being a totally different conductor and band trainer to Major Kenney".

Denzil conducting at the Royal Albert Hall

Denzil recalls that "National success did not come easily", but added, "the Cory Band always gave good performances at both the National Championships, London and the British "Open" Championship contests. It was gratifying for the Band and me to eventually beat the famous and long established Black Dyke Band, by winning the European Championships in 1980 at the Royal Albert Hall playing *The Land of the White Cloud* (Sparke) and *Triumphant Rhapsody* (Vinter). The Cory Band had during that year, reached a great contesting standard, having won 11 out of 13 contests, including the Pontins' Brass Band Festival. The 1980 European win certainly made up for coming second to "Black Dyke" at the 1979 European Championships the previous year".

Cory had qualified for the 1980 European Championships by virtue of becoming Champion Band of Wales in 1979 when they won all six of the Welsh Brass Band Association's ranking contests. It was the first time that this remarkable feat had been accomplished. They finished five points clear of their nearest rival in the final contest and were presented with the crown at the Pontypridd Contest in December 1979.

The 1980 National qualification was a different story altogether as Cory upset many bandsfolk in the Principality by accepting an invitation to compete at the National Championships even though the Welsh Associations were in bitter dispute with the National Contest organisers. Cory won the Welsh Brass Band Association Contest held in Treorchy in the March by a massive six point margin and then headed for London even though every other band in Wales boycotted the contest. Not competing in the National Championships might well have compromised their chances of success in the European Championships, especially as both contests took place over the same weekend, in the same venue being sponsored by the same company, Boosey and Hawkes Ltd., the brass instrument suppliers.

DENZIL'S MOMENT OF GLORY

Denzil Stephens, of the Cory Band, receives the trophy at the end of the Winter Contest at Wembley, from Amanda Tinsley, a representative of Grand Metropolitan Hotels, who sponsored the contest. This was the second time in four months that the Welsh band had scooped a £1,000 prize. They won the Pontin's event last November.

Denzil winning more silverware

Quite possibly it was the controversy of accepting the National Championships invitation that spurred the players on to work even harder than usual. Jim Davies recalls that the Band felt thoroughly prepared for both contests: "Our own choice selection for the European Championships was Vinter's *Triumphant Rhapsody* and we also enjoyed working on the set work, *Land of the Long White Cloud* by Philip Sparke. In addition to these two major works we also had to prepare Geoffrey Brand's sparkling new arrangement of Dvorak's *Carnival Overture* for the Nationals too! There was plenty of hard work to do and I remember the Band increasing the frequency of rehearsals from two to three per week."

"Much of the preparation was down to the players and we always tried to improve standards amongst ourselves. We were a solid band, with no stars but plenty of great players who were just as solid and secure on stage as they were in the practice room! We didn't feel in awe of bands such as "Black Dyke", but we certainly respected them and even when players from the top bands asked us how things were going, we were honest, directly telling them that some parts of the piece were difficult. Something they never used to admit!"

The final preparation for the weekend went well until disaster struck on the Friday night before the contest, when one of the Bands' BB♭ tuba players - Selwyn Lewis suffered a heart attack. "That came as a shock to us all", said Graham Sheppard. "Thankfully, Selwyn made a full recovery, but that meant we had to secure a replacement at short notice for the European Championships. We actually played with just three basses on the Saturday at the National Championships performing the test piece *Carnival Overture*.

Cory were awarded sixth place at the National Championships on the Saturday, but the relative disappointment of this result was soon put behind them as they prepared for the European event the following day. Cory had a rehearsal in the Irish Guards Barracks early in the morning, whilst "Black Dyke" used the Welsh Guards Barracks just across the road from them. Jim Davies recalls, "We were happy with the ways things went."

The Band had drafted in Brian Davies on E♭ Bass, Brian stepping into the breach at short notice. He was a student studying in London. It all seemed to come together on the day, said Graham Sheppard who readily recalls "Jim Davies was the key, what a superb player he was on stage. He organised everything in the Band room and made sure nothing was left to chance. We had such confidence in him. He was never arrogant, but self-belief in his ability just flowed from him to the rest of the Band. He played quite astonishingly on both test pieces, especially the Vinter."

Jim Davies doesn't remember a great deal about the performances though. "We seemed happy enough. We had drawn number two on the set work and then number three in the afternoon on the own choice selection. It was a long day and "Black Dyke" had a great draw playing Eric Ball's *Journey Into Freedom* in the afternoon. However we had done enough to win it and that's all that mattered."

In fact, Cory had taken an all important lead on the set work in the morning, being placed ahead of the Swiss representatives by two points, with "Black Dyke" a further point behind.

In the afternoon, Black Dyke certainly turned up the heat, winning the own choice section by three clear points with Cory in second position to tie on the overall points awarded for both events. Cory's win in the morning – the compulsory set work, meant that the title headed to South Wales. At the time one of the judges wrote in his remarks on the set work "A quite brilliant performance and taken at such a remarkable pace."

We had a fantastic time celebrating, insists Graham. "We had a few drinks after the result and then, phoned our local, the Pentre Hotel to tell them that we would be back with the trophy as European Champions, and to wait open for us. We also had fantastic coverage in the local press and great support from the local authority to recognise the Band's achievement."

Winning the 1980 European was the high water mark for the Cory Band under Denzil Stephens' direction, and he remembers the period with fondness saying, "All in all, I enjoyed training and conducting the Cory Band, proving that with the co-operation of the players, it is possible to achieve success even with a mix of experienced and less experienced players. The team spirit is so important to accomplish this. It also needs experience in man management, as well as being

Winning the European Championship in 1980

fully supported by the training and conducting techniques of the conductor. I am indeed proud to have been associated with this fine Band."

Graham Sheppard has fond memories of this period – "Denzil was an excellent band trainer and always knew what he wanted us to do on stage. He was a military man all right with the discipline that is symptomatic of this background, and that was perhaps what we needed at that time to make the most of ourselves on the contest stage. The Cory Band has a great deal to thank him for. There was an aura about the Band that Denzil instigated and developed. This later flourished when Major Kenney returned to direct the Band.

Jim Davies said: "The European win was a great achievement for the Band and Welsh banding. We certainly worked hard for it and the players deserved it. It was a significant highlight for me in my playing career, although I used to also enjoy the contest when it was staged overseas. It was however, so gratifying to win on United Kingdom home territory in 1980 though!"

Defending the title the following year Cory were awarded their sixth place. The famous Denzil Stephens/Cory partnership ended in 1982 when Major Kenney returned to mastermind their famous hat trick of National wins.

On the following pages there is a poem written about the players in the Band.
The author signs his name: - 'A foreign music lover'.

The Cory Band 1979-1980

Deep in the Rhondda there's a band named Cory,
Who over recent years, have been covered in glory.
Founded last century, now mature to the full,
their standard of playing ensures them a "Bull".

Rich with friendship and quality of sound,
their music makes the world go round.
Feet are a tapping after the very first beat,
by every listener in their concert seat.

Denzil Stephens is the man with the stick,
as composer, arranger he misses no trick.
His ear for music keeps the Band on their toes,
and he is respected and liked wherever he goes.

Glenys Stephens is the Bands number one fan,
Travels to see them whenever she can.
No matter what distance be it near or far,
She'll always he seen traveling in Denzil's car.

Jim Davies, Principal Cornet, takes the very first seat,
a musician you'd willingly go a long way to meet.
His triple tonguing is a joy to each ear,
and his melodies could cause many to shed a tear.

John Neathey, the man with the very fair hair,
Tall, good looking and plays with flair.
First started on cornet when just half a score,
And will play for the next thirty years or more.

Richard Dix, third down, he's also quite tall,
Loves making music, says, "He's having a ball".
A subtle comedian, he keeps a stern face,
Enjoys his contesting, helps win the race.

Mr. Hedditch, or to all his friends Paul,
Being front row, he certainly walks tall.
At triple piano he plays such a sweet note,
that one day the onus of principal he'll tote.

Gwyn Thomas, back row, instruments the "Sop",
Recognised by many as being the top.
In "Candide" his playing causes many a flutter,
and demi semi runs go with nary a stutter.

There's many a Jones but this Jones is Howard,
when playing Rep. he's far from a coward.
No matter how many black notes there are to a bar,
He'll play the lot and not be driven too far.

Ian Jones, the joker, of a very large pack,
Full of fun and of jokes he don't lack.
He's the third generation of the Trotman kin,
And as pleased as "Punch" with the National win.

A relative new face, that is Gary Price,
Who smiles on Dame Fortunes' roll of the dice.
"A Cory player" it's a dream come true,
Playing grand music, it's like starting anew.

Ralph Morgan's another who is tallish and fair,
Seated with honour along the back tare.
As important a member as he who plays solo,
His music sheet reads that he must play low.

Another Jones and this one's named Greg,
A back row position that many would beg.
Modest and quiet until cornet is in hand,
He then plays his part in a very great Band.

Just one more Thomas and this one is Jeff,
Who goes with a flugal, as with Rugby with Ref.,
His solos come forth with so much feeling,
That the audiences think
it's with Pan they're dealing.
Top man on HORNS was christened Wayne Cook,
His cadenzas earn him many an admiring look.
Gifted with the ability to produce a good sound,
there's few in his class for miles around.

Robin Davies is a civil servant by trade,
yet as a musician his future is made.
The Tenor Horn, she's the lady of brass,
Rob treats her so, as if she were glass.

Jeff Sheppard's the third of the trio of horns,
would sooner play music than mow any lawns.
Blonde haired and smiling, the Horns leading joker,
who after a prank has face straight as a poker.

Chairman Don Tanner, a great solo Trom.,
Never worries who the next score is from.
Be it classic or "Pop", he'll make it sound rich,
Like Tommy Dorcy, he has the sound and the pitch.

Terry Lambert, another who "Stretches his arm",
and produces notes that a snake would charm.
'His favourite bar would include a Gliss,
and plenty of these, to him, is sheer bliss.

John Jones, an ex member of the Royal Marine Band,
Who sits in front of a Cory sheet stand.
Oscillates his slide both correctly and sure,
And in his element playing "Troms to the fore".

Gareth Keys delights with "The Pink Panther" theme,
Just one of the pieces of this winning team.
Whatever he plays the rendering is great,
A musician that all would be proud to call "Mate".

Roy Roberts, he plays the Brass Band's Cello,
His harmonising is both rich sounding and mellow.
When it comes to a solo much feeling is there,
And those runs on his Euph leave him gasping for air.

Brian Davies another person. who revels in runs,
In the "Ninth of January", he's going great guns.
Like all those around him, he pulls his weight,
and is ever eager for the next contest date.

Third of the Euphs, is Watkins, Huw,
His timing is perfect, comes in dead on cue,
A very quiet lad who is quite unassuming,
But the sound from his Bell is certainly blooming.

Stuart Lewis, you'll see him with his pipe,
Quiet, serious looking, but the very best type.
Nimble fingers floating over the valve tops,
A hard working Bandsman, would play till he drops.

The other Bard. is hailed Phillip Wicks,
Enjoys his playing, gets up to no tricks.
Nice personality, a very pleasant Chappy,
A contest win makes him very happy.

Huw Williams plays Tuba, now there is a treat,
No more confident player will e'er take a seat.
Plays his 'Eb' as though twas a cornet,
And his sting in the tail is that of a hornet.

Selwyn Lewis, civil servant, who's worthy of note,
There's a good pun, so it must surely be wrote.
A versatile player who once played Bass Trom,
Now it's the Tuba that his notes come from.

John Trotman; yes he is dear Tom's son,
The Bands longest player, he still finds it fun.
Another pipe smoker and he does have pipe dreams,
To win Belle Vue Open and hear yells and screams.

The Bandmaster, he's known as Graham Sheppard,
Good on the Bass, could play the spots off a leopard.
You'll never miss him, he's the one with the beard,
A terrific character who was musically reared.

Clayton McCann, now he plays the drums,
Keeps the pace marked for all of his chums.
Be it a roll, or triplets, it's all very neat,
Its drumming perfection down to the last beat.

Alan O'Leary, ex cornet, now makes the Timps hum,
A quaveror crescendo strikes the audience dumb.
He makes percussion his own personal delight,
And that "Beam" on his face is a wonderful sight.

The Secretary's a grafter by the name of Ron Pryce,
Forever writing letters and giving advice.
A great asset to Cory, though he doesn't play,
And each Band win really makes his day.

Brian Privet, well he's assistant Sec.,
His help saves Ron being a nervous wreck.
Serving his apprenticeship and getting better,
For when the time comes he writes every letter.

Clifford Rees he tends the "Bees and Honey",
This being cockney rhyming slang for money.
Treasurer would be the very formal term,
And Cliff will keep those purse strings firm.

Harold Hearne lovingly nicknamed Uncle Fester,
In his time was the Bands number one jester.
The oldest living ex member of bygone Cory,
If its an anecdote you want, he'll tell you a story.

Tom Trotman to all was the Band's very first Dad,
His zest to play starting when he was a. lad.
His recent death was a great loss to the Band,
But his name will be remembered throughout the land.

Gwyn Dackins, too, was a great character of note,
Who's popularity, bandwise, would win many a vote,
Alas, like, Tom Trotman, he has passed away,
But his presence is felt each time the Band play.

We mustn't forget the men's girlfriends and wives,
Those marvelous women, alone best part of their lives.
Musical widows who let out one big scream,
As the adjudicator announces that Cory were CREAM:
(n-b. Cream is always at the top.)

So here we have just some of the Band story,
National Champs, seven four, is part of their glory.
Who's to pay what the next contest will bring,
If it's the Belle Vue Open - THEY'LL BLOODY WELL SING

Finally, what is music?, there's food for thought,
Can it really be notes put together, as taught?.
To go into detail could be quite a long time,
But to hear pure music ---GO: LISTEN TO CORY.

Signed. A foreign Music Lover.

Chapter 9

The Thrills & Spills of the
Glorious Hat-Trick Years

Denzil Stephens' tenure as Musical Director ended in 1982 after five very fruitful years, with the Band having been successful in many of the major entertainment contests during this period. Denzil Stephens also left the Band with a legacy of popular and good quality L.P. Recordings, also a successful 'single' called *Stop The Cavalry,* which was a collaborative project with 'The Gwalia Singers'. The contesting highlight of this era was the award of second place at the National Championships, London in 1979 and being crowned European Champions at the Royal Albert Hall, London, in 1980. Returning to Cory in 1982, Major Kenney was disappointed with the Band's mediocre performance of Herbert Howells' *Three Figures* at the British 'Open' Championship resulting in the Band gaining a lowly fourteenth place. Disappointingly the performance failed to reflect the way the Band had been playing and the quality of the depth of sound that was always apparent within the Band. Just a few weeks later, they travelled to London to compete in the National Championships of Great Britain. As ever, Cory Band were well prepared and determined to improve on the recent British "Open" contest result.

Written in 1973, Wilfred Heaton's *Contest Music* had been chosen as the test-piece having been previously rejected as a National Championships test-piece on the grounds that the music was too contemporary in character. Not surprisingly, the composer had disagreed, contending that the work followed a tradition of similar type music for brass band. He compared *Contest Music* to music written by Elgar, Holst and Ireland in placing the musical content first and instrumental virtuosity second. What a perceptive evergreen description! Heaton also wrote that the music exists solely for itself and allies itself with 18th and 19th century classicism in the wider musical context. Whatever anyone thought of the music, when even in 1982 it was regarded as 'modern', certainly it was new to the Cory Band and Major Kenney. Cory had a late order of play at number 17. They began their performance with steely determination, all the soloists performing confidently, especially the stylish cornetist Jim Davies who negotiated the treacherous solo line that includes a one and a half octave descending leap from top C sharp, near the end of the second (slow) movement, with consummate ease. The Band played superbly and literally "brought the house down!" It was indeed an unbeatable performance that clinched the title. The Cory Band under the magical baton of Major Arthur Kenney were once again National Champions of Great Britain. A title they last won under the same conductor eight years previously in 1974.

Bass player John Prosser joined the Cory Band in 1981, serving the Cory Band for the past twenty eight years. Having achieved stalwart status, he has seen many accomplished players come and go from the Band. He joined Cory from the nearby Markham Colliery Band and was immediately astonished by the high level of playing and commitment of the Band. John fondly remembers the Major's time with the Band and still wonders at the M.D.'s infectious enthusiasm for new music. "The Major had high expectations of all his players and, not surprisingly, they worked hard to fulfil them." The preparation for *Contest Music* was involved and intense "It was gong extremely well and although the Major was a super interpreter of all kinds of music, he was particularly sensitive to the flow and phasing of slow music. Sitting in the Bass Section at the back of the Band and listening to the emotive passages in the second movement of this fine music was simply breathtaking during rehearsals. Every phrase and nuance were captured and exploited to the full by the Major.

Cory - now best of British bands

One down, two to go in 1982

1982 was John's baptism of fire; it was the first time for him to play at the Royal Albert Hall and he still cringes at his relative naivety. "I can remember going into the hall with high expectations to listen to the famous Black Dyke Band playing. After their performance I turned to my friend Jeff Thomas and whispered, 'we can beat that!' In retrospect, I wish I'd said nothing, because my lasting memory of our winning performance on *Contest Music* was me splitting a top note that appeared to sound forever – a flaw in the performance that was duly mentioned in the written adjudications.

Flugel Horn soloist Jeff Thomas also has uncomfortable flashbacks to the 1982 performance, "It was during the slow second movement I became aware that I was one beat adrift of the ensemble. The Major simply leaned over and said 'don't panic'. We carried on as if nothing had happened; so the overall impression was obviously quite stunning with the adjudicators thankfully dismissing my fleeting mishap."

The third movement was full of power and accuracy, leading John to savour his bitter sweet start to his long playing career with Cory Band!

Full results on the victorious day were:

CORY	1st	194 points
BLACK DYKE MILLS	2nd	193 points
BRODSWORTH COLLIERY	3rd	192 points
CAMBORNE	4th	190 points
EVER READY	5th	187 points
FAIREY ENGINEERING	6th	186 points

The adjudicators on that occasion were Dr. Roy Newsome, Arthur Butterworth and Noel Cox. Here are their respective remarks on the Cory performance:-

1. *An excellent start. Fine control, attention to dynamics, detail, phrasing etc. Splendid sound also in all areas. A real climax at M and great delicacy from P.*

2. A beautiful cornet line and troms make themselves an integral part of the music. A-All soloists of high quality – though horn a shade under, and a slight blemish in flugel. E, played with great feeling, though with some blemishes – if only slight!

3. A fine lively start, but basses slightly rough before B. F. very effective. Good build up. Splendid from H. and good basses at I. Good climax at L. Balance and dynamics controlled in this performance. Molto Animato very fast but most effective. A very good performance.

Roy Newsome.

1. Good! A bit impetuous though. A neat overall shape to the phrasing of the bars – they hang together quite convincingly. Technically most assured. A smooth ebb and flow of controlled sound. Good quality of tone colour in individual sections providing a good contrast of timbre. Percussion rather ponderous at times. Most shapely and musical.

2. Excellent, refined opening. Trombones have an air of quiet mystery and remoteness. This movement – like the previous one – has musically conceived shape to commend it. Some ravishing sombre colours and a melancholy that is most compelling indeed. Most convincingly conveyed to the alert listener for sure!

3. The iron hand in the velvet glove? The suppressed power of this opening was electrifying. This conveyed a sense of the music's symphonic structure and overall shape. The cross rhythms were excellent! The dynamic contrast cunningly contrived. Only the ending was a bit misconceived – the ritenuti exaggerated – knocking the note values out of shape from that intended by the composer – no 'pause' really last three bars.

Arthur Butterworth.

1. A very loud opening with one or two overplayed bass accents but it had a splendid clarity in the quick soft quaver tonguing - affluent performance which seemed along with real confidence, the playing was in excellent health and spirits.

2. Quite a slow tempo, but very well held and it was both expansive and spacious – the chords accompanying the euphonium solo were most impressively soft. Much atmosphere was created in this performance – a very fine niente at the end-most musical.

3. Not always impeccable in tuning but with enough excitement in the rhythms to create a feeling of panoply and splendour. A fine sonority (well balanced) at L and thereafter and a most thrilling build up to the ending.
A very fine performance.

Noel Cox.

There is a Chandos recording of Cory's actual live performance conducted by Arthur Kenney from the Royal Albert Hall. It's a double L. P. (BBRD 1017/8) and features the Saturday night Gala Concert with the massed bands of Carlton Main Frickley Colliery, Desford Colliery, Leyland Vehicles and Whitburn. It also features the winning band from the National Championships (Cory) playing Contest Music and the winning band from The European

Brass Band Championships (Black Dyke) playing *Journey Into Freedom* by Eric Ball. As well as featuring Cory's super performance of Elgar Howarth's *Fireworks* which they played the following day as their own choice, as part of the European Brass Band Championships. Cory were beaten into second place by their arch rivals from Queensbury, the Black Dyke Mills Band.

The following year Cory Band were quite busy playing concerts and in January travelled to Stroud to take part in the long established Stroud Brass Band Festival. This festival featured concerts by top class bands throughout the year. The 1983 season featured Cory Band, Fairey Engineering, James Shepherd Versatile Brass, Besses o' Th' Barn, Desford Colliery and Fodens Motor Works. Cory presented a mixture of classical arrangements with original compositions; they also featured a fine array of soloists. The concert began with a rendition of the National Anthem *God Save The Queen* and then the resident compere for the series Mr. W. J. S. Burnt introduced the items. They began with Arthur Kenney's superb arrangement of *Fanfare for Rocky* by Conti which led to another work by Major Kenney, this time a composition dedicated to, and named after his wife *Barbara*, the work being in the style of a waltz. The programme featured five soloists:

> Jeff Thomas (flugel horn) played Bacharach's evergreen *Alfie,* arranged by Denzil Stephens,
> Wayne Cook (solo horn) played Hamlish's *Memories,*
> Jim Davies (cornet) featured a Rafael Mendez favourite *Chipanecas,*
> Gareth Key (trombone) played *Fandango* and
> Roy Roberts (euphonium) featured Godfrey's evergreen *Lucy Long.*

Cory closed the first half of their demanding programme with Frank Wright's arrangement of the overture – *Carnival Romain* by Berlioz. Other items included: *Barn Dance and Cowboy Hymn,* Sparke, *Serenade,* Bourgeois, *Habbeytak Bessayf,* Kenney, *Mephistopheles,* Douglas and *Dance of the Tumblers,* Rimsky Korsakov. Cory played wonderful concerts to full houses throughout the entire year at widespread venues such as Victoria Hall, Crewkerne and their favourite recording venue – the Brangwyn Hall, Swansea where they also promoted a Brass and Voice Concert with guests 'The Gwalia Singers' and 'Rhos Cwmtawe Male Choir'. Unfortunately their contest record for 1983 again displayed varying fortunes, being placed thirteenth at the British 'Open' Championships in September, playing Edward Gregson's *Connotations* despite a competent performance. However, as in previous years, the situation changed dramatically one month later at the National Championships of Great Britain at London's prestigious Royal Albert Hall.

This year the organisers had commissioned Joseph Horovitz to write the test piece. He titled the work *Ballet for Band.* It was a delicate work using the individual instruments of the Band to display characters in an imaginary ballet. It was a great vehicle for the Major to show his supreme musicianship and for him to showcase the ability of the Cory Band and its wonderful team of soloists. *Ballet for Band* was particularly demanding for the soprano cornet and flugel horn with both Gwyn Thomas and Jeff Thomas (no relation) delivering stunning individual contributions.

Similar to the previous year, Cory were fortunate to obtain a favourable draw. Playing off number nine, the Band gave a memorable performance to again win the title Champion Band of Great Britain for the second successive year. *Ballet for Band* posed totally different musical and technical challenges to the previous year's test piece *Contest Music*. Again, the Major and the Band responded to these challenges in fine style. John Prosser relates the story that – during a band rehearsal prior to the contest, Major Kenney's wife Barbara gave the Band her ideas on what the characters would be if *Ballet for Band* was a real ballet using male and female dancers. "Barbara attended most rehearsals and her insight into the imaginary characters of *Ballet for Band* was fascinating. She had obviously spent hours listening to the music and choreographing the whole performance in her mind. Whether this had any impact on Cory's winning performance one will never know but it did stimulate the players' imagination and gave several of the soloists' helpful interpretative ideas."

The concept of a 'Instrumental Ballet certainly resonated with Roy Newsome's wife Muriel. In reminiscent mood Roy, who was a member of the adjudicating panel at the National Championships at the Royal Albert Hall on two of the three hat-trick winning performances of 1982, 83 and 84 – all directed by that wizard of the baton, Arthur Kenney, vividly relives his memories of the 1983 event. "The test piece was Joe Horovitz's 'Ballet for Band', and I was in the adjudicators' box with Eric Ball and the choral specialist – Sir David Willcocks. We all felt there were two outstanding performances, and these proved to have been given by Black Dyke and Cory. We thought long and hard about which should be declared the winning performance. But having read, then re-read our written comments and discussed the two performances thoroughly, we were unanimously of the opinion that one just had the edge. I doubt if we could have put into words why this was so. It was what my friend Bob Childs would call the 'X-factor'. The winning band was, of course, Cory. Unbeknown to me at the time, a conversation was also taking place in the hall, between Harry Mortimer CBE (HM) and my dear wife, Muriel. HM asked Muriel what she thought, and she was adamant that Cory's would be declared winners. She even went so far as to say that if they weren't she wouldn't live with me for the next month! Harry wanted to know why she thought Cory's would win, maintaining that Black Dyke had also given a superb performance. She agreed wholeheartedly, but pointed out that Black Dyke's performance had been 'grand opera', whereas that of Cory's was pure 'ballet' – in keeping with the work's title. I always said that Muriel was the best judge that never entered an adjudicator's box."

John Prosser remains adamant that "No matter how musically imaginative a performance is, it also needs a high level of technical assurance and Cory's performance on *Ballet for Band* was virtually flawless. We pulled off the double, something most of the Band didn't think was possible. From my earliest playing days I have never gone into the hall to listen to contest results and the results ceremony at the Royal Albert Hall in 1983 was no exception. I was with a couple of other Band members sitting in the dressing room nervously awaiting the results. As we sat there, Stuart Lewis the Band's solo baritone player was reflectively smoking his pipe, he turned to me and said "John I think we have got this one", no sooner had he said it than we could hear Greg Jones our third cornet player screaming the result as he was running through the circular corridors of the Royal Albert Hall.

NATIONAL BRASS BAND FESTIVAL

1983 Champions

UNDER the direction of Major Arthur Kenney, the Cory Band retained the title of National Champions in the 1983 Finals. What a magnificent way to enter their centenary year of 1984. With Major Kenney is Cory secretary Ron Pryce, one of the long-serving members of the famous South Wales band.

Two down, one to go!

Full results were:

CORY	1st	197 points
BLACK DYKE MILLS	2nd	196 points
G.U.S.	3rd	195 points
GRIMETHORPE COLLIERY	4th	194 points
FODENS O.T.S.	5th	193 points
JONES & CROSSLAND	6th	192 points

The adjudicators were: Eric Ball, Dr. Roy Newsome and Sir David Willcocks. Here are their remarks on Cory's performance.

The fanfares first rate. Bass duo properly humorous and from the grazioso all goes well. Lento tranquillo-flugel and other soloists do well and the flowing pulse of the music is impressive. Moderato thro' 15-17 first rate-and so it goes on. Allegro thro' 20 to the end: a very fine performance – technically sound; all details in proper focus, including percussion. Quite stirring.

Eric Ball.

A most convincing opening section. 5 also fine and the grazioso had everything. Lento just beautiful. Slight intonation in close. Excellent work through 14, 15, 16 and 17, with a magnificent full band sound in climax after 18. Allegro a tremendous climax to a superb performance.

Roy Newsome.

A stunning performance – accurate and well controlled – but more important perhaps was a ready appreciation of the widely varying moods of the piece. The playing was also colourful and full of character. Great care was taken over balance to ensure not only that melodies were given their due prominence but also that counter melodies were given their value and that chords were 'complete'. Every accent, every nuance was noted. The tempi were beautifully judged and though the players were kept on a tight rein they were given freedom for expressive utterance. P. 19 first five bars – Soprano cornet just a shade sharp but otherwise admirably controlled. An admirable 'sound' from all departments with a corporate brilliance in ff and warm richness in pp and ppp. Bravo to conductor and each player.

Sir David Willcocks.

The following year the Band were full of eager anticipation and the expectancy of the brass band public was high given that Cory had won the National Championships two years in succession. 1984 was to be a special year for the Cory Band as they were also celebrating their Centenary. The Band had produced a Centenary booklet and also produced a Cory Band Centenary Tea Towel. They had recorded an L. P. in December 1983 which they intended promoting throughout the celebratory year. The record featured *Land of the Long White Cloud* by Philip Sparke and Vinter's *Variations on a Ninth*. The highlight of the Centenary celebrations was a concert held in Cardiff on 2nd June. The Cory Band invited 'Bingham and District Choral Society' to be their guests and together they performed Gilbert Vinter's intriguing oratorio *The Trumpets*. William Mackay was the bass soloist, John Fussell

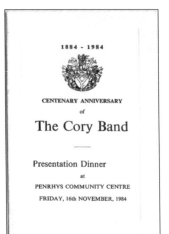

of Swansea's Brangwyn Hall fame was the organist with B.B.C. presenter Robin Boyle the compere for the evening. Cory had commissioned Philip Sparke to write a major work for them called *The Year of The Dragon* and the Band gave the world première of this work at the same concert. The evening also featured Jim Davies (cornet) playing *Hungarian Dance No. 5* by Brahms. The whole Band was showcased in W. Hogarth Lear's spectacular *Mr. Lear's Carnival*.

Cory Band's Centenary year was off to a flying start. However, at the end of the summer period, the adjudicators at the British "Open" Championship contest hadn't read the script and placed then a lowly thirteenth bringing the Band crashing down to earth. The test piece at the British 'Open' was *A Comedy Overture* by John Ireland and just like the previous two years, the Band members and the Major were happy with their performance but very disappointed with the result. How could a Band achieve such good results for October contests and such poor results for contests held in September? Some of the Band were talking about possible conspiracy theories, whilst others constantly muttered, "That's banding!" There was little doubt that each year, the disappointment of the British 'Open' acted as a catalyst for determination, dedication and focus towards the National Championships held in the following month.

Edward Gregson had been commissioned to write the test piece for the 1984 National Championships of Great Britain. The work was titled *Dances and Arias*. Although constructed in one continuous movement, as the name suggests, the music is a series of alternating fast and slow sections. Gregson's fascinating work strayed from the conventional scoring pattern for brass bands requiring two flugel horns. One of the back row cornet players needed to double on both cornet and flugel horn. Under the tutelage of the Band's experienced flugel horn soloist (Jeff Thomas); 2nd cornet player Phillip Harris did a sterling job. Again allotted a favourable order of play at number fourteen, Cory produced a brilliant performance to take

the coveted cup back to Wales for the third successive year.
The results were as follows:

CORY	1st	197	points
SUN LIFE	2nd	196	points
LEYLAND VEHICLES	3rd	195	points
FAIREY ENGINEERING	4th	194	points
BRIGHOUSE AND RASTRICK	5th	193	points
BLACK DYKE MILLS	6th	192	points

The adjudicators were: William Relton, James Scott and Sir David Willcocks. Here are their remarks on Cory's hat trick winning performance.

 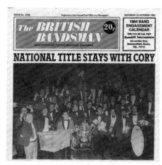 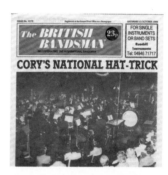

British Bandsman covers 1982, 1983, 1984.

Fine fiery opening, good balance and a real difference between f and ff (3). Good and fine cantabile from unison horns. (6) Excellent playing but a sustained bass line as this somehow makes the cornets hurry. (8) Excellent solo cornet, small slip in solo horn. (9) More solo horn please, a real duet – good unison cornets. (10) Fine bass line – and good Eb Bass solo. Slight trombone split before (11). Schezo good speed. 5 after (15) a slight rock in the ensemble – miraculous playing here up to (21) – euphonium safe – well spaced and flugel full of character. Matching at (24), not quite so neat. (25) Well paced and such a fine tight rhythm, also the great difference between f and ff so skilfully managed.

William Relton

Very fine sound – and everything so committed. Playing of a high level indeed – with all parts logically in their place, though there is a slightly ponderous feel in the ffs. Good entry into (8) – which has very fine cornet playing – horn does not quite match this – tutti cornets play the difficult (9) plus 3 so well. From (10) is beautifully played by all. Your scherzo has excellent tempo, and a true scherzo feel to the music. (15) plus 5 rocks a little in the rhythmic figures. (17)-(18)-(19) is superb – and (26)! (22) Competent euphonium, with muted cornets well balanced. (23) plus 3 is superb. Flugel plays with just the right style here, and the 2nd does well, though not absolutely in tune with the first. At (25) you display extreme competence, with a fine sense of rhythm – the playing is so exact. (33) is superb, leading to a most exciting ending.

James Scott

An excellent start – rhythmical and incisive playing – with scrupulous attention paid to dynamic markings, with the result that every detail was clear. Excellent technique in semi-quaver tonguing. (8) vibraphone inaudible. A good solo cornet on (16)/(17), but thereafter secure, (21) atmospheric – a fine Eb bass solo with subtle accompaniment. Scherzo – a good speed, allowing for clarity of detail. (12) +1. – Horns not quite together in (dotted figure), but there were few such instances of ragged ensemble. (43) onward – splendid euphonium, with impressive asides from muted cornets and vibes. Sensibly the euphonium player took time over his recital. (47) a flugel solo – imaginative – with sombre trombones accompanying. A lovely duet (49)/(50) which prepared the way for the brilliant final section. The Band (and of course the conductor) display a splendid rhythmical sense – the changing meters being absolutely clear because quaver always equalled and groups of three quavers were never hurried. An outstanding performance. Bravo!

David Wilcocks

A quote from the Brass Band News, November 1984 gives lasting testimony to Cory's rare and splendid achievement:-

"Hat-tricks are rare and popular, the upward thrusting fist of the diminutive Major Kenney as he came on stage to accept the award, embodied an explosive exhilaration which was shared by the vast majority of the audience."

On stage at the RAH 1984

Peter Lambert, Arthur Kenney, Ron Pryce and Ashley Rayburn

Celebrating the historic Hat-Trick

John Prosser, the Cory Band's celebrated Eb Bass player recalls discussions on the coach on the way to London. "We had pushed Black Dyke into second place the two previous years and it was strongly rumoured that they were not playing *Dances and Arias* very well. Of course, as fellow competitors we took this to be a hint of brinkmanship on their part. I can remember our performance well but the moment that really sticks in my mind was sitting on the stage with all the usual chatter around the hall. The Major strode to the podium, turned to the audience, then to the Band and lifted his baton; it was so quiet, I thought it impossible for such a large crowd to be totally silent. It was really scary! We started the performance and as the performance progressed, the Band and the Major grew in both stature and confidence. At the end the audience erupted into tumultuous applause, a sound that will live with me forever!"

Currently, still a valued member of the Band, Philip Harris joined Cory in 1980. His ability and experience remains highly regarded. His most vivid memory of the 1984 performance of *Dances and Arias* was the first rehearsal. "I can remember going to the Bandroom to learn that the test piece needed an extra flugel horn player, Howard Jones (repiano) was given first opportunity, but after one rehearsal and a short discussion with the Major, the job was mine. I had previously played flugel horn with Lewis Merthyr Band for a period of four or five years, so I was happy to accept the responsibility. What most of the Band didn't know was the near disaster that occurred on the day of the competition. As usual, the Band rehearsed in the Irish Guards bandroom, then it was back on the coach for the short drive to the Royal Albert Hall. It wasn't until arrival there that I realised I had left the flugel horn at the barracks, but luck was on my side. My cousin Mike Jones, was playing in H.M. Band of the Welsh Guards stationed at Chelsea Barracks, so a quick phone call and a taxi ride and disaster was averted!"

In December 1984, the Cory Band recorded a CD album entitled *Dances and Arias*. They featured their winning test-piece *Dances and Arias* by Edward Gregson and although it was not the actual live performance from the competition, it nevertheless acts as a true testament of the Band's outstanding maturity and musicianship. Also featured on the disc is the composition the Band commissioned for their Centenary celebrations, *The Year of the Dragon* by Philip Sparke. The sleeve notes state the recording is, 'both a momento of, as well as a tribute to, the Cory Band's recent spectacular accomplishments.' Other items on the recording are: *Continental* and *Doyen* by Goff Richards, *Men of Harlech* by German, and *Siegfried's Funeral March* by Wagner. During this extremely successful period in the Band's history the momentous achievement of winning the 'Hat-Trick' of firsts at the National Championships of Great Britain can easily overshadow the other worthy podium places obtained under Major Kenney's dynamic direction. Cory Band's record at the European Championships remained at a consistently high level confirmed by the following results:-

1982 at London placed 2nd
1983 at Kerkrade placed 3rd
1984 at Edinburgh placed 2nd
1985 at Copenhagen placed 2nd
1986 at Cardiff placed 3rd.

The achievements of Major Kenney and the Cory Band are synonymous, clearly emerging from their mutual respect for each other. The Major immortalised his emotional attachment to the Band when he wrote an article for the Band's Centenary Booklet, published in 1984:

"When I arrived on the scene in the autumn of 1970 I was tremendously lucky in that I inherited a Band which over the years had gradually grown like a seedling and was nearing maturity. I began to mould them into my way of thinking and from nothing there came an affinity between us which cannot be put into words. It is as if they knew what I was thinking and I could feel just what was needed from me in order to produce from them an inspired and uplifting performance. The first year brought dazzling success and as I and the Band grew together we reached the great climax of the National Championships in 1974. I was compelled by circumstances beyond my control to part company with the Band for a few years, but what a marvellous reunion came when I was asked to resume the position of Musical Director in 1982.

I feel very proud to be with the Band again yet at the same time I feel very humble in the company of players who are able to produce musical sounds which one would never imagine amateur brass players could produce. Their technical ability is beyond question, but I also know that at times I make demands from them which in lesser bands would be termed impossible, yet they turn up trumps every time. To conduct the Cory Band is to enjoy a musical experience which words cannot describe. The dedication and response in both rehearsal and performance is something which I personally have never experienced anywhere else or at any time since I started conducting in the Army as far back as 1942. Yet in this dedicated approach to the job in hand, there shines through a tremendous sense of humour plus a will to help one another in times of personal adversity.... a true family Band. *CORY, I SALUTE YOU"*.

Major Kenney relinquished his position as Musical Director for the second time in the late 1980s to return once more to conduct the Band in 1992. His recall was to take the Band to the National Championships in London, and although by this time his health was failing, his musical brain was as alert as ever. The test piece was New Jerusalem by Philip Wilby and required an off-stage cornetist to play three separate fanfares. The Major asked John Southcombe to play the part but with a difference? The Major wanted John to play the three separate fanfares from three different parts of the hall. There were logistical problems, not least in negotiating the corridors of the Royal Albert Hall. John was escorted by an official to the three solo positions, each one chosen by the Major. Despite Major Kenney's failing health and the obstacles involved in executing such an outrageous musical idea he remained musically inventive and unique to the end.

Chapter 10
The Disastrous Bandroom Fire
and the Gloomy 1990's!

In an article written in The Times newspaper John Trotman said, "During the seventies and eighties the Cory Band had a big, round sound and then, we gradually lost it. By the time we got to the 1990's, I didn't think things could get worse; two principal players left, two long serving bass players also left. Then the conductor, Major Arthur Kenney, who'd taken us to four National wins retired following a heart attack. Finally, to cap it all, on the 11th May 1990 the Bandroom burnt down."

A fire engine outside the bandroom

A fireman fighting the blaze

The fire was a disaster for the Band. The biggest financial loss apart from the building itself was the value of the instruments, which amounted to many tens of thousands of pounds. Clayton McCann took photographs the day following the fire, quickly realising that his entire percussion equipment had been totally destroyed. However, it was the irreplaceable items such as memorabilia that had progressively adorned the walls since the formation of the Band, which would be missed most by the Band members and the many visitors to the Bandroom, many from far off places. Banners from their National wins and trophies from contests, photographs dating back to the inception of the Band were prominently displayed throughout the Bandroom. Soprano player Gwyn Thomas said that the place was more like a museum of achievement than a bandroom. The Band had also accumulated an eclectic library of more than 5000 sets of music, some dating back as far as 1884. It was estimated that seventy-five percent of the contents of the library were completely destroyed in the blaze, with the rest being badly damaged.

The library after the fire

Gwyn Thomas in the burnt out bandroom

Ironically, it was a member of the Band who first noticed palls of smoke billowing from the former colliery lamp room on Llewellyn Street, the building used as a Bandroom by the Cory Band. Andrew Howells was delivering gas containers at 2.20 pm on Friday 11th May 1990, when he saw the dense plumes of smoke; he immediately phoned the fire brigade. They sent six fire engines and more than forty firemen fought the blaze until it was brought under control. Some firemen remained on the scene until late into the night.

Graham Sheppard, the Band Chairman at that time, was one of the first Band members on the scene. He remembers seeing two tubas and one burnt out kettle drum rescued from the blaze just standing forlornly on the pavement opposite the building. Within minutes the word spread to other Band members and by the time Assistant Secretary, Glan Lewis arrived, there were several highly distressed musicians with tears rolling down their cheeks standing helplessly, watching the fire really taking hold, being totally unable to take any action to salvage any equipment. Ron Pryce, Secretary of the Band who lived less than a mile from the Bandroom said, "It was a dreadful sight. Never before had I seen grown men crying." The road through the village was completely closed for many hours as firemen fought to control and then dampen the blaze.

Vandals were believed to have been responsible for the fire. A spokesman for the Mid-Glamorgan Fire Service said they were treating the cause of the fire with suspicion.. Graham Sheppard said that the few instruments that were recovered were smeared in paint and the locks on the instrument cases had been forced open.

The following day, Band members carefully and laboriously sifted through the rubble to try and salvage what they could; but it was tragic. Trophies that once stood proudly were reduced to lumps of melted silver. Charred picture frames which used to surround irreplaceable photographs and the ashes from the library of what was once a comprehensive and valuable library of music littered the floor. The metal tubes of chairs and severely buckled music stands were cluttered everywhere. One of the players managed to save just a single damaged music stand banner, that had been made by the Ladies' Committee.

Clayton McCann, principal percussionist and librarian said, "It was a truly poignant moment when I found a framed picture of one of Cory's

A Cory banner saved

most loved and respected stalwarts, the late Mr. Gwyn Dackins. Miraculously the picture was untouched by the flames." Clayton added, "It may be prophetic, but I also rescued a sodden but uncharred score of Eric Ball's *Resurgam,* the title of which means *I Shall Rise Again.*" This biblical phrase has much emotive significance when there is the realisation that the Band has subsequently risen to the pinnacle of world prominence in accomplished brass playing.

The nightmare of every percussionist, especially Clayton McCann!

Within hours of the announcement of the fire offers of help were pouring in from other bands and organisations. Local bands loaned instruments to Cory, to enable them to fulfil a concert just two days later. The Band were also able to compete in a competition at Ebbw Vale, the following week. Only hours after the fire had been quelled, news of the loss was announced at a concert taking place in St. David's Hall, Cardiff. Immediately, the sponsors of the concert, Barclays Bank, made a donation of £500 and ordered a collection for the Band which raised another £1000. Novello and other brass band music publishers donated music. Treorchy Male Voice Choir donated £1000 with many other musical organisations, 'pubs and clubs' dipping deeply into their pockets to help the Band. Not surprisingly, the Band had to withdraw from a National Competition held in Doncaster. Glan Lewis said, "We need specialist instruments for that contest and new music, so we have decided not to go. It would have been impossible to get things together in time."

The Band initially sought refuge for rehearsals in the vestry of Jerusalem Chapel, in Ton Pentre. Band President and local MP Mr. Allan Rogers, set up an Appeal Fund, which in only a few weeks reached a staggering £17,000 pounds. The Band had a peripatetic existence practising in schools, workingmen's clubs and at a 'state of the art' factory on the Gelli Industrial estate in the Rhondda Valley; the latter loaned to them by the Welsh Development Agency. It took the Band just sixteen months to locate, purchase and renovate a new home and on Thursday, 16th September 1991 they opened a new bandroom situated less than a mile from their former home. The new bandroom was located behind the Post Office in Ton Pentre. The opening was a grand affair with the late Harry Mortimer CBE performing the opening ceremony. Denzil Stephens conducted the Band and the event was supported by local dignitaries, including the Band's President, MP Allan Rogers. A celebratory evening followed in Ton Pentre AFC Social Club.

Harry Mortimer CBE opening the new Bandroom, 1991

As recorded earlier in this chapter, the Band were at a comparatively low ebb after the departure of Major Arthur Kenney, being placed 18th at the National Championship Finals in 1988. The Major subsequently left because of ill health in 1989. During the next six or seven years there was a virtual procession of conductors in what was a very unsettled period for the Band, using a veritable series of both resident and professional conductors with just a few names only making an impression on the Band's personnel. Of the numerous different conductors, John Prosser the long serving Bass player explains, "Brian Howard was a quiet unassuming conductor, he was only with the Band for a short period but produced some fine performances. He conducted on the *Brass from the Valleys* recording and also at the 1989 European held in Bergen, then steering the Band to 3rd place overall." Howard's tenure with the Band was just short of one year, which was the average time that a conductor stayed with the Band during this very unsettled period. In 1990, Nigel Seaman took control of the baton. He gave the Band the benefit of his orchestral experience from his position as Principal Tuba player with the BBC Welsh Orchestra (now the BBC National Orchestra of Wales). Nigel possessed an excellent conducting technique with a scrupulous attention to detail.

Malcolm (Mal) Brownbill also worked as professional conductor with the Band for a short period in 1990 when Nigel was the resident conductor. Malcolm was with the Band during a most difficult period because his first rehearsal was the night before the Bandroom burnt down. In fact Malcolm's tape recorder was a casualty of the tragedy. Every rehearsal he attended after the fire was held at a different venue. Mal conducted the Band at several local competitions; and BBC Broadcasts, during his period of tenure.

In July 1991, the Brass Band World magazine ran a front and centre page spread on the Cory Band and interviewed Denzil Stephens. Who better to lead the charge at the start of this decade than the man who had brought them European success in the early 1980s. Denzil Stephens returned to Cory and once again was hungry for the one title that had eluded him. During his interview with Andrew Baldock of Brass Band World, Denzil had stated that his objective was to win the National Final at the Royal Albert Hall, London. He regarded this aim as a personal goal. Denzil's earlier period with Cory is well documented, but it should be noted that he left the Band in 1982, just a few months before Major Arthur Kenney won the National Finals, (the first win of the Band's historic hat-trick). Denzil had an up-hill battle to try and emulate Kenney's success. Euphonium ace Lyndon Baglin had resigned to re-join arch rivals the Bristol based Sun Life Band and Chris Thomas, the virtuoso trombonist left to join Williams Fairey Band, another arch rival based in Stockport. Bass player Graham Sheppard, veteran with over thirty years of service was adamant that this was the most difficult period he had experienced during his entire time with the Band.

Denzil Stephens conducted Cory at the Welsh Regional Championships in 1992 on Michael Ball's *Frontier* gaining second place to Tredegar Town Band directed by Nigel Weeks. However, by the end of the year, David Thomas who had started to forge a conducting career in the Bristol area, had been appointed conductor with Arthur Kenney making a guest appearance to conduct the Band in a winning performance of Derek Bourgeois' *Blitz* at Treorchy thereby re-gaining the Welsh Championship and ensuring that the Band qualified to represent Wales at the European Championships to be held in Plymouth the following year. There were still more setbacks to come in 1992. The Band lost stalwart, Stuart Lewis who had played baritone since 1976 having been a member of the Band for almost forty years. The Band's long serving secretary, Ron Pryce relinquished his administrative role and the Band lost its sponsorship with the furniture manufacturers, Christie Tyler, in the same year.

During the next two years (1993-1995) Michael Antrobus arrived, a former conductor of the Black Dyke Mills band, to conduct the Band. Although his presence in the Bandroom was intermittent, he was regarded as a classy conductor, possibly the nearest thing in musical intensity to Major Kenney. Nevertheless the Band was slow to perform consistently at the high standards of previous years, consequently contest results proved the Band were still considerably underachieving during these lean years.

Under the baton of Michael Antrobus, Cory were placed 3rd at the European Championships in 1993, playing John Golland's *Sounds* and Philip Sparke's *Harmony Music*. Michael also conducted the Band the following year winning the Welsh Annual Regional Championships. Unfortunately an early draw at the National Finals in October coincided with Antrobus and Cory gaining a lowly 14th position. Throughout 1994, the resident conductor was Dennis Mahoney.

Stuck in this perpetual downward spiral, Graham O'Connor was engaged to conduct the Band during the 1994-95 period. Through his determination and raw enthusiasm, he was instrumental in halting the serious decline in the Band's historic levels of performance. He led the Band to a winning performance at the Grand Shield on Gilbert Vinter's *Spectrum*, thus heralding the start of a revival of fortunes on the contest platform. Winning the Grand Shield meant that the Band were promoted into the British 'Open' Championship after an enforced absence of five years. Disappointingly, Graham O'Connor's magic wand deserted him and the Band failed to qualify for the National Finals in 1995, and Michael Antrobus disappointingly just managed to steer the Band to a mid-placed 13th position at the British 'Open' Championships later that year.

Melvin White conducted Cory in 1996, although this relationship did not last. Melvin lived in Kent and the commute to and from the Band was simply not sustainable. Melvin conducted Cory at the British "Open" Championship in 1996 on Philip Wilby's *Revelation* where the Band were placed in a lowly 19th position.

Jeremy Wise arrived next on the scene to conduct Cory from 1997-2000. A talented all round musician, a fine cornet player and a promising conductor, Jeremy had a distinctive pedigree (his father Peter Wise had been a noted euphonium player and Professor of Euphonium at Kneller Hall Military School of Music). Jeremy proved to be an effective band trainer ably carrying on the re-building process started by Graham O'Connor. Even though he was more successful in competitive events than his predecessors in this decade – wining the Welsh Regional Championship in 1998 and 2000; his record at the British "Open" Championship, the National Championships and European contests didn't compare with Kenney or Stephens and some found his style of communication with the players rather abrupt. In an article in The Times newspaper he is quoted, during a rehearsal (conducting Dvorak's *Carnival Overture*), as suggesting that the only way the Band will learn this music is by "Going out into the garden and smashing yourselves in the face with a spade". Later in the same rehearsal, reporter Peter Martin wrote that "Jeremy dropped his hands in despair and asked the Band if they had just played the crap version or the very crap version!"

Throughout the eleven years between 1989 when the Major left due to his ill health and the year 2000 when Jeremy Wise departed, the Cory Band had experienced a sequence of thirteen professional conductors! Performances remained inconsistent, with contest results confirming that as well as being demoted from the British 'Open' Championships, they only qualified for the National Championship Finals on three occasions. This was certainly not a true reflection of the ability of the aforementioned conductors, as none of them were given full control of the Band during this low point in the Band's fortunes. Indeed most of these were directing winning performances with other bands whilst they were assisting Cory to re-build.

Obviously such a dire situation required drastic and direct action to stop the rot and there are characters who quite simply thrive on cheating adversity. Such a person was Bass player Austin Davies. Elected to lead a newly formed committee and aided and abetted by his right hand support – another long serving professional person – John Southcombe, Austin brought a new dynamic thrust and purpose to the committee. He is an inclusive man who believes in the powers of effective communication. Austin and John quickly gathered around them a team of officials that had a wide range of complementary yet diverse skills. Together and in a very short timescale they laid down both short and long term strategic plans aimed at achieving and then consolidating the future success and well being of the Band. That is another story!

Chapter 11
Sponsorship – Money Matters!
Sponsorship Safeguards Success

Sponsorship for the Cory Band started as long ago as 1895, when Sir Clifford Cory offered to provide financial assistance to find suitable employment and accommodation for a first class conductor. On the strength of this generous offer, the Band changed its name from the Ton Temperance Band to the Cory Workmen's Band. This essential support was ever present for many years whilst the collieries were privately owned. Such support continued for several years after 'vesting day' in 1947, which was the date the government nationalised the entire coal industry to form the UK wide National Coal Board.

Cory Band and Gelli Colliery Lodge started a Tote Fund in 1955 believing this was a successful and secure method of raising revenue for the Band. Every member was expected to sell at least one book of 'tote tickets' per week, although most sold many more than that. Every ticket that was sold generated monies for the Band. Although there are no records available that record the accurate income from the Tote Fund, Ron Pryce describes it as a substantial income stream. He recalls the Band loaning £1000 to Pen-y-graig Rugby Club in the early 1970's with the agreed method of repayment being the sales of Band tote tickets. Ron said, "They paid the loan back to us within three weeks!"

The Band stopped selling tote tickets in the mid 1980's when it started a new "money making" scheme known as The 200 Club. This scheme was based on the premise of 200 people paying £1 a month. Each week a number would be drawn and £100 in prize money would be paid out, thus generating a secure income of £5,200 per year for the Band. The 200 Club still operates today and it is compulsory for every Band member to contribute £1 per month.

In addition to the Tote, another fundraising scheme was introduced in the 1950's when it was common place for colliery bands to approach their local trade union mineworkers' lodges to request that their membership pay a weekly levy or subscription towards their local bands. In the Rhondda valleys there were about eight bands including:-

Coedely Colliery, Lewis Merthyr Colliery, Mid Rhondda, Parc and Dare Colliery, Treherbert Colliery, Tylorstown Colliery, Ynyshir & Tymawr Colliery, as well as Cory Workmen's Band.

They all received sums of money from the collieries, the money being deducted from the mineworkers' weekly pay. This income varied considerably; the workers supporting Cory Band paid half a penny a week towards the Band, while just a few miles up the valley the Parc and Dare Band received a full penny, twice as much per worker. This income also fluctuated according to the size of the individual colliery's workforce. Nevertheless, this was a steady and secure source of income for Cory Band to build on, whilst the mining industry remained in existence.

In return for these 'subscriptions' the Band would undertake a number of community activities including marching under their respective colliery banner at the annual National Union of Mineworkers (NUM) Gala Day held at Sophia Gardens, Cardiff. Also leading the parade on Armistice Day. The subscription lasted as long as the Colliery was working, so it's no coincidence that many Colliery Bands throughout the UK disappeared with the mass closures of the mines during the 1960's and 1970's. Cory Band survived financially following the closure of the Gelli Colliery in 1962, but found it very difficult to find a replacement source of income until the formation of the hardworking Ladies Committee in the mid 1970's.

People often say that, 'Behind every great man is an even greater woman'. That statement is the absolute truth for Cory Band from the mid 1970's, when the Band was totally self funding being heavily reliant on the Ladies' Committee to ensure that the Band remained financially viable. This dedicated group of women made up of wives, mothers, girlfriends, sisters, aunties, and other female friends of the Band, raised an amazing sum of £41,446 over a period of approximately twenty five years.

Their fundraising activities were many and varied, ranging from jumble sales, raffles, Christmas fayres, duck races, car rallies, social evenings, ladies "make up" parties and even a sponsored swim! The ladies had a totally separate committee to the main Band committee, and all the money they raised through their functions was held in their own bank account. If the Band required financial support from the ladies for a particular project, the

The Ladies Committee celebrates another win.

elected officers of the Band had to meet with the elected officers of the Ladies' Committee and put forward their case for the funding. The officers of the Ladies' Committee would then consider the request, verifying the decision with the other members in response to requests from the Band committee. Just picture the scene, Jeff Thomas, Chairperson of the Cory Band, Graham Sheppard, Secretary, and Gwyn Thomas having to go "cap in hand" to their wives:- Margaret Thomas, Barbara Sheppard, and Helen Thomas to ask for money! Brownie points had never been so vital!

In an interview for the Sunday Times, Dot Tanner, a leading member of the Ladies' Committee said, "I just can't imagine there not being a Cory Band, we are all so proud of their achievements". Barbara Sheppard, another member said, "The "boys" are all so dedicated, it's impossible to plan a family wedding without consulting the Band's diary". The reporter asked Dot if she ever got fed up with the Band and the amount of time it took her husband away from her. She answered, "I'd rather play second fiddle to a trombone than a blonde any day!"

In 1982, the year that the Band won the National Championship for the first victory of the historic hat-trick years, the Band could not have afforded the coach to travel to London (there was also two nights in a hotel), if it hadn't been for the fundraising by the dedicated Ladies' Committee. Barbara Sheppard said they regularly sold homemade cakes, sandwiches and teas, held countless Tupperware parties and organised fayres. Susan Southcombe said, "Since we formed in 1976 we were sometimes raising up to £3000 per year". John Trotman remained adamant, but very grateful that where ever the Band was due to play, they were certain that the women would help to get them there. Helen Thomas was very matter of fact, "The boys prepared the music for contests and we organised the fundraising for these important events." Jeff Thomas was more realistic for the long term - "We need a sponsor, we don't need a lot of money, £12,000 a year would be great, and we'll do the rest".

Cory will always be forever thankful to everyone who has played some part in the fundraising activities of the Ladies' Committee throughout this period in the Band's history. Margaret Thomas, Helen Thomas, Barbara Sheppard, Pat McCann, Dorothy Tanner, Susan Southcombe, Lynette Jones, Joan Curtis, Doreen Trotman, Betty Pryce, Julie Roberts are just some of the many ladies that were at the forefront of this dedicated supporting effort, to help finance the Band. There are many more that contributed. An unqualified and sincere "Thank You, Ladies!"

The Ladies Committee 1983

In 1987, Jeff Thomas's wish was granted when local firm Christie Tyler contacted the Band. Graham Sheppard recalls the sequence of events that led to the development of this partnership. "1986 was not a successful year in contesting terms. We still had a full concert diary but the need to raise the profile of the Band

The Ladies Committee in the 1980's

was glaringly obvious, else the concert engagements would fade away. There was also a growing tendency to seek financial assistance from the Ladies' Committee on a more frequent basis. Obviously, without a concerted effort to seek a meaningful sponsor, the Band would soon run into serious financial difficulties. A subcommittee was convened with the aim of producing a Marketing Portfolio for the Band, which could then be used to attract potential sponsors.

At that time Don Tanner's (Solo Trombone) daughter Jill, worked as an editor with a local free magazine. We discussed our plan with her and within a short space of time Jill created our first Marketing Portfolio. With an explanatory letter, and the help of many people possessing administrative and secretarial experience, we proceeded to produce and send out a hundred of these portfolios to various companies within South Wales. Fortunately, Christie Tyler (International Furniture Makers) was one of them. Nigel Phillips, Christie Tyler's Sales and Marketing Director contacted Jeff Thomas, and a meeting was convened. One of the significant marketing strategies of Christie Tyler at that time was their Furniture Fortnight, when once a year they would invite major customers to visit South Wales for a few days to be

New stand banners

entertained alongside a tour of their various show-rooms. Nigel's plan was for the Band to perform each night during this fortnight. This was agreed, (the terms were beneficial to the Band) and the outcome was a major success for the Company. Christie Tyler subsequently contacted the Band to co-operate with them on similar promotional events in the future. It was at this stage that the Band considered it timely to raise with them the possibility of sponsorship.

After brief negotiations, they offered the Band an inclusive sum of £10,000 per year, to be reviewed after two years. We readily agreed and entered into partnership with them, consequently from 1988 until 1992 we were known as Christie Tyler Cory Band.

Christie Tyler Cory Band c. 1989

Acquiring this sponsorship meant that we were able to apply to the Welsh Arts Council for a Pairing Grant. The application was a success and we were awarded the Grant, which effectively doubled our income. Throughout this period we performed at Christie Tyler's Furniture Fortnight, the 'Leekes' Welsh Squash Classic Tournament, a Concert in St David's Hall, Cardiff, and at a range of functions at smaller venues that only required an ensemble from within the Band. Unfortunately, our contest results failed to improve at the desired rate so we encountered several major changes of personnel. This added unwanted fuel to the Bandroom fire of 1990. A traumatic experience that thrust us into a difficult nomadic existence for several years.

Nigel Phillips, our crucial link with Christie Tyler left the Company, so our sponsorship ended. This was almost a blessing in disguise because the Band were becoming increasingly disenchanted with the direction that the partnership was taking during a period when Christie Tyler was refocusing their Marketing strategy. Nevertheless, the Band will always be extremely grateful for the support they received from Christie Tyler, during such a difficult period for the Band. It would not have been possible to have obtained our current Band Room had it not been for their generous support.

In the intervening years between the lapsing of the sponsorship deal with Christie Tyler and the development of the partnership with 'Just Rentals', the financial support given by the Ladies' Committee continued to be invaluable, but sadly it was inevitable that eventually the funds would become exhausted.

In April 1998, Cory was successful in securing the Champion Band of Wales title when their performance of *Montage* found favour with Lt Colonel Frank Renton at the Annual Welsh Regional Championship contest at the Brangwyn Hall, Swansea. This success also secured Cory's invitation to represent Wales at the European Brass Band Championships that were being held in Munich in May 1999.

Much prestige and esteem is connected with an invitation to represent your country at any hobby, pastime, or sport and the feeling when walking onto a platform knowing you are representing not just your own Band, but the whole country, fills Musical Directors and players with an immense feeling of pride. However, the European invitation doesn't come without its challenges and is somewhat of a double edged sword. There is little doubt that the sharpest edge of the sword is the financial outlay required to attend these annual European events. For the visit to Munich in 1998, Cory had to raise £12,000 and that was travelling by coach, not flying!

Such projects are significant undertakings and invariably result in a subcommittee being formed to look after the specific logistics of the Band's attendance at the competition. The European event in 1999 continued the task of raising funds and organising the visit of the Band to Munich. This was delegated to John Southcombe, a long serving solo cornet player with the Band, but in his professional life, a software sales executive.

John was tasked by the Band's committee to research and find potential organisations that would be prepared to provide financial support to assist Cory in their quest to represent Wales in Munich. With some trepidation, but much enthusiasm John recalls the extent of his task, "Initially, I visited Treorchy Library, searching through several directories of local and national trust funds as well as charity organisations to identify suitable candidates. Eventually I amassed four A4 pages of addresses and telephone numbers of potential candidates. It was a fairly arduous process because each trust and charity specified different criteria that had to be met. For example, each had special areas of interest they were prepared to support, such as the arts, sport, local community and environmental projects. This was coupled with the constraints imposed by the geographical areas for which they were responsible. Finally and impartially there was a maximum amount that they were prepared to offer for single projects that they adjudged to be worthwhile."

This was quite time consuming research resulting in some thirty letters requesting financial help being sent to organisations. John advised that "The letters I wrote were basically appealing to the Trusts and Charities in Wales, the content focusing on the heritage of the Cory band and its strong roots in the mining industry. I also described the undoubted honour to the locality of a village band in a deprived area being invited to represent Wales at a major European Music Championship – in other words the pride of the valleys going to do battle with the cream of Europe."

The approach paid dividends and responses started to come back through the post. As anticipated "We had more rejections than successes, but the success we received in financial terms amounted to the value of £3,000. Nevertheless, we still needed to raise £12,000 to get to Munich but this funding helped us to make a great start, but we still had a long way to go"

As always, the Ladies' Committee members were ready to 'roll up their sleeves' and help as much as possible. Even with their immense support and all the additional engagements that the Band was able to accept it was clearly apparent that the Band needed a major sponsor to get to Munich.

The Band's 'local hostelry' was the Ton Pentre Football Club. Cory Band is renowned as a 'family' band and after rehearsal on a Thursday night, most of the players, along with wives, girlfriends, and partners would congregate at the club to socialise and talk about anything and everything, including brass bands. It was during one of these nights at the football club, when the Band members were enjoying a "congenial pint" that the fundraising for the 1999 European contest became the focus of attention and it became clear that a strategic change in outlook was now overdue.

It was thought, rather than looking for support to address the short term challenge of getting the Band to Munich, why not look for a major 'blue flag' sponsor to help level the playing field with the other sponsored bands from the North of England.

The seed was sown and the task of identifying potential candidates for such a partnership was underway. The criteria was pretty straightforward and required a company with local roots in the South Wales Valleys, or Wales in general, with a strategic growth and expansion plan, a shared vision of success and a significant leader in their field. Such a company would probably hold community values high and understand the heritage of the valleys and the critical role brass bands played in the community. The prospective company would need to be financially sound, forward thinking and open to building a successful partnership with an amateur music organisation. A number of companies made the shortlist but only one stood out head and shoulders above them all.

Just Rentals PLC was the brainchild of two very successful self made businessmen and entrepreneurs; Bernard Jones OBE and Gerald Coleman were co-owners of the company. Just Rentals was established in1972, and had grown to become the largest independent electrical retailer in Wales, and the market leader in coin meter television retailing. The cornerstone of the company's success was its reliance on traditional values and the delivery of unbeatable standards of customer service.

Stand banner 1998

Just Rentals' whole business ethos was built around caring about its customers and the community it served. Both Bernard and Gerald strongly believed in supporting the people that supported them, and they consistently provided financial assistance of over £700,000 to specific community initiatives covering Education, Health, Crime Prevention, Drug Awareness, and Sports on an annual basis.

On 8th April 1998, John wrote a letter to the Chairman of Just Rentals, Bernard Jones outlining the recent success of the Band and their impending visit to Munich. The main body of the communication detailed the financial outlay required and posing the question, what could be offered in return for any assistance Just Rentals might provide?

Also included was a paragraph relating to major sponsorship of the Band which finished with the following sentence "The Band currently ranks in the top 10 brass bands in Great Britain and it is strongly felt throughout the Banding fraternity that Cory will, in the near future, win one of the coveted 'majors' and this could be achieved carrying your company name"

This obviously resonated with Bernard and a response was sent advising that the letter had been forwarded to Maurice Padfield, who was then Community Affairs Director of the Company, with the possibility that a meeting could be arranged to discuss the proposition by furnishing more detail.

On 30th April 1998 John walked into the headquarters of Just Rentals, Dinas Isaf House in Williamstown, deep in the Rhondda Valley! Carrying a laptop computer, he was going to meet with Maurice Padfield and deliver a presentation that the Band hoped would help secure its future at the very top of the brass band tree. The initial presentation went extremely well and it was apparent early on that a relationship was being struck between John and Maurice. The presentation outlined a number of key areas of how the Arts and Business could work together to their mutual benefit. The presentation covered key areas such as:

- The Cory Band Heritage
- Vision and Mission Statement
- Key Benefits that a partnership with a world class brass band could bring to Just Rentals
- Maximising commercial funding through the Arts and Business (Cymru) Pairing Scheme
- Existing successful partnerships between the Arts and Business
- Commercial Proposal
- The potential PR exposure

For the final slides of the presentation, John used his professional skills from the printing and graphics art industry to create four newspaper headlines using the banner of the local newspaper, The Rhondda Leader. The headlines read:

- *Just Rentals Help Cory Achieve National Success*
- *Just Rentals Cory Band Win National Championships of Great Britain*
- *Just Rentals Cory Band Take British Open Title Back to Wales for the First Time*
- *Just Rentals Cory Band Conquer Europe*

Little did he realise that the presentation he had just delivered would prove to be the catalyst of a relationship that would help shape and consolidate Cory's future. Nor was there any crystal ball that could predict the future. However, in the first fourteen months of the partnership between Just Rentals and Cory Band they managed to rewrite the record books and deliver the British 'Open' Championship title to Wales for the very first time in the competition's history. This was closely followed five weeks later by the Champion Band of Great Britain trophy returning to Wales over the Severn Bridge for the 5th time – Yes, all in the first 14 months!

Maurice was true to his word and indeed he presented the Band's commercial proposal to the board of Just Rentals. Subsequently, a meeting was then arranged for John to meet with Bernard Jones and Gerald Coleman in Dinas Isaf House.

"As part of my business life, I meet with many high level executives, however, for some reason the day I met with Bernard and Gerald there was a little more tension than normal. When you're representing your friends, family, and people who give up a lot of their own personal time to achieve the extremely high standards that are expected to play in a Band like Cory, this meeting took on a whole new perspective." says John.

As it turned out, the whole two hours flew by, with the majority of conversation taken up reminiscing about brass bands. Before their business ventures had taken off, both Bernard

Gerald Coleman and Bernard Jones

and Gerald had been former players in brass bands. Gerald had in fact, spent a short time as a cornet player and member of the Cory Band, whereas Bernard had been a tenor horn player for many years with the Mid Rhondda Band. As their business grew into a market leading force in the coin meter sector they, unfortunately, had to leave their playing days behind them, though they always kept an eye on proceedings from a distance.

The time that was spent discussing the Band's proposal centred on the benefits that could be attained by partnering with the Band. As an organisation, Just Rentals received a lot of requests for financial assistance and a significant amount was given each year through the community initiatives they supported. However, something different was needed to capture the imagination of Bernard and Gerald that was more than just headlines in a newspaper and general media exposure. At this particular time, the company were looking to expand their business into the North East of England, Yorkshire, the Midlands and the North West. The timing was perfect for Just Rentals to connect with the communities in these new regions through a brass band. In Cory they had one of the best known bands in the country. Through numerous concerts in Morley, Huddersfield, Brighouse, and Leeds, the Just Rentals Cory Band could carry the Company's name wherever it travelled, helping to build brand awareness in regions that were synonymous with brass bands.

Just Rentals Cory Band, pictured outside The Royal Albert Hall, October 1998

Obviously, there was commercial benefit to be gained from a partnership with the Cory Band but deep down it was the love of brass bands and the knowledge that they would be associated with the best that helped Bernard and Gerald come to a decision. On 27th July 1998 a letter was sent by Maurice Padfield of Just Rentals to John Southcombe stating:

"Dear John,
Further to the recent meeting which was held here at Just Rentals Direct head office, I am delighted to confirm formally to you that Just Rentals Direct will sponsor the Cory band for an initial period of 3 years.
The level of sponsorship is to be at the sum of £15k per annum, and an additional cost to Just Rentals Direct to provide uniform items for the Band, which will include a new formal concert dress and a walking out uniform"

The media wheels started turning almost instantly with press releases hitting both digital and physical brass band publications. The local press also got in on the act.

On Wednesday August 19th 1998 under the heading ....

"Neil Jenkins's audition for the Cory is a nice try!"

. ... it was reported that Neil Jenkins the famous rugby player and Wales' outside half had 'auditioned' for the Just Rentals Cory Band in front of a Western Mail photographer!

"Just Rentals, the market leading television and electrical goods Rental Company based at Williamstown in Rhondda Cynon Taff, has entered into a sponsorship deal with the Cory Band.

When the deal was announced on Monday night at Ton Pentre Football Club, Wales outside half Neil Jenkins sportingly submitted to an audition for a place in the Bands prize winning line-up.

Jenkins is a public relations executive with Just Rentals as well as one of international rugby's great place kickers of all time – but the Band decided he didn't quite make the grade as a brass player."

For many years, Just Rentals had been the main sponsor of Pontypridd Rugby Football Club which just happened to be Neil Jenkins' club side. As a PR executive for the Company, he seemed an obvious choice to use as the talisman to announce the new partnership to the Welsh public.

Such a long standing history and heritage of the Cory Band did cause some problems for the media in the initial stages of the partnership. There were numerous telephone conversations between Maurice and John during those early days. The media insisted on referring to the Band as Cory Band and not Just Rentals Cory band. Both parties had worked hard to ensure that the right message was getting to the publishers and editors but it seemed as if old habits died hard. These were mere teething problems that were easily resolved.

There were also changes that the Band personnel and the Banding public needed to embrace. As part of the sponsorship package, Just Rentals had committed to providing new stage uniforms as well as walking out uniforms. The blazers were quite straight forward and would remain the Band's traditional navy blue with a change to the badge to reflect the new name of Just Rentals Cory Band. These would be accompanied by a new tie in the Company's corporate colours and grey trousers.

The changes to the stage uniform were however somewhat more radical. Cory had been synonymous for years with their navy blue stage tunics with maroon lapels and black trousers. As soon as they took the stage everyone knew it was Cory. However, it was agreed with Bernard and Gerald that to ensure maximum impact and representation of the Just Rentals brand, the new stage tunics would be in the corporate colours of Just Rentals which were red with green trim. This did not sit comfortably with some of the traditionalists on the Band's committee. It was further discussed and agreed that this was a necessary change to move the Band forward into the 21st Century and to allow competition on a level playing field with the top bands in the country.

With this news, the Band's immediate future was financially secure. What's more, not only did they have enough capital to attend Munich, they could also start on other projects that had been put on the 'back burner' until finances were more stable. One of the main priorities was the upkeep of the Band room; with the additional finances, they were able to give it a face-lift.

To maximise the funding opportunities available to the Band, it was agreed with Just Rentals that John Southcombe would look into matched funding through the Arts and Business Pairing Scheme. This is a cash award scheme promoting business sponsorship of the arts and has three primary objectives:

- To encourage businesses to sponsor the arts for the first time
- To foster strong, lasting partnerships between business and the arts
- To develop wider access to the arts through high quality business sponsorship

The pairing scheme is an incentive scheme for business sponsors, not simply another source of public subsidy for the arts. It helps both businesses and the arts get the most from their partnership by providing additional money. This is given on the basis that it is used by the arts organisation to supply extra benefits to their sponsor which would not otherwise be available.

The application process required some detailed responses from both Just Rentals and the Band; however, the time invested proved to be fruitful and match-funding was granted by Arts and Business (Cymru) to the Just Rentals Cory Band.

The Band did quite well in their first outings as the Just Rentals Cory Band gaining 1st prize at the Royal National Eisteddfod of Wales and 6th place at the National Championships of Great Britain. Bernard and Gerald were present in the audience at the Royal Albert Hall, London and the day brought back mixed emotions for them, both having played there themselves years before.

Bernard and Gerald were fantastic sponsors because they took a real and knowledgeable interest in the Band, but placed few reciprocal demands. In 1999, there were just two requests for the Band to perform. The first date was 11th November 1999 at the Just Rentals Hall of Fame Sports Award Luncheon, the second was at the Just Rentals Children's Christmas Party.

The following year, the Just Rentals organisation went through a process of re-branding which resulted in the company changing its name to Buy As You View Ltd. The Band was happy to be part of the re-branding and immediately became known as the Buy As You View Cory Band. The new Buy As You View Cory Band won the first four contests it entered with its equally new conductor Dr Robert B. Childs. The wins included the historic 'Double' in 2000.

Buy As You View Cory Band, pictured outside the company headquarters in Llantrisant after their historic 'double win' in 2000

The year 2000 also proved to be successful for Buy As You View Ltd, as a result of their sponsorship of the Band. Each year, Arts & Business Cymru present awards celebrating creativity and excellence in partnerships between business and the arts. 2000 represented the seventh in the Arts & Business Cymru series of awards and Buy As You View, were nominated by the Band in the category 'Best New Sponsor'. All the criteria were met - businesses were eligible to enter in this category within the first three years of arts sponsorship. The award recognised an outstanding and imaginative partnership between an arts organisation and a new sponsor. It was with great pride that Maurice Padfield took the stage at St. David's Hall, Cardiff to accept the award of 'Best New Sponsor 2000' on behalf of Buy As You View.

It also represented the second year of the initial three year sponsorship deal with Buy As You View. John Southcombe was then asked to put together a business case and commercial proposal for the coming year. John recalls, "I knew that 2001 was going to be an expensive year for the Band as we had qualified again for the European Championships, this time in Montreux, Switzerland". John submitted the proposal as requested and was delighted when Bernard agreed to increase the Band's sponsorship and introduce a rolling year on year agreement rather than the initial three year package.

In 2004, Bernard and Gerald sold their shareholdings in Buy As You View and effectively, this was the beginning of the end of the Band's sponsorship. Bernard's final act on behalf of the Band was to negotiate a further three

The inauguration of Gerald Coleman (left) as High Sheriff of Mid-Glamorgan in 2002

year sponsorship package for the sum of £350,000. The partnership between the Band and the new owners of Buy As You View was working and the relationship between Bob and Bernard was still very warm, however there was a niggling problem that was beginning to upset everyone involved in the new partnership. This was the continued reluctance of the brass band press, commentators, programme printers and the BBC to fully embrace the new name of the Band. They continually abbreviated it from the Buy As You View Cory Band to Cory Band. The final straw was delivered during the European Championships in Glasgow in 2004. Not only were the Band on the end of a shocking result, but the organisers printed the Band's name in the contest programme as Buy As You View Cory Band and most unfortunately the contest controller and BBC presenter referred to the Band as Cory from the stage on several occasions!

This was totally unacceptable! Bob Childs and the Management of the Band agreed to change the name to the Buy As You View Band, hoping that this might give longevity to the association with Buy As You View well beyond the agreed three year package. The change of name didn't go down at all well with some of the past players of the Band, but it was the same decision, based on the same rationale that the Ton Temperance Band took in 1895 when they changed their name to Cory Workmen's Band! The decision was taken with the knowledge that the traditional Cory name could always be readopted if, and when, the association with Buy As You View ever ceased. Buy As You View didn't extend the deal beyond Bernard's three year plan and the Band did revert back to its traditional name in 2007. Since then the Band has received continued financial support from Bernard via The Desna Robbins Jones Charitable Foundation. This Foundation was set-up in the name of his late wife.

The Cory Band have subsequently developed several significant working partnerships with business and education, currently having healthy relationships with:-

- Bergerault Percussion,
- G.K.Graphic Design vof,
- Hercules Music Stands,
- Prima Vista Musikk,
- Royal Welsh College of Music and Drama.
- Thomas Coaches of the Rhondda
- World of Brass.

Bernard Jones OBE

Nevertheless it is still the warm generosity of the Band's President - Bernard Jones OBE which allows the Band to function and compete on a level financial playing field with other sponsored brass bands in the United Kingdom.

Chapter 12

Childs Play!

Austin Davies, Chairperson of Buy As You View Cory Band describes events leading to the appointment of Dr Robert (Bob) Childs to the Band, "I had been speaking to 'Nick' Childs and discussed the possibility of him coming to conduct the Band on a regular basis. At that time he could not give us the commitment we wanted because he was conducting Fodens Band. We were looking for someone to conduct us at the Ebbw Vale Contest, Nick couldn't do it, so he asked his brother Bob if he was available. At this point we had nothing to lose and Bob was engaged to take us to the Contest on a one-off basis."

Dr Robert B. Childs

Bob Childs remembers the sequence of events very clearly, "In 2000, I got a phone call from my brother Nick who had been approached by Cory to take them to the Ebbw Vale contest. They had chosen to play Bailey's - *Diadem of Gold*, Nick was unable to take them, so I agreed to take Cory and set about preparing for the contest. I asked Nick about the strengths and the weaknesses of Cory and the strengths and weaknesses of the main opposition at the Contest. Nick told me that Tredegar Band were on a high at this time with Iwan Fox on Soprano and Ian Porthouse on Principal Cornet. I knew that if we were going to win we'd have to work really hard. We would have to beat the other bands and the dreadful acoustic of the notorious Ebbw Vale Leisure Centre! I set about the rehearsals with thorough preparation. Ian Williams (solo cornet) and Steve Barnsley (soprano) played superbly and adjudicator Malcolm Brownbill put us three clear points above the rest..... We won!

At the same time, conditions were beginning to deteriorate at Black Dyke. "We had just lost our sponsorship from Bradford and Bingley Building Society and the conductor - James Watson was on the verge of resigning. I had played at Black Dyke for almost ten years and was thinking about a change. I really enjoyed conducting Buy As You View Cory at the Ebbw Vale contest so I subsequently mentioned to Austin Davies that I would be interested in taking the Band on a full time basis. I had been conducting Black Dyke a little at that time, and after taking Buy As You View Cory I easily recognised their great potential. I remember saying to my brother, "this band could beat Black Dyke". Austin was delighted, but felt he couldn't ask me to give up my playing and my role at Black Dyke. I reassured Austin that I thought Black Dyke was going through a transition period. James Watson was about to leave and I had always played under his direction, not just at Black Dyke, but also at Brighouse & Rastrick, I was one of the older players in Black Dyke and had been around the circuit for some time. I was now looking to make the transition from player to conductor. In June Austin Davies and I arranged a meeting to discuss the idea further. We met at the Bandroom in Ton Pentre, there were about seven or eight committee members present including Austin Davies, John Southcombe, John Prosser and John Trotman. I was quite nervous and had written everything I wanted to say on a piece of paper. It was rather like a "sales pitch". It included my thoughts and plans for the Band and described why I thought I was the right man for the job.

This is the basis of the presentation made by Bob for the challenging position of Musical Director of Buy As You View Cory:-

Education
Everyone knows Bob Childs the euphoniumist, but it's been my plan to eventually swap from the euphonium to the baton for over ten years. That's one of the reasons I've studied music in such great depth as a mature student. I spent three years with Dr Philip Wilby at Leeds University gaining a Masters Degree, then continued developing my skills by doing a Post Graduate Degree in Education with the Open University. During the same period I also gained diplomas from both the Royal College of Music and the London College of Music. I am currently considering a Doctoral programme at Salford University. All a big step from leaving school at 15 and going to work at Ebbw Vale Steel Works!

Conducting
I first started conducting when my dad was ill, helping to fulfill his commitments with Brodsworth and Thoresby Colliery in the 1980's. Since then I formed a band in Hull and took them from the 4th Section to the Championship Section in 6 years, culminating in being placed 8th at the Royal Albert Hall, London on Isaiah 40. The Band's rise was not dissimilar to David King and Swinton Band. Since then I've conducted lots of bands on a one-off basis (due to commitments at Dyke) Yorkshire Imps, Brighouse & Rastrick and Fodens. Opportunities have arisen in the past with other bands, but the time or the situation didn't seem right for me to sacrifice what I had at Black Dyke.

Black Dyke
I have been at "Dyke" for 10 years as a player and latterly 4 years as associate conductor and have recently been made a Trustee of the Band. I've won the European, National, British 'Open', Yorkshire Regional and Spennymoor Entertainment contests. I've conducted concerts with guest soloists Susana Walton, Lesley Garret, Evelyn Glennie and Phil Smith the American trumpeter. I have been the person hiring and firing players for the past 3 to 4 years, as well as negotiating individual retainers and concert fees.

Why Buy As You View Cory?
I was very impressed by the Band in the preparation for the Ebbw Vale Contest. I think the Band has great potential and an attitude to match. Working with the Band also reminded me that I am Welsh and coming back to my roots is also a major attraction. There is no doubt that to compete at the top level, you need good musical resources but you also need financial assistance, Buy As You View Cory seem to have both these aspects sorted out.

How can I see this relationship working?
I will have to resign my position at Black Dyke. This would mean losing my retainer, concert

fees both as a player and associate conductor. It would also mean resigning my post at St Mary's College, Hull where I teach one and a half days a week. So, obviously there are important financial implications to overcome.

Long Term Goal
To be the Musical Director of the Band, a role similar to Nick Childs at Fodens, David King at YBS, and James Watson at Dyke. This would mean relocating and finding additional work in Wales.

Short Term Aims
To be the Professional Conductor and work with a resident conductor. This is <u>not</u> so musically fulfilling, but could be a starting point.

Aims both Long & Short Term
- **Contests:** Winning the Nationals, European, British 'Open' and Kerkrade World Music Festival/World Champion Band. To be ranked No 1 in the world. To be consistent at major contests (winning can never be guaranteed). To lift the position in the Band's World Rankings. Whit Friday March Contest. I'm <u>not</u> keen on this!
- **Recordings** CD's Video: Buy As You View Cory has little or no recordings available. I would like to fund some recordings and make the Band one of the most recorded Bands in the country, producing: Popular selling also CDs/ Premiere Recordings/ CDs promoting Soloists from within the Band and possibly a link up with a publisher?
- **Premier Band in Wales** Lots of top Welsh players have drifted to play with bands in the North of England. I'd like to entice them back and use their expertise and experience to make and consolidate Buy As You View Cory as the Premier Band in Wales.
- **Tours: UK/ European/ (USA ?)** Music commissions: Peter Graham, Philip Wilby, Ken Downie, John Pickard (Bristol).Either arrangements suitable for concert work / entertainment contests or Test piece for European 2001.
- **Joint Concerts:** Brighouse/Dyke in Yorkshire. CWS in Scotland / Concert Uppermill Civic Hall.
- **Contempory Music Festivals:** Fishguard, Huddersfield, Cheltenham Festival.
- **Conclusion:** Taking the Buy As You View Cory Band is something I really want to do. You've seen me working and I've heard you play. I honestly think that working together could bring us both unparalleled success and that this decade could be ours. But it is a massive decision to make for us both and one which will send shock waves through the Banding world. I am obviously giving up a secure and prestigious position to come to Buy As You View Cory and I have to be sure you really want me.

Bob continues the story, "The meeting went well and I was reassured that Buy As You View Cory had the platform to be successful, not only regarding personnel, but also financially. I rang Nick and told him that I wanted to leave Black Dyke to take Buy As You View Cory. I told him that if he wanted the job I'd obviously retreat. Nick said that he could never take Buy As You View Cory full time because his main priority at that time was Fodens. He advised me to accept the position and wished me all the best. I was officially appointed Musical Director of the Buy As You View Cory Band in June 2000 and regularly travelled from Hull to Ton Pentre until I relocated to Wales the following year."

After a successful result at Ebbw Vale, Bob and the Band followed that up with a win at the Welsh National Eisteddfod, held at Llanelli in August. Preparations were then in full flow for the start of the major contest season. Firstly the British 'Open' in September; this was to be Bob's debut conducting at the British 'Open'. The test piece was *Ceremony* by Michael Ball. Buy As You View Cory and Bob produced a stunning performance resulting in another first prize. However this wasn't Ebbw Vale or Llanelli. This was the British 'Open' Championships and was the prize that had eluded the Buy As You View Cory Band throughout their long 116 year history. It was also the first time any Welsh Band had won in the contest's 148 year history. Three contests and three wins, the perfect start, but could it continue?

Once the celebrations had ceased the hard work began again, this time for the National Finals at The Royal Albert Hall, London. The test piece was a new commission by Peter Graham called *Harrison's Dream*. The members of Buy As You View Cory Band were beginning to find out that Bob's contest preparation left no stone unturned. The Band's Principal Cornet player Ian Williams commented, "Bob's preparation was a revelation; we had never experienced such a meticulous approach before". Bob describes his preparation methods; "Conducting the Band full time means I need to be both the resident and professional conductor. To do this, I make a copy of my score and physically touch every dynamic with a red pen. I also circle all the interesting parts I want to bring out. Then I take this fully marked up score to band and rehearse the Band knowing exactly what I would like to hear. I am a hundred steps ahead of the Band which means I can pace rehearsals exactly how I want.

Usually about a week before the contest when I have the piece technically perfect, I transfer to the original score and start working from a totally different perspective. I play all the parts on my euphonium and look for natural intuitive expression, I look for awkward fingerings to see what I can make easier, if it's a big blow, I can work on stamina building leading up to the final performance. By discarding the copied score and reverting to the original one, it's like swapping from being a resident conductor to being a professional conductor. I find myself saying different things and using a different vocabulary. This is a methodical system which I have used since being with the Band. I have rather an obsessive approach and the only way not to miss something is to keep checking the score all the time."

Contest day soon arrived and the Buy As You View Cory Band gave another fine performance. The year was complete and the combination of Buy As You View Cory and Bob Childs was cemented by winning the National Championships of Great Britain and thereby attaining 'the seldom achieved Double.' The Buy As You View Cory Band and Robert Childs had shocked the Banding world by winning its two most prestigious contests in the first year of their relationship.

Cory Band, Dyffryn House, 2000

The Buy As You View Cory Band Personnel for the winning performance at the National Championships of Great Britain 2000 is shown in Appendix C

Bob remembers shoals of congratulatory letters arriving the following week. "An A4 packet arrived and inside was a green card signed by the whole of the Black Dyke Band obviously instigated by my brother Nicholas. Thanks Nick!"

Bob also reflected on the instant success and gives a few reasons as to why it may have happened; "I think that maybe it was that I was new to conducting at the top level and had nothing to lose. I had been watching people work for the last 20-30 years, people like Major Peter Parkes, Dr Roy Newsome and James Watson. I took the best of what I'd seen and put it into practice. Maybe some of my musical decisions were a bit cavalier and I have a tendency to overdo things. Nevertheless, they are always decisive. When I listen to the performances of *Harrison's Dream* and *Ceremony* now, I do think that possibly they were overdone, however times change and so do styles and interpretations.

Professor David King frequently referred to Buy As You View Cory Band as the 'Mighty Cory Band.' I think what he was referring to was the massive volume the Band produced. We were a very loud Band. At times, very very loud, bordering on harsh. However, halls like the Royal Albert Hall, London and Symphony Hall, Birmingham will take high volume and reduce the harshness. We are certainly not as harsh now, but we are probably not as loud either, we have cultivated a more mellow tone over the years.

I was also fortunate that both my first British Open and National test pieces with Buy As You View Cory were new pieces of music. What I have discovered about myself is that on new music, I do not have to try and invent new approaches. I just look for what's on the score and bring it out, and certainly my record with Buy As You View Cory on new pieces reflects this. So, had the year 2000 been two established test pieces, who knows, it might have been a different result. The fact was that *Ceremony* was a very complicated and technical piece that needed some major decisions-making in terms of balance, and *Harrison's Dream* was an equally difficult and complicated work that needed rearranging for my players at the time; this all worked to my advantage with the way I approach preparation for performances."

Ian Williams sums up in his own opinion of why the new partnership worked so well, "Bob allowed the Band to play as a Band. Before Bob arrived we were a group of individuals: Bob joined us all together. I relate our rise to that of Welsh Rugby. It took us some time to grasp the professional era, but like Wales, Buy As You View Cory was shown the way by Bob and the Band seized the opportunity with both hands."

John Southcombe identifies some of Bob's strengths; "Bob is a very structured person, and every rehearsal is planned and disciplined. Bob treated the Band room like a church and so we soon treated it the same way. We were a group of individuals and Bob turned us into a team. We were a 'middle of the road Band' with the occasional top six finishes. Bob's freshness and new approach realised our dream of being a top Band."

John Prosser also cites discipline as the catalyst for success, "The key word for me was discipline. Bob had no messing about in rehearsals. He was very approachable and built confidence within the Band. We didn't realise how good we were, Bob brought that out. We had the raw talent and with Bob's phenomenal work ethic, we became World Class."

David Cornelius placed encouragement high on the list, "Confidence is everything when playing at the top level. Bob identified players who needed encouraging. The preparation was so structured, more than any other conductor I have played under. Bob dissected every piece to the last semi-quaver and knew exactly where each part would sound best. Some swapping of parts created amazing performances."

The same words are used to describe Bob's approach to contesting, Andrew Williams (bass trombone) also referred to discipline and planning, "Discipline and more focused rehearsals, concentration in each rehearsal was intense: when you finished rehearsal you knew you had worked hard. Before Bob arrived the rehearsals were like a farmyard. Bob's experience and discipline solved this straight away. Everyone knew what was happening within a performance. When we played *Ceremony* at the Open, I was surprised how well the Band played: we just did what we had been doing in the rehearsal room. Meticulous preparation and respect for the conductor was the key."

Bob Childs also introduced open rehearsals prior to a contest. This aids preparation by adding a little extra pressure on the players with a live audience present. It also allowed the Band to play in a bigger acoustic. 2001 started with a shock 4th place at the Annual Welsh Regional Contest, adjudicator James Scott placing the Band 4th after a superb performance of *Jazz* by Philip Wilby. This was quickly followed with a stunning performance of *Montreux Wind Dances* at the European Championships in Switzerland. The performance was good enough to win the set test piece section but not enough to take the overall title from David King's fantastic Yorkshire Building Society (YBS) Band.

Bob puts most of the success the Band has achieved over the past decade down to team-work and continued support from their sponsors. Bob speaks very highly of former Buy As You View, Chairman, Bernard Jones O.B.E. and his co-owner, the late Gerald Coleman. "They always supported me and the Band. When I first started conducting the Band, I was travelling down from Yorkshire and staying over night. The Band paid my fees and I initially stayed in modest bed and breakfast hotels. I remember having had an effective planning meeting with Bernard and Gerald just after the Band had achieved the 'Double' when they asked me where I was staying. I told them. Bernard was shocked, and a few minutes later I had been booked into a leading five star hotel in Cardiff. Within a week, I was an employee of Buy As You View Company with my own company car. Since then my salary has always been paid via Bernard and not the Band.

Whenever I needed to do Band work I was given an office at Buy As You View Headquarters and also given access to any equipment I needed, I used to love chatting to Bernard and Gerald. In fact it was Bernard, Gerald and myself who planned the Classic Brass recordings Volumes I-IV. Gerald was always whistling tunes from test pieces and asking me what they were and if the Band could record them.

A 'classic' recording session in Aberdare

'Ty Rhondda', the Headquarters of Buy As You View was a significant building with state of the art offices and a massive warehouse. There were large revolving doors at the entrance and the first display to attract the attention of visitors when entering the building was a picture of the Buy As You View Cory Band. Not a standard sized picture, it covered the entire wall, 2 metres tall and 3 metres wide. That picture said it all to me. What fantastic support!

Can you imagine the disruption it must have caused when I asked Bernard if the Band could practice in the warehouse just because I wanted a more generous acoustic for the Band?

We even did concerts in the warehouse. These were not ordinary concerts, but top class stylish events. The

Letter from Buy As You View Chairman, Bernard Jones OBE

BWRJ/PAT

9 June 2003

Mr. Bob Childs,
Ty Cerdd,
13 Parc Plas,
Highfields,
Blackwood,
Gwent,
NP12 1SJ.

Dear Bob

Thank you for your letter and the CD – the Band are sounding absolutely fantastic. Benvunuto Cellini is magnificent and I have to say that the Les Preludes' performance is exquisite.

Your choice of classics for Vol. 3 is mouthwatering and it would be great to meet at your convenience to consider adding to the list. This time it will be lunch if that is convenient.

Keep smiling.

Kindest regards and very best wishes.

Yours sincerely

BERNARD JONES O.B.E
CHAIRMAN

NB: I had an opportunity to speak to Gerald on the telephone this weekend and like me he is over the moon at the standard of playing on the disc.

evening would begin with a champagne reception in the executive offices. The invited audience dressed in dinner jackets and black tie would enter the converted warehouse, the floor would be temporarily carpeted especially for the event and I remember that we bought white tuxedos for the Band. There was no hint that we were actually in a room that usually housed more than a thousand televisions. Bernard, Gerald and I would choose the programme and the music would usually include classic test-pieces; Epic Symphony, A Downland Suite, Life Divine are just some examples. Great times, great people! There are so many examples of their kindness and generosity, but time and space will not permit me to tell all. However, if I had to choose two words that appropriately summed up Bernard and Gerald they would certainly be "style and class".

Sadly, Gerald died in 2004; the Band played at his funeral and also played a memorial concert in the Parc and Dare Theatre, Treorchy, in May the following year. Since then Bernard has continued supporting me and the Band. He has become a good friend and confidante. We often meet for lunch and chat about the Band. In all the time I've conducted the Band, Bernard has never refused me anything. He is a great supporter but without his business guidance, the Band wouldn't have achieved so much, so quickly.

As well as totally reforming the Band's approach to contesting, Bob Childs has also revitalised the Band's concert work. When asked what programmes the Band had been playing in recent concerts, the librarian replied, "Whatever is in the pad. We always have about 20-30 pieces in the pad and we choose the programme from that." Bob Childs soon changed Buy As You View Cory's attitude to concerts and made them much more of a priority in the musical output of the Band. Commenting on concerts, Bob said, "Having played with Grimethorpe, Black Dyke and Brighouse & Rastrick, I had seen firsthand how professionally they were run and I suggested that if Buy As You View Cory wanted to, I could offer them a much more professional approach. My visions for the Band were to win contests, but also to lift their profile through concerts, recordings and performing contemporary pieces outside of the contest arena. Up until this point they had only played modern music at contests. We had great players, I don't know any Band who worked as hard as Buy As You View Cory, but they needed to lift their expectations in performing concerts, producing CD's and delivering new repertoire. Denzil Stephens and Major Kenney both worked hard in these areas, but over the years standards had slipped. Concerts were not a priority to them: winning contests was the "be all and end all", with Welsh Contests being the biggest priority.

Deciding not to attend local contests was probably one of the most controversial decisions I have made. Likewise the name change brought about considerable friction between the Band and past members. However, the latter was out of my hands, the Band needed substantial financial support to compete and the sponsors insisted on the name change. This was a committee decision that I supported. The decision to perform more concerts and recordings and to withdraw from local contests was greeted with dismay by other Welsh bands and the Welsh Brass Band Associations. My argument was that Black Dyke, Brighouse & Rastrick, Fodens, Fairey, YBS and Grimethorpe didn't attend their local contests, so why should we? When you are cultivating a sound to fill the Royal Albert Hall, London, Symphony Hall, Birmingham and all the other wonderful halls we visit as Welsh representatives competing in the European Championships, it's difficult to down-size to suit local acoustically unsuitable Leisure Centres. Top banding is a business and we have to balance our books. It makes more economic sense to earn a significant fee for performing a concert than paying an entrance fee to enter local contests where prize money is understandably minimal. I would also argue that playing a two hour concert in a receptive concert hall is musically much more rewarding than playing in a local contest. The Band had been on a resident and professional conductor route for a long time and accepted the status quo far too easily. As soon as you go to a 'One man, one band' situation, then you can plan a lot more in advance and you get to know your players much better. With a resident and professional relationship, the professional knows what he is going to do before a contest but the resident is just running through pieces for the rest of the time. You can be more focused in your approach and exercise better forward planning by adopting my way."

Apart from Philip Sparke's *Year of the Dragon* which was commissioned in 1984 for the Cory Band's Centenary celebrations, the Band had not commissioned any other music until Bob Childs came along. When you look at the pieces the Band has commissioned, the output has been quite immense. All this has helped the Buy As You View Cory Band to develop musically, outside of the contest field. In 2001, they appointed Dr John Pickard as their 'Composer in Residence'. John Pickard's tenure with the Band ended in July 2005 when the Band made history by giving the première performance of his *Gaia Symphony* at the prestigious Cheltenham International Festival. The *Symphony* was broadcast live on BBC Radio 3. Lasting over an hour in duration, it is currently the largest scale original work in the brass band repertory. The Band is dedicated to new music, raising the profile of the brass band genre, and keeping music alive in Wales. They have an active commissioning policy and have performed works by many of Britain's leading contemporary composers namely John McCabe, Judith Bingham, Elgar Howarth, Edward Gregson, Alun Hoddinott, Karl Jenkins, Gareth Wood, David Bedford, as well as John Pickard The Band's current 'Composer in Residence' is Welshman Gareth Wood. Since Gareth's appointment he has written three large scale works for the Band; *A Tear in the Fabric of Time*, *Concerto for Tenor Horn & Band*, and *Actaeon – Symphony for Brass & Percussion*.

One of the major projects Bob wanted to accomplish when he relocated to Wales was to conduct the National Youth Brass Band of Wales (NYBBW). He remembers ringing Keith Griffin the Director of the former Welsh Amateur Music Federation – now known as Ty Cerdd Music Centre, Wales, that had formed the Band in 1982, saying he would like to conduct a summer course with the NYBBW. Bob was ecstatic when Keith invited him to become the Band's new Musical Director, a ten year tenure which sadly concluded in 2009.

Bob Childs and members of NYBBW 2006

Bob said, "It was a great honour to be the Musical Director of the NYBBW, following in the footsteps of founder Musical Director Edward Gregson and James Watson. I also saw a possible link between the NYBBW and the Royal Welsh College of Music and Drama, Cardiff, that could benefit Welsh banding in general. I initially approached Chris Mowatt (Head of Brass) at the College with a view to starting a Brass Band course, the strategic thought was that the young talented musicians in the NYBBW would progress to the Royal Welsh College of Music to embark upon undergraduate studies thereby stemming the trickle of talented Welsh players migrating to England to study. The links with the NYBBW and the RWCM&D, as well as the Composers in Residence initiatives have brought an added dimension to the Band. I suppose Buy As You View Cory Band committee engaged me to win as many contests as possible. I'm sure they can now see the benefit that all these other connections are making for the Band too. In 2001, together with the BBC National Orchestra of Wales we were appointed as resident ensemble to the Royal Welsh College of Music and Drama."

It should not be assumed that the new direction Buy As You View Cory's were taking made contesting any less of a serious business. In fact, the triumph of the British 'Open' win in 2000 was repeated in 2002 when the Band won their second British 'Open' title. The piece was *Maunsell Forts* by John McCabe. After the competition, the composer wrote a letter to the Band saying how pleased he was with our playing. He said that he found the performance, 'Utterly compelling from beginning to end.'

Morfydd Childs (left) and her family 2002

The Buy As You View Cory Band Personnel for the winning performance at the British Open 2002 is shown in Appendix C.

Also in 2002, the Band were selected to play in London for the Queen's Jubilee celebrations and have since performed in many of the world's finest concert venues including the Grieg Hall, Bergen, Norway, Stravinsky Hall, Montreux, Switzerland, the

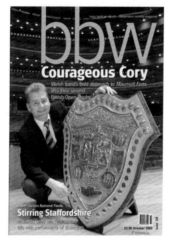

Royal Albert Hall, London, the Welsh Millennium Centre, Cardiff and the Symphony Hall, Birmingham. The Band regularly appears at the prestigious Welsh Proms series and has had the pleasure of sharing the 'Last Night' with both the Royal Philharmonic and Royal Liverpool Philharmonic Orchestras on several occasions.

2003 started with a win at the Annual Welsh Regional Championship Contest, followed by two stunning performances in the European Contest in Bergen, Norway. The Set Test Piece, *Aubade -The Magnificent Birds* by Torstein Aagaard Nilsen and a truly stunning performance of Wilby's *Revelation* in the Own Choice Section, especially the Euphonium duet from David

Childs and Nigel John that impressed both the audience and the adjudicators. Buy As You View Cory were disappointed to learn they had come second once again with exactly the same points as YBS, who were pronounced overall winners by virtue of a higher placed set test piece performance. Next came the British "Open" Championships where the Band came 6th on Holst's *Planet Suite*, followed by 3rd place at the National Championship Finals on *Enigma Variations* by Elgar. The following three years from 2004 – 2006 saw the Buy As You View Cory Band win the Annual Welsh Regional Championship three times, finish 2nd, 3rd and 6th at the Annual European invitation contest and runners-up three times at the British "Open" Championship with two 4th and one 3rd placing at the National Championship Finals, a 3rd place at the prestigious Brass in Concert in 2005 and a runners-up position at The All England International Masters contest the same year.

2007 started with another almost predictable sixth win in a row at the Welsh Annual Regional Championship Contest. This was followed later that year with a collaboration between the Cory Band, Karl Jenkins and Only Men Aloud (Cantorian) Choir to produce a CD (with EMI) of Karl Jenkins' compositions and arrangements. The Band was elevated into the limelight with numerous TV appearances, briefly becoming film stars for the accompanying promotional video. The CD enjoyed great success and entered the Top 10 on the Classic FM Chart, making Cory the only Brass Band ever to have achieved this honour. Shortly after recording the Karl Jenkins CD, the Band took the stage at Birmingham's Symphony Hall to try and win the British 'Open' for a third time in the decade. Cory had to follow a great performance from the Black Dyke Band for which Bob had wisely kept Cory in the warm up room. Bob explains "I knew Dyke would put on a stunning performance and I did not want my players to be psychologically affected by this, so I made a conscious effort to keep my players away from

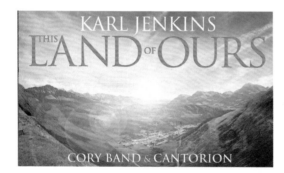

Filming on top of the Bwlch Mountain

Joanne, Owen, Dave, Lisa and Darren

Cory Band and Karl Jenkins, Brangwyn Hall

tensions in the warm up room." It worked to perfection and Cory went on to play a faultless performance of *Visions of Gerontius* to again win the British 'Open' Championship Title. The win was even sweeter when both Bob and brother Nick were also awarded the Iles Medal of the Worshipful Company of Musicians for services to Brass Bands.

The Buy As You View Cory Band Personnel for the winning performance at the British Open 2007 is shown in Appendix C

The third British 'Open' title for Cory meant that the Band was awarded the World of Brass / 4barsrest / Rankings Trophy for being the No. 1 band in the World at the end of the year. The Band consolidated these successes by continuing their innovative programming away from the contest arena, with a film crew from the BBC following the Band for several months producing a documentary called 'The Brass Factory'.

When questioned about his unique management style that has brought so much success to the Cory Band, Bob Childs replied, "I am totally dedicated when rehearsing, but I am a disciplinarian rather than a martinet. Many conductors can be quite ruthless in their management styles, but I don't sack many people. If someone has a genuine problem, then I don't just dump the player. Instead, we consider what the Band can do to help. The Band is the most important thing in my life apart from family and friends, so I appreciate that although people will put the Band first as much as they possibly can, they also need to look after their family and their careers. If their families and careers mean that they can't give the commitment I need for the Band, then we probably have to part company, but I fully understand the player's individual priority. I remember my Dad conducting Tredegar Band and it was a week before a big competition, the Eb soprano cornet player said he couldn't come to the weekend rehearsal because he was getting married, so my Dad asked what time he was getting married: he said twelve o'clock. My dad said, alright we will have band rehearsal at 3pm. I remember the guy at rehearsal in his suit with his wife in a white bridal gown sat in the Band room for the rehearsal. To me that was unreasonable but that's the way it was!

Wales is a small community when compared with England. We don't have as many good bands in one area so, in a way it is difficult for a player to lose his temper and say, 'well that's it! I've had enough! I'm off!' and walk out. Brighouse & Rastrick is just eight miles from Black Dyke, and in a radius of less than twenty five miles there are several top class bands in Yorkshire. It is the same in Lancashire. At Cory, if a player loses his head and falls out with me, where are they going to go to play at the same level? The same is true for me. If I have a difference of opinion with one of my star players at Cory, where am I going to find a suitable replacement? World class players don't grow on trees! We are a family and we have to work through our problems. What makes Cory special to me is that they are a Welsh band. I don't think you ever forget your roots, in spite of the fact that before I left Yorkshire, I had lived in the North of England longer than I had previously lived in Wales. I left Wales when I was 17 moving back in 2000 when I was 43 years old, but I still felt Welsh and coming back to conduct Cory was a real attraction to me. To be a successful conductor with the best band in your own country is just like managing your National football or rugby team. It is very special.

I also think that although Welsh people have a demeanour of being confident, they are not 'Big headed,' whereas the alleged typical Yorkshire stereotype, (which I have to say I have not found to be a true cliché), is that they speak their mind - "You can always tell a Yorkshire man, but not very much" is one such cliche. Welsh people are different, they always tend to understate things and then over perform, so if someone said to a Welsh person, 'You're a good player, aren't you?' They would say, 'Well I'm alright', and then would take their cornet out of its case and dazzle you. That's what's so special about them. The Cory Band remain a real family, not just that we have several families within the Band, but I feel that the Band is itself a family, so we all have a close affinity for each other. Having my own children, David and Lisa in the Band with me is very special. Being a conductor can be a lonely existence but having my family by my side to bounce ideas off and use as a sounding board is very special. I also have an extremely tolerant wife. Lorraine has always supported me in my music. Without her I'd be a lesser person than I have become.

During my career, I have played with some fantastic bands where I have observed a range of problems. Factions exist within bands, where the cornets won't speak to the euphoniums, or the basses try to manage the Band. It's not like that at Cory, we create a secure environment to work in. I try to build on that and we always talk about ourselves in the plural. I like the Welsh mentality and I work well with it because I am Welsh. My brother Nick has cultivated a similar working environment at Black Dyke. It is something that leaders of people can do. People underestimate the power of an effective leader. There is a small margin between winning and coming second or being in the top three and being in the fourth to sixth positions at competitive events. It is the camaraderie and that feeling of tightness, looking out for other players, the nod and the wink simply encouraging people that makes the subtle difference."

2008 didn't start too well for the Band, after a stunning performance of *Festival Music* by Eric Ball at the Annual Welsh Regional Championship Contest, Cory were awarded an extremely disappointing 3rd place. This only put fire into the stomach of both conductor and Band. This contest, affords the first placed band to compete at the following years' European Contest. Having come third, the only way to qualify for the "2009 Europeans" was to win the 2008 European Contest at Stavanger. The Band rehearsed hard as usual, but with an added hunger for success and a near perfect performance of the set test piece *Brass Blot* led to a standing ovation from a packed auditorium. The next day, the Band played *Music for Battle Creek* (Sparke) and after a fine display retired to the local music bar. When the phone call came through it was down to two bands Grimethorpe and Cory, 'and in first place..... The Cory Band' the players erupted. At last, the curse of the Europeans was lifted after so many near misses. This win was extra special! The Cory Band were Champions of Europe. Bob still jokes with his old friend Alan Morrison because if he hadn't placed us 3rd at the Annual Welsh Regional Championship, (a result that will never be understood!) we might not have had the hunger and drive that clearly propelled us to our first European win under Bob..... Thanks very much Alan!

The Buy As You View Band Personnel for the winning performance at the European Championships Stavanger Norway 2008 is shown in Appendix C

After two great performances in the British 'Open' and National Championships with podium finishes at both events, it was left to the popular Brass in Concert entertainment competition, held at The Sage in Gateshead, to round off the contesting year. The Band put in a great deal of work and concentration, both with the music and choreography and were rewarded with 1st place gaining 199 points out a possible 200 for musical performance (virtual perfection), with the added bonus of David Childs winning the Solo Prize. This win placed the Band once again at the top of the World Rankings. The Cory Band ended the year as No.1 in the World for the second year in a row. What a way to close on a decade of direction by "Bob Childs"

Registered players who played in Cory Band under Bob Childs between 2000-2009 are listed in Appendix D

Cory Band 125th Anniversary Concert, St. Davids Hall, 2009

Chapter 13

2009.......That was the year, that was!

2009 was always going to be a memorable year for the Band as it marked our 125th Anniversary. On 27th January a Working Party from the Band including Austin Davies, Neil Blockley, John Southcombe, Chris Turner, Lisa Fitzgerald-Lombard, Bob, David and Joanne Childs, met at the Tredegar Arms, Bassaleg to cement our plans for the year. This book was on the agenda as was a Gala Concert at St David's Hall and a Jubilee Reunion Concert in Swansea. If we had known then what a successful year 2009 was going to be, I don't think any of us would have believed it.

Bob Childs describes how the year unfolded, the Band's our first engagement was a joint concert helping our friends, the Bratton Silver Band, celebrate their 150th Anniversary. "The celebrations began with workshops performed by the Cory soloists and myself, culminating in a massed band concert on Saturday 30th January, with a grand finale of Tchaikovsky's 1812 Overture. The following week the Cory Band and I were awarded The John Edwards Memorial Award for "outstanding contribution to Welsh Music" by the Welsh Music Guild. This was a particularly special honour as The John Edwards Memorial Award, named after the Guild's founder, is the most prestigious non-competitive award given in Wales for services to the nation's music. Composers, including Alun Hoddinott, John Metcalf and Grace Williams, performers ranging from Osian Ellis to Bryn Terfel and institutions including the Royal Welsh College of Music and Drama, the Vale of Glamorgan Festival and the Lower

Letter from Welsh Music Guild

Machen Festival are among its distinguished recipients. We were presented with a framed certificate which read:- *The John Edwards Memorial Award is presented to Robert Childs and the Cory Band for their outstanding contribution to Welsh Music."*

February was a busy month the Band travelling to Northern Ireland for a fantastic weekend of music making and socializing in Strabane. A very rewarding workshop helping young brass players from the Rhondda was held and then a memorable concert at the Hawth in Crawley. This event was memorable for several reasons; Ian Williams, our Principal Cornet couldn't attend because of work commitments, so we engaged our friend Phillip Cobb as guest Principal Cornet for the evening. Little did we know that later in the year he would be appointed Principal Trumpet of the London Symphony Orchestra, arguably the youngest principal in the history of the orchestra I also engaged Bert Van Thienen (Belgium) to play Eb soprano cornet with us as a 'run-out' for the Annual Welsh Regional Championships the following month, so we concluded the first half of the concert with Gilbert Vinter's, *Salute to Youth*.

On St David's Day, the Band repeated their successful Royal Albert Hall 1000 Voices concert in the Welsh Millennium Centre under the baton of the inimitable Welsh Choral Conductor - Haydn James. The concert was organised by the London Welsh Society and was a sell-out. Two weeks later we were competing in the Welsh Regional Championship of the National Brass Band Championships of Great Britain, affectionately known as the 'Area Contest'. The Band has a terrific record at this contest and since I've been with the Band (2000), we've won on six occasions during my nine year tenure. Nevertheless, you can never take 1st place for granted and we never do! The test piece was Gilbert Vinter's *Salute to Youth* and it suited the Band immensely. A technical first movement with plenty of florid cornet work, an expressive second movement and a third movement with a sting in the tale; "a wall of death" euphonium solo that could have been especially written for David Childs, the Band's talented Principal Euphonium. We drew number ten and won the contest for the seventh time in nine attempts. This win was particularly sweet because the Band's President, Bernard Jones O.B.E. was present to witness the success at first hand. The adjudicator, David Read MBE, commented that it was the best performance of the piece that he had ever heard and wrote in his remarks that it was, 'a truly outstanding performance'. David Childs was also awarded best instrumentalist of the day, a richly deserved added bonus.

Our first contest of the year went to plan; now we needed to focus on defending our European title, but not before the biggest 'gig' of the year, for the Childs' family, Bob's daughter's wedding. On 4th April she married French horn player Oliver Fitzgerald-Lombard. Bob's brother Nick conducted Cory and David played solos. It was a great day!

One of the most successful trends at the European Championships is to have a new work specially written for a Band to play in the own-choice part of the competition. Peter Graham was asked if he would write music suitable for Cory to play at this event and he kindly agreed. The work is in three movements and called, *On the Shoulders of Giants*. It was exceptionally difficult; a real tour de force for the Band, so Bob knew that if we played it well, it would take some beating. However, we had the test-piece to play first - a fantastic piece written by Belgian composer Jan Van der Roost, titled *From Ancient Times*. This was even more difficult than the Band's own choice selection.

We drew number eight and the Band played superbly well. All the soloists played "out of their skins" and the audience went wild. Bob knew we were in contention so all we needed to do was to focus and perform at the same level the following day. Bernard Jones was kept informed by telephone and was told that the Band were fifty percent on the way to success. He asked Bob to convey his best wishes to the Band for the following day. That performance was superb and special mention should go to the wonderful contributions from Chris Thomas (trombone) and Joanne Childs (flugel horn). Their solo playing was "from another planet". Peter Graham was in the audience and he joined with them in giving us our second standing ovation of the weekend. Two great performances 'done and dusted', now all we had to do was wait. However, because we were the reigning Champions we were involved in the Evening Gala Concert that took place before the announcement of the results. Bob claims that he doesn't remember much about the concert, since he was so drained, mentally and physically, from the contest performances and the prior preparation. In fact he was virtually on automatic pilot, but he does remember that after the concert and before the results, he left the hall and went for a short walk to the Doyen Recording Van that was showing live coverage of the results. Stepping inside he listened to the result from there. Not understanding much because the presenter was not speaking English, he heard the name Cory and a massive cheer. We'd won for the second year in succession and by the time Bob got back inside the hall the whole Band were on stage singing the Welsh National Anthem, a truly fantastic moment, one that none of us will never forget. The Band was elated and many players were totally overcome by the emotion of such a landmark achievement. Although it was late, the day wasn't complete without phoning our President Bernard Jones. He was clearly "over the moon" with the result and sent hearty congratulations to all.

European Trophy

Robert and his wife, Lorraine, 2009

When the details of the result became known it transpired that we had actually won both sections of the competition, achieving 98 points in each of the two sections, so our nearest rivals were a massive 8 points behind. Iwan Fox of 4barsRest wrote, "The Cory Band, directed by Dr Robert Childs were crowned the 32nd European Brass Band Champions in Ostend this weekend, after delivering two scorching performances that comprehensively beat the multi-national field of rivals. Cory's massive 8 point winning margin was the largest in the contest's recent history, beating the 6 point margin the YBS Band managed in the same country back in 2002."

A packed Kursaal complex on the Ostend seafront had enjoyed playing of the very highest class from all the contenders over the two days of the event, but Cory still managed to take their playing to another level, comprehensively taking the combined 9,500 Euro first prize ahead of Treize Etoiles from Switzerland'. Here is what the adjudicators wrote:

From Ancient Times - Jan Van Der Roost

Great atmosphere to begin. Playing of the highest class. Well shaped soloists. Excellent sounds. Well crafted performance.

Garry Cutt

Very Enthusiastic performance. Good musical expression. Splendid colours & technique.

Jan Hadermann

In spite of the many difficulties, the music making was just brilliant. Grand !

Franz Cibulka

On The Shoulders of Giants - Peter Graham

Wow! Beautiful! Fabulous! Bravo & thanks.

Ray Farr

Good start - excellent. Soloists superb. Technique fantastic! Fanstastic soloists. Fantastic. MERCI!

Blaise Heritier

I am very impressed by this performance. Very, very beautiful. Thank you! very much!

Rob Goorhuis

Cory Band Personnel – see appendix C

After such a magnificent win, the Band was ready for fresh challenges. The next projects on the agenda were two CD recordings for Doyen; a popular light recording featuring most of the winning 2008 Brass In Concert material plus some solos. The CD was entitled Enter the Galaxies. The other recording which is much more musically substantial features *Triumphant Brass* by Gareth Wood (this is a piece he wrote for us as a 125th birthday present), *On The Shoulders of Giants* by Peter Graham, *From Ancient Times* by Jan Van der Roost. We recorded all the music on the weekend of the 5th-7th June at one of our favourite local recording venues, Ysgol Gyfun Rhydywaun, Aberdare.

Our 125th Anniversary Concert was held at St David's Hall, Cardiff on 20th June. The concept of this concert stemmed from an idea of David Childs. In fact, he played an enormous role in coordinating it too! He had been playing in Australia at the Melbourne International Festival of Brass, when he met an amazing trombonist called Wycliffe Gordon. David suggested to me that we promote this concert ourselves and ask Wycliffe to be the guest soloist. He was also keen to promote the traditional side of Welsh music making, so in addition we invited a male voice choir to join us. I remember chatting to Bernard Jones, and mentioning the idea to him, and he suggested that we invite the famous Morriston Opheus Male Voice Choir.
In the initial stages, the concert was going to be promoted and funded by David and Bob Childs'. David booked Wycliffe and Morriston Orpheus and Bob booked St David's Hall. However, later in the development of this celebratory event, World of Brass were attracted

to the event and they took control of its promotion. They filmed and made a DVD of the Concert and also sold it to the BBC who made two 'Listen to the Band' programmes. The Band commissioned Philip Sparke to write a piece especially for the event called *Hail The Dragon*. He had composed *The Year of the Dragon* for the Band's Centenary Concert held at the same venue in 1984.

The entire programme is listed below:
Cory Band
Hail The Dragon   Philip Sparke
Overture Ruslan and Ludmilla   Glinka
Cory Band & Morriston Orpheus
Myfanwy   Parry (arr Jenkins)

Guest Soloist Wycliffe Gordon accompanied by Cory Band

Sweet Georgia Brown   arr Dewhurst
Me We   Gordon
Cory Band & Morriston Orpheus
Danny Boy   Trad (arr Jenkins)
Cory Band
On The Shoulders of Giants   Peter Graham

Interval

Cory Band & Morriston Orpheus
Cantilena   Jenkins
Cory Band
Aspects of Adiemus   Jenkins
1.   Adiemus
2.   Song of the Spirit
3.   Vocalise
4.   Song of the Plains (joined by Morriston Orpheus)

Guest Soloist Wycliffe Gordon accompanied by Cory Band

Wonderful World   Armstrong
Hallelujah Shout (joined by Morriston Orpheus)   Gordon
Cory Band & Morriston Orpheus
Shenandoah   American Trad
Cory Band
Sing Sing Sing (joined by Wycliffe Gordon)   Louis Prima
American Tale (joined by Morriston Orpheus & Wycliffe) Dan Price

Massed Encore: Rhythm of Life (new arrangement for Band, Choir and Soloist)

Commemorative plaque

Alun Horgan, Simon Brittlebank and Gavin Pritchard play the stools

The night was a resounding success and Wycliffe Gordon's playing was particularly special. Simply spectacular! Morriston Orpheus Male Voice Choir's contributions were wonderful, and as a result of the collaboration, Cory are appearing at Morriston's 75th Anniversary Concert in 2010. The Band's President; Bernard Jones OBE gave a moving speech documenting the Band's landmark achievements throughout its history. The compere for the evening was the BBC Radio Wales' immensely popular presenter Roy Noble who as usual had the audience "eating out of his hand!"

Phenominal trombone soloist Wycliffe Gordon with Cory Bnad

July is normally a month when the Band personnel begin to think about summer holidays and how to re-charge their batteries ready for the British 'Open' Championship in September. However, 2009 was a special year, so we were thrilled to accept an invitation to enter the World Brass Band Championships in Kerkrade, Holland. Already Welsh Champions and European Champions, the lure of also becoming World Champions was the stuff of fairy tales. Like the European Championships, the contest is in two sections; a fixed test-piece followed by an own choice concert programme. Peter Graham's *Harrison's Dream* was chosen as the fixed work (a piece I knew well as we had won the National Championship with it in 2000). The programme for the own-choice had to be forty minutes long, and needed to include a major work so our choice was:

> *Into the Light* - Philip Wilby
> *The Mist of Arfon Forrest* – Gareth Wood
> *Brillante* – Peter Graham (Soloist David Childs)
> *From Ancient Times* – Jan Van der Roost

The Band members travelled by coach on Thursday 9th July and breaking their journey performed a joint concert with Bert Van Thienen's Brass Band Heist in Belgium. Unfortunately, Ian Williams (Principal Cornet) couldn't play with the Band due to work commitments, so Bob invited Nicholas Walkley to substitute for Ian. This concert provided a pleasing warm-up for him before the main event. The following day the Band drew number 5 and played *Harrison's Dream*. Just as in 2000, it went like clockwork and Nick Walkley played beautifully. We knew we had to play well because the Treize Etoiles Band from Switzerland were also competing and they had a score to settle, after coming second to us at the recently held European Championships. The National Band of New Zealand was also taking part and they were rather an unknown quantity. They had a Band full of star players, hand-picked from the length and breadth of New Zealand, so we couldn't afford to slip-up. An added pressure for us was the presence of a television company from Wales who were travelling with us to make a documentary programme about the Band. Naturally we wanted their film to have a happy ending too!

On the Saturday, we drew number 2; Bob remembers telephoning Bernard and telling him that the draw for order of play was a little early! Nevertheless the Band took the stage as the audience were cheering and shouting, Bob lifted his arms to start the first piece and you could have heard a pin drop, the audience were full of expectation after their super show the previous day. Bob glanced to his left and saw that Nick Walkley was looking cool and ready for business. The Band and Nick rose to the occasion and delivered a scintillating show. There must be a special mention of the Band's secret weapon - Repiano cornet specialist Richard Davies - Dickie (as he is affectionately known) - is good enough to sit Principal Cornet with any band, his tone is one of the best in the business and his phrasing is so sensitive. Over the years, Richard has accrued many points for the Band playing the lyrical cornet solos in most of the test-pieces. It was up to Richard to start our programme in Kerkrade with an off-stage unaccompanied solo that he delivered with both style and panache. Tom Brevik, one of the adjudicators thought that our performance of *From Ancient Times* surpassed that of the one given a few months earlier in Ostend.

For me, the highlight of the programme was *Brillante*. David's euphonium sang like a bird and his technique dazzled like "polished gold" on a summer's day. The audience simply wouldn't stop applauding and Bob was genuinely concerned that the extra time taken would push the Band over the forty minute limit which might incur penalty points. There was no need to worry, Cory won comfortably gaining 97 points on *Harrison's Dream* and 96 points with the concert programme. We were victorious by 3.5 points and the television crew was delighted with the fairytale finish to their documentary. Equally thrilled was Bernard Jones, he sent me a long text message which I relayed to the Band and it set the scene for a night of great celebrations.

Iwan Fox of 4barsrest reported the win by saying, "The Cory Band has added the World Championship title to its 2009 CV after a stunning victory in Kerkrade. Cory's domination of the Banding scene continued last weekend with their comprehensive victory to become World Champions in Kerkrade.

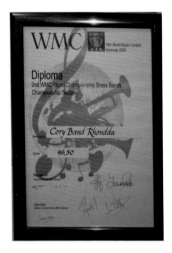

Their performance of the set work, *Harrison's Dream* on the Friday night followed by a stunning 40 minute concert programme on the Saturday, gave the reigning Welsh and European champions their first ever World Championship title. Cory's concert programme included David Childs on spectacular form with Peter Graham's *Brillante*."

Winner's sash

Here are a few selected comments from the Adjudicators:

Harrison's Dream
> *Maurice Hamers*
> *This performance had everything; effective technique, music making, great soloists and a superb interpretation.*
>
> *Ian Porthouse*
> *Superb performance, technically great with all the risks coming off.*
>
> *Jan Van der Roost*
> *That was a most excellent performance.*

Concert Programme

Jan de Haan
Outstanding performance, a joy to listen to

Tom Brevik
Thank you from the depths of my heart for some outstanding playing!
For me, From Ancient Times was even better than Ostend!!
A pure joy to listen to you.

Frank Renton
Great Band, great sound, wonderfully accomplished performance.

Unfortunately, Bob missed some of the celebrations, because from Kerkrade he had travelled to Japan and from there back home to conduct the National Youth Brass Band of Wales. However this remarkable achievement is all captured on film for us to savour for many years to come.

The Cory Band Personnel for the winning performance at the World Championships Kerkrade Holland 2009 is shown in Appendix C

Cory Band, conductor Bob Childs, St. Teilos Church, Cardiff, 2009

After a short summer break for the Band, Cory began preparations of Herman Paul Huber's *Titan's Progress* for the British 'Open' Championships. As I worked on the piece I was almost scared to contemplate what everyone else was asking... Can Cory win the Open too?

Before we started preparations in earnest on the British 'Open' Championships test piece, we took a short tour to Holland. Gerard Klaucke and his wife Gerda are great friends of the Band; in fact Gerard designed all of the Band's 125th Anniversary stationery and produced our celebratory programmes as a gift to the Band; we also use his company G.K. Graphic Design to produce the art work for our CDs. He was in charge of this tour, so we knew we were in for a treat. From the time we arrived until the time we returned home we were treated like Royalty. The Tour was funded by Brass Info Management which consists of, Gerard Klaucke, Jappie Dijkstra and Michael van der Schaaf. They had organised a concert on the Friday evening in a picturesque church in Schoonhoven, so Gerard and Bob took the opportunity to choose a programme which included quite a lot of Salvation Army music to fit the beautiful surroundings. The following day we performed a much more flamboyant and traditional programme in Drachten. During the concert, Bob Childs was presented with the BUMA International Brass Award, which was a real surprise and significant honour particularly as Professor Philip Wilby, the noted British composer, had won it the previous year. The certificate reads:

> *To Robert Brynley Childs for his remarkable contribution to the development of International Brass Music. With admirable energy and effort for a long period. Robert Childs has crossed many frontiers and contributed significantly in the development of brass music in the modern era.*

Before the Band flew home on the Sunday they performed a short concert in a Salvation Army Citadel in Amsterdam. Brass Info Management had commissioned Professor Philip Wilby to write a new work for the tour, *Into the Light*, sub-titled *Fanfare With Echoes*. It's a super work, one we have been playing ever since. In fact, it's the opening track on the new CD to be released in 2010. As part of our British 'Open' Championships preparation, Bob programmed the test-piece *Titan's Progress* in Holland. The Band played it well, but they had no idea how much it would improve by the time it was performed in Symphony Hall, Birmingham on 12th September.

Speculation was rife before we travelled to Symphony Hall, Birmingham. All the brass band media were wondering if we could win the British 'Open' Championships and add to our already bulging trophy cabinet. The open rehearsal at St Teilos Church, Cardiff, went well, Bernard Jones was present and he really liked the piece. As usual, he wished us all the best and gave all of us kind words of encouragement. On the big day we drew number six, which statistics show, is a little too early to win the coveted Gold Shield. Nevertheless, it took the pressure off us just a little. We played a great performance. It had never gone better and once again the audience really showed their full appreciation of our performance. Bob listened to several Bands that followed us on stage and he was convinced that we had a chance. However Black Dyke conducted by his brother Nick had the favourable draw, playing off number 16, so Bob was keen and went in to listen. From the very first note to the last, their performance oozed quality, style and musicianship. When they finished, the audience went crazy for them too! Bob had butterflies in his stomach, but didn't have to wait long for the result. It seemed we couldn't do anything wrong in our 125th year, so for the fourth time in ten years, the coveted Gold Shield was on its way back to Wales and Bob had been awarded another Mortimer Maestro Trophy for his personal trophy cabinet. Not surprisingly, his brother Nick was the first to congratulate him and the Band. Within a few days, we had received an official congratulatory letter from Black Dyke Band, what a magnanimous gesture from a truly great Band.

Rodney Newton, writing for the British Bandsman reported:

> Last Saturday, in a tense playoff between the nation's top-ranked Bands at Birmingham's Symphony Hall, Cory Band moved to the brink of making history by adding the British Open crown to those of the Brass in Concert, Welsh, European and World championships that the Band currently holds. It was the scrupulous attention to detail that has marked recent previous wins by Dr. Robert Childs and Cory that characterised a well-nigh unimpeachable reading, with a refined quality in the tutti passages and faultlessly executed solos that won the day. Impressive among these were the all-important chorale melodies for solo cornet, which were played with calm assurance by repiano player Richard Davies. "Our Band is all about teamwork," said Principal Cornet, Ian Williams, speaking to BB afterwards and it was teamwork that surely paid off last Saturday. With dynamics held firmly in control, Cory gave a finely nuanced account of the first episode of the piece, an immaculate farandole and a haunting rendition of the interlude in which Ian Williams and solo euphonium, David Childs, who were placed at the very back of the platform were interrupted by an impudent landler from the flugel horn (Joanne Childs). Dr. Childs gave this passage a little more space than many of the other conductors and it had the effect of making time seem to stand still for a moment. The other featured soloists - Bert Van Thienen (soprano), Owen Farr (solo horn), Sue Thomas (baritone) Chris Thomas (trombone) and Simon Howell (Eb bass) - were no less outstanding, and were solidly supported by the other members of the Band to produce a homogenous whole that satisfied in every way.

The British 'Open' Championships win saw Cory Band extend their lead at the top of the World Rankings by 757 points over the Grimethorpe Band, who was in 2nd place. The following day the Band enjoyed a short concert in Symphony Hall, Birmingham as part of Bram Gay's successful Festival of Brass series. The Festival concluded with massed Bands of Cory and Black Dyke with the Childs' brothers sharing the conducting. They both commented afterwards that it was most enjoyable and something that they should do more often.

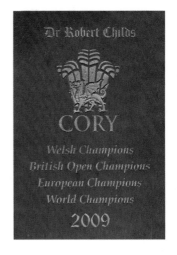

The Cory Band Personnel for the winning performance at the British Open **is** shown in Appendix C

Unfortunately, the year didn't quite have the perfect ending in contest terms, although we did secure podium finishes in both the National Finals and Brass In Concert (3rd prize in both). Nevertheless, we still had our Jubilee Concert to look forward to. This was officially the last celebratory concert in our 125th Anniversary 2009, and what a great day it turned out to be. The concert was held in the superb acoustics of the Brangwyn Hall, Swansea and it began with a tribute to Karl Jenkins and included the World Première (brass band version) of his *Euphonium Concerto*, a piece written especially for David Childs. David gave a brilliant account of the work and whilst Bob really enjoyed conducting the performance, Karl was enticed to the stage to take his well earned applause. The Band managed to persuade him to stay and conduct his own arrangement of *Eventide*. Again a very special moment for Cory.

The second part of the concert featured new arrangements, including *Tribute to the King of Swing* which showed off our amazing percussion section. The final part of the concert was a Cory Band reunion and there were at least 80 players on stage. We invited Denzil Stephens to conduct the *March - Castell Coch* by Tom Powell, *Bugler's Holiday* by Leroy Anderson and his own arrangement of *Myfanwy*. Bob then concluded the concert by conducting a marvellous rendition of Tchaikovsky's *1812 Overture*. The sound of the massed Band was tremendous, the atmosphere was electric and the occasion was so very nostalgic. Whilst he was conducting the Finale it was surreal to see Cory legends in front of him;-

Gwyn Thomas on Eb soprano cornet,
Jeff Thomas on flugel horn,
Clayton McCann on percussion, and
Graham Sheppard on BBb Bass

to mention just a few, but to have John Trotman, the Grandfather of the Band on tenor horn was simply an unbelievable treat for everyone!

The concert was doubly special as this was the last concert that Principal Cornet player Ian Williams played with the Band. He had led the Band with distinction and much aplomb for 20 years and was a fine example of cornet playing and dedication to the Cory Band - a time served stalwart! He led the Band through 'thick and thin' and played a significant part in the Band's recent successes. Cory presented Ian with an inscribed cornet, listing all the successes he'd been part of during his tenure with the Band. It was then great to see Ian Williams, Tom Hutchinson (our new Principal Cornet) and John Southcombe (another past principal) performing *Bugler's Holiday* in the concert.

Just as 2009 began with Cory playing the 1812 Overture, it was a fitting finale to close the year too, and what a year it had been. All that was left was our Christmas Awards Dinner, which was held at the Vale of Glamorgan Leisure Resort. We all enjoyed the evening, basking in our glory and remembering the great performances from the year. There were however a few surprises left. The Band's President Bernard Jones announced that 4barsRest readers had voted Cory - Band of the Year, and myself - Conductor of the Year. He also reminded us that for the third successive time we had been awarded the World of Brass World Ranking Trophy for being number one in the World. Finally, to cap it all, we were announced, the Band of the Decade!!

Contest record 2000 – Present. Conductor Dr. Robert Childs

	Open	National	Welsh Regional	European	Brass in Concert	Masters	World Championship
2000	Winners	Winners					
2001	3rd	5th	4th	2nd			
2002	Winners	2nd	Winners	DNQ			
2003	6th	3rd	Winners	2nd			
2004	2nd	4th	Winners	6th			
2005	2nd	3rd	Winners	2nd	3rd	2nd	
2006	2nd	4th	Winners	3rd			
2007	Winners	3rd	Winners	3rd			
2008	3rd	3rd	3rd	Winners	Winners		
2009	Winners	3rd	Winners	Winners	3rd		Winners
2010			2nd	Winners			

Chapter 14

A Glittering Array of Super Soloists

Cory Band has always relied upon their soloists to provide something special in both concert and contest performances. The 'wow' factor that a soloist elicits from an audience when playing faster than imagined or the feeling of the hair standing up on the back of your neck when a soloist shapes a beautiful phrase is absolutely exhilarating.

Over the years the Cory Band has had numerous teams of virtuosi soloists who have complemented each others' abilities. Some players excel when playing technically dazzling "air and variations" style solos; whereas others feel more at home playing lyrical solos. There have been, and still are, players in the Cory Band that prefer relaxed jazzy solos. Then there are the comedians! The clowns of the Band that not only deliver great solo performances, but make it look even easier by adding an entertaining dimension to their performance. Throughout the Band's illustrious history there have been some soloists who have shied away from the limelight and preferred not to stand and deliver at the front of the stage. They have been happier specialising in the all important solos within test-pieces, overtures and other repertoire. They have often been referred to as great 'band players' and their contribution to Cory's continuing success must not be diminished.

It's fair to record that over the years, the number and nature of prominent soloists within the Cory Band have changed according to the repertoire of the time. In the early days of Mr Dobbing's Cory Band, a staple diet of operatic transcriptions formed the basis of major contest and concert repertoire. Principal Cornet, Tenor horn, Trombone and Euphonium soloists were referred to as 'the corner men' and the solos of varying styles and complexity within these operatic selections and orchestral transcriptions were mainly played by them. This was also reflected on the concert platform.

Reg Little's Cory Band had many more identifiable soloists, partly due to the Band fulfilling regular and frequent BBC Broadcasts and the need to be inventive with the programme content. Reg Little frequently featured xylophone and harp soloists, although they were not registered players with the Band. By the time Walter Hargreaves conducted the Cory Band in the late 1940s, original compositions were much more frequently featured and composers like Eric Ball and Denis Wright were writing dedicated pieces for 'stand up' soloists to play, whilst at the same time expanding the role of the other instruments such as the Eb soprano cornet, who up until that time had not been considered a soloist at all.

Aaron Trotman, T.J.Powell and John Harrison witnessed considerable changes to the role and use of the traditional set of 'corner men' as they experienced the development of original repertoire for brass band and the increasing amount of percussion being utilised. However, the biggest change in terms of perceived soloists took place during the tenures of Major Kenney, Sq Leader Denzil Stephens and the current Musical Director, Dr Robert Childs. One wonders what Mr Dobbing would have thought about featuring the flugel horn, or a set of back row cornets in a 'stand up' solo feature? Did Reg Little have an opinion on the beneficial use of percussion in the Cory Band? Would he have imagined a time when in addition to his solo xylophonist, a virtually full complement of orchestral percussion would be featured at the front of the stage? Did any of the early conductors have the vision of Denzil Stephens to realise the full potential of the Eb Bass as a soloist?

In the Cory Band today every player can be called upon to play a 'stand up solo from memory' and are frequently used in this way! Times have changed and although there are still star players who thrill and excite audiences, it's not unusual for most players to experience the "buzz" of standing up and playing some sort of solo contribution at some point during a two hour concert. Here is a list of the conductors, their dates of appointments and the team of soloists associated with them. In truth, a veritable Who's Who of the Band's star players for almost the past century. Their names have been identified from existing photographs with the help of John Trotman, the most dedicated and longest serving member of the Cory Band:

J.G. Dobbing 1911

Mr Dobbing's soloists included, Moss Davies, the Band's long serving Eb Soprano Cornet player, he lived at Pleasant Street, Pentre and had the reputation of being a "bit of a character". Apparently, he would take a large suitcase away with him on all Band engagements, irrespective of whether the concert was for one night only, or a week! He was also known for his virtuoso playing and in particular, how he managed to do such a good job wearing false teeth. He made a pair of springs that sat between his top and bottom molars that kept his teeth firmly in position whilst he played. The Davies' were a close family unit, with Moss's brothers; Will Ruth (euphonium), Bill (euphonium/flugel) and Edgar (horn) also playing in Cory Band.

Aaron Trotman, (John's uncle) was a superbly talented Principal Cornet player in Dobbing's band, although John remembers him as being very strict and always very sure of himself. One of his favourite solos was *Hailstorm*. He had a fast triple tongue, but was equally at home playing slow melodies. He lived with his father on Partridge Road (near Llwynypia Hospital). Aaron was also the principal trumpet for the BBC Welsh Orchestra. This caused a few problems from time to time, not only because he had to miss Cory Band rehearsals when there was a clash of diary dates, but also because at that time professional musicians were not supposed to play in brass bands. For this reason the Band would frequently engage the services of Alwyn Teasdale who deputised for Aaron and also played solos such as *The Nightingale*, *Perfection* and *Shooting Star* in concerts. Another deputy for Aaron was Horace Davies - he later transferred to Eb soprano cornet. The Band's assistant Principal Cornet, Jack Carter was also a fine player and enjoyed playing duets with Aaron.

Jim Hearn played solo horn and he lived at Bronllwyn Road, Gelli. Like many of the Cory players he worked underground at Gelli Colliery. He was an accomplished player and later became treasurer of the Band. John Trotman remembers that Jim was a short man with severely bowed (bandy) legs. Jim's brother Dick played baritone in the Band, as did his nephews - Gomer, Charlie and Harold. The later became secretary and gave a total of forty years service to Cory Band.

George Howell played solo trombone in the Band and always displayed a professional standard of performance. One of his favourite solos was - *In Native Worth* by Haydn. John recalls that George was quite a character as well as a great player, although he added that George certainly wouldn't have been allowed to play in the earlier named 'Temperance' band! George left the Cory Band and joined the Glyn Samuel Dance Orchestra who were the resident entertainers at the Esplanade Hotel in Porthcawl. He died in tragic circumstances, drowning in the sea as he took an early morning swim in Porthcawl. His funeral is documented in a locally published book - The Rhondda.

Tom Trotman (John's father) was both a long serving Solo Euphonium and Band Sergeant and there is a long list of solos performed by him including: *Longing For Home* (Hartmann) *Love Is Immortal* (Hardy) *Annie Laurie* and *Gypsy's Warning* (Hartman), also *Land of Hope and Glory,* Tom Trotman also liked playing duets with his friend Will-Ruth Davies. One of their favourites was *A Night In Venice* (Lucantoni).

Two other soloists who were featured in Mr Dobbing's band concerts, although they were never members, were xylophonist Mr R. Tasker and harpist Mr M. Davies whose repertoire included: *Il Papagallo*, *The Minstrel's Adieu to his Native Land*, *Gwenith Gwyn*, *Morfa Rhuddlan,* and *The Rising Sun* all arranged by Mr J. Thomas.

Other players in Mr Dobbing's Cory Band included: Sid Willoff (Eb soprano cornet before Moss Davies), Will Armstrong (baritone), Dick Hearn (baritone), Will Pickings (Eb Bass), Mr Summers (BBb Bass), Will Adlam (BBb Bass), Aaron Trotman senior (BBb Bass) and Charlie Smith who was also the Treasurer of the Band.

Reg Little 1940

Reg Little's main soloists included a young but emerging Emlyn Bryant on Eb soprano cornet. He became one of the finest soprano cornet players of his generation. He never seemed to over blow, but could always be heard at any dynamic. His sound was typically likened to being "the icing on top of a cake". Interestingly, he walked with a severe limp as a young man, this was operated on when he was middle aged and totally rectified. Many of the top bands had talent scouts that attempted to lure talented players to the "top" Bands in England. Emlyn was eventually enticed to join Luton Band later moving to the join Fairey Aviation Works Band. However, it was with Munn and Feltons Band under the baton of Stanley Boddington that Emlyn really made his reputation as a top soprano cornet player. For many years, he was a household name in the Banding fraternity.

Stan Williams was a great servant to the Cory Band and was for many years Principal Cornet. Stan began his playing at Pentre Salvation Army and left the "Army" in his early twenties to join the Cory Band on solo cornet. Stan was famous at Cory Band for his performances of *Post Horn Gallop*, he also played many other solos including *Cleopatra* and *The Nightingale*. He was particularly well known for his stamina and his sight-reading prowess, causing T.J. Powell to comment on Stan's high standard of reading when the Band first ran through Lalo's *Le Roi d'Ys*. As well as his very high standard of playing John Trotman enthused about his

Stan Williams (cornet)

demeanour, "Stan was everyone's friend and he never said a bad word about anyone." Leaving the Band for a short time to conduct Lewis Merthyr Band, Stan returned to play tutti cornet until his retirement.

Steve Trotman was a long established solo horn and his tenure in the Cory Band spanned several conductors. He is John Trotman's uncle and like all the Trotmans, he had a razor sharp technique and was featured as a stand-up soloist on many occasions. One of his favourite solos was *Iona*. He also led the horn trio *Horns in Harmony* (especially written for the Band by Arthur Kenney) with John Bowen on 1st Horn and Ceri Lewis on 2nd Horn. Steve worked at Gelli Colliery for a while but after passing several examinations at the School of Mines in Treforest he moved to Parc Colliery to work as an overman – a senior operational management role in the coal industry.

Arthur Bryant was the brother of Emlyn Bryant and played solo trombone in the Cory Band. He was quite a character and enjoyed playing the *Acrobat* and the *Joker* in concerts. During the war John Trotman remembers the Band travelling in three taxis from the Rhondda Valleys to Blackwood for a concert in the Miners' Institute. When they arrived they set the stage behind the curtain. Just before the start of the concert, the Band took their seats, but Arthur didn't realise how close he was to the edge of the stage. He moved his chair to the left a few inches and fell through the curtain, off the stage and into the audience, completely wrecking his trombone. Arthur was cursed with quite a bad stammer and all he could say to the Band who were all convulsed with laugther and in stitches was….. "lo lo lo lo look at my trombone, lo lo lo lo look at my trombone!"

Other notable players in Reg Little's Band were: Gwyn Davies (cornet), Gwynfor Davies (cornet), Don Hendy (cornet), Stan Brown (cornet), John Trotman (flugel horn), George Roderick (horn), Charlie Smith (horn), Tommy Roberts (baritone), Ossie John (bass trombone), Bill Davies (euphonium), Jackie Combes (euphonium), Tom Trotman (Eb Bass), Eddie Moore (Eb Bass), Idwal Jenkins (BBb Bass) and Caradog Davies (BBb Bass).

Walter Hargreaves 1947
Many of the soloists in Reg Little's Cory Band continued their roles through to Walter Hargreaves Band including: Emlyn Bryant (Eb soprano cornet); Stan Williams (cornet) and Steve Trotman (horn). Ivor Jones joined the Band on solo trombone and often enjoyed playing solos in concerts. Tom Roberts replaced Tom Trotman as the solo euphonium. Both were reliable, good all round players and never missed a practice. Tom Roberts was a cousin of John Trotman, both living on Tyntyla Road, Ystrad Rhondda.

Other players in Walter Hargreaves' Band were: Gwyn Davies (solo cornet), who was later appointed Principal Cornet to the famous Morris Motors Band in Oxford. Horace Davies (solo cornet), Steve Trotman who had moved to repiano cornet), Jimmy Hargreaves (Walter's son and 2nd cornet), Don Hendy (cornet), Sid Hendy (Don's brother. cornet), John Trotman (horn), George Roderick (horn), Vic Maggs (baritone), Harry Baker (euphonium) Ernie Hendy (Don's brother. baritone), Arthur Bryant (trombone), Ossie John (bass trombone), Dick Davies (Eb Bass), Tom Trotman (Eb Bass), Will Ruth Davies (BBb Bass), Idwell Jenkins (BBb Bass) and Dilwyn Davies (Band Sergeant and Mace Carrier)

Aaron Trotman 1956

By the time Aaron took up the baton, Horace Davies was sat in the Eb soprano cornet seat. Stan Williams and Steve Trotman were still Principal Cornet and solo horn respectively. Don Tanner was the new solo trombone player and became a real stalwart of the Band. He was an underground mineworker for most of his life, and sadly died of the mining related illness - emphysema. He was a great soloist, playing slow ballads as well as technical show pieces. Some of his favourite pieces were *Scarborough Fair, I wish You Love* and *Fiorella*.

Don Tanner (left)

George Davies

George Davies was now solo euphonium and became another long serving member of Cory Band. George, like John Trotman is still a supporter and regular visitor to the Bandroom. The current M.D., Bob Childs frequently phones George to discuss their common love of the euphonium. Bob remembers George playing with Cory and has long playing records of him performing solos. They include; *Arabella, Spanish Serenade* and several more. George also became the Chairman of the Band.

Other members in Aaron Trotman's band were: Gordon Evans (cornet), Laurence Davies (cornet), Dewi Evans (cornet), Don Hendy (cornet), Gwyn Davies (cornet), Ralph Morgan (cornet), Alan Hawkins (cornet), Tommy Roberts (baritone), Haydn Lawthum (baritone), Steve Trotman (horn), Billy Jenkins (horn), Alun Roe (horn), Denis Jenkins (trombone), Ossie John (bass trombone), Tom Trotman (Eb Bass), John Trotman (Eb Bass), Idwal Jenkins (BBb Bass) and Huw Williams (BBb Bass). The two timpani in the photograph were just for show!

T. J. Powell 1960

Most of the soloists in Aaron Trotman's Band remained in position when T.J Powell took over as conductor. Roy Williams learned to play euphonium with the Ogmore Band and lived in Ogmore Vale. He moved up to the North of England for a short period to play for the CWS (Manchester) Band. When he returned to Wales he joined Cory Band on solo euphonium. Roy played all the demanding florid euphonium solos including *Jenny Jones, Rule Britannia,* Weber's *Last Waltz* and many more, sadly, Roy died in 2008.

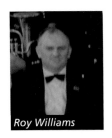
Roy Williams

Huw Williams

Huw Williams had transferred from BBb Bass to Eb Bass, a position he was later to make his own both as an accomplished player and featured soloist. Some of his favourite pieces were: *Bombastic Bombardon* (Siebert), *1st Movt. Concerto for Tuba* (Williams), *Dear To My Heart* (Siebert), *Albertie* (Stephens) and *Rondo Rotondo* (Stephens).

Other players who played in T.J. Powell's band were: Laurence Davies (cornet), Selwyn Prothero (cornet), Steve Trotman (horn), Ceri Lewis (horn), George Roderick (horn), Bill Davies (flugel), Roy Williams

(Euphonium), George Davis (euphonium), Tom Roberts (baritone), Harold Gay (baritone), John Gorman (trombone), Ossie John (bass trom), Huw Williams (Eb Bass), John Trotman (Eb bass), Idwell Jenkins (BBb bass) and Gareth Cousins (BBb Bass).

John Harrison 1965

Young Gwyn Thomas had joined the Band when John Harrison was appointed conductor and Gwyn stayed with the Band throughout the Kenney and Stephens years. He eventually moved on to Eb soprano cornet and played a massive part in the National contesting successes of the Band, as well as touring overseas with the Band. He was a much admired player and a true gentleman.

Gwyn Thomas

Stan Williams, Steve Trotman, Don Tanner and Roy Williams also played for John Harrison, alongside Richard Dix (cornet), Colin Stokes (cornet), Laurence Davies (cornet), Selwyn Prothero (cornet), Ralph Morgan (cornet), Darryll Morgan (cornet), Alan O'Leary (cornet), Steve Trotman (horn), Ceri Lewis (horn), George Roderick (horn), Bill Davies (flugel), Roy Williams (euphonium), George Davies (euphonium), Tom Roberts (baritone), Harold Gay (baritone), Ivor Roberts (baritone) John Gorman (trombone), Ivor England (trombone), Ossie John (bass trom), Huw Williams (Eb bass), John Trotman (Eb bass), Idwal Jenkins (BBb bass) and Gareth Cousins (BBb bass).

Major Arthur Kenney 1971

Colin Stokes was still ensconced in the Principal Cornet chair when Arthur Kenney arrived in the Rhondda Valleys, However by time the Band had won the National Finals in 1974, the cornet virtuoso Jim Davies had arrived. Jim is arguably the most famous principal solo cornet player the Band has ever had. He played all the contemporary and popular "wow factor" solos specialising in the Rafael Mendez "Latin" style. He led the Band with panache and style throughout both the Kenney periods and the Stephens' years. Some of his favourite and spectacular solos were:

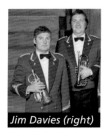

Napoli Il Silenzio (Celeste/Brezza), *El Cumbanchero* (Mendez), *Rule Britannia* (Hartmann), *Concerto* (Denis Wright), *Elfride* (Swift), *Sonia* (Swift), *Rule Britannia* (Rimmer) and many more. Jim also liked playing *Allegro Preciso* (Eric Hughes) a cornet and euphonium duet which he played with George Davies Throughout the 1970's and 1980's Jim Davies' name was synonymous with Cory Band and their success. Jim was widely known as an outstandingly talented "top flight" soloist.

Jim Davies (right)

Jeff Thomas was a star flugel horn player for the Band, frequently playing solos in concert and in recording sessions. These included *Nocturne and Interlude* (Barry), *Adagio* (Rodrigo), *Y Deryn Pur (Pure Bird)* (arr Stephens) and *Alphie* (Bacharach). Jeff also played a massive part in the Band's series of successes at the National Finals under Kenney and Stephens. He also became Chairperson of the Band.

Other players to play under the magical baton of Major Arthur Kenney in the early days were: Ken Williams (Eb soprano cornet), Colin Stokes

Jeff Thomas

(cornet), Richard Dix (cornet), Malcolm Picken (cornet), Glyn Jones (cornet), Stan Williams (cornet), Paul Arthur (cornet), Gwyn Thomas (cornet), Jeff Shepherd (cornet), Ralph Morgan (cornet), Selwyn Protheroe (cornet), Graham Lewis (cornet), Jeff Thomas (flugel horn), Steve Trotman (horn), John Bowen (horn), Ceri Lewis (horn), Ivor Roberts (baritone), Colin Radford (baritone), George Davies (euphonium), Roy Roberts (euphonium), Don Tanner (trombone), Ivor England (trombone), Norman John (bass trombone), Huw Williams (Eb Bass), Roy Parsons (Eb Bass), Alan Cleary (BBb Bass), Graham Sheppard (BBb Bass) and Bryan Davies (percussion).

Sq Leader Denzil Stephens 1975

Many of the soloists transferred from Arthur Kenney's National winning team to become Band stalwarts in Denzil Stephens' era. Jim Davies's popularity continued to flourish and Denzil wrote and arranged several solos that became synonymous with Jim's flair and panache. Denzil also developed Huw Williams as a featured Eb bass soloist, writing solos especially for him. Jeff Thomas remained a prominent soloist in the Denzil Stephens era.

Other players who played under Denzil Stephens included: Gwyn Thomas (soprano), John Neathy (cornet), Richard Dix (cornet), Paul Heddich (cornet), Howard Jones (cornet), Ian Jones (cornet), Gary Price (cornet), Greg Jones (cornet), Ralph Morgan (cornet), Jeff Thomas (flugel horn), Wayne Cook (horn), Robin Davies (horn), Jeff Sheppard(horn), Stuart Lewis (baritone), Philip Wicks (baritone), Huw Watkins (baritone), Roy Roberts (euphonium), Brian Davis (euphonium), Don Tanner (trombone), John Jones (trombone), Terry Lambert (bass trombone), Gareth Key (bass trombone), Huw Williams (Eb Bass), Selwyn Lewis (Eb bass), John Trotman (BBb bass), Graham Sheppard (BBb bass), Clayton McCann (percussion) and Alan O'Leary (percussion)

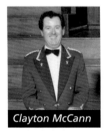

Clayton McCann

Major Arthur Kenney 1983

During the mid 1970's and through the 1980's, the Cory Band remained a settled team and there were very few changes in the line-up of soloists. Roy Roberts was established as a great band player, also featuring as an euphonium soloist on several long playing recordings, including virtuoso solos like *Lucy Long* (Godfrey) and the contrasting tranquil *Swan* from Saint Saens' *Carnival of the Animals*. Gareth Key had successfully moved from bass trombone to become an effective solo trombone. Jim Davies, Gwyn Thomas, Jeff Thomas and Wayne

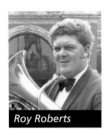

Roy Roberts

Cook were all renowned for their quality and success, being long established soloists.

Philip Sparke wrote *The Year of the Dragon* for Cory Band (originally in four movements) and it was Gareth Key on solo trombone who played the beautiful slow movement.

Other players to play under Arthur Kenney's second period with the Band and taste more National contesting success were: Gwyn Thomas (soprano), Richard Dix (cornet), Paul Heddich (cornet), Ian Waite (cornet), Howard Jones (cornet), Paul Lavender (cornet), Philip Harris (cornet), Greg Jones (cornet), Steve Harris (cornet), Jeff Thomas (flugel horn), Wayne Cook (horn), Robin Davies (horn), Keith Curtis (horn), Stuart Lewis (baritone), Philip Wicks (baritone), Roy Roberts (euphonium), Derek Andrews (euphonium), Gareth Key (trombone), John Jones (Trombone) Don Tanner (trombone), Terry Lambert (bass trombone), John Prosser (Eb bass), Paul Evans (Eb bass), Philip Privett (BBb bass), Graham Sheppard (BBb bass), Clayton McCann (percussion), Alan O'Leary (percussion) and John Trotman (percussion).

Gareth Key

Dr Robert Childs 2000

The Band Robert Childs inherited in 2000, had great potential and some accomplished great players. The front row cornet section had all been Principal Cornets in championship section bands. Steve Barnsley was on Eb Soprano cornet and could "sing like a lark". He also had the ability to play very softly and delicately; an ability which undoubtly helped to win him the 'Best Instrumentalist' award at the 2003 National Brass Band Championships of Great Britain, due to his contribution to Cory's performance of Sir Edward Elgar's *Enigma Variations*.

Steve Barnsley

After Steve resigned from the Band, he was replaced by Michelle Ibbotson, who was much more of an extrovert player. Michelle certainly enjoyed the limelight of playing solos with the Band, making a joint solo album with Joanne Childs (Flugel Horn) in 2008. The Band's current soprano player for competitions is Bert Van Thienen. He is one of the 'strongest' players that Conductor Bob Childs has ever heard. He is so reliable and his high register knows no limits. He also delights in playing solos.

Bert van Thienen   Michelle Ibbotson

Jeff Fear was playing Assistant Principal Cornet in 2000, and was as solid as a rock. John Southcombe was playing 'third man' and as a past Principal Cornet and Eb soprano cornet player with the Band, he brought a wealth of experience, expertise and total commitment to his playing. John still occasionally plays with the current Band but sadly his work commitments remain too onerous to allow him at attend every rehearsal. Bob Childs relies heavily on John's guiding hand and always consults him with regard to all administrative matters.

Darren Thomas was on 'fourth man' and had a similar approach to Jeff Fear; reliable, strong and consistent. He left the Band for a few years to develop his solo playing, but has since returned. He is now a significant contributor to the sound and style of the current Cory cornet section. Darren's father Jeff played flugel horn with the Band for many years, so it has become a family tradition to play for Cory. Nigel Guy was very much an asset in the role of the Band's 'secret weapon' sitting on repiano cornet. He was a very lyrical player with an intuitive sense of phrasing born out of years of playing at and winning, slow melody contests. His tone and fast vibrato was very much in vogue at the time and he had the inherent ability to really 'turn heads' during a contest performance.

The person charged with the responsibility of leading this strong 'top end' was Principal Cornet player Ian Williams. Ian is one of the most talented cornet players of his generation, always leading by example. His intuitive and phenomenal technique is legendary and recognised internationally. Bob Childs has said in many interviews, "He is my right hand man and is such a stabilising influence on the whole Band. He was here when I joined and he has never played less than brilliantly for me." Ian has played many solos with the Band including; *Napoli, Chipanicas, Charivari, Mexican Hat Dance, Paragon.* His contest performances have always been impeccable.

Ian Williams   Tom Hutchinson

Sadly, Ian retired from the Band at the end of 2009 due to work pressures. His successor is the talented Mr Tom Hutchinson – cornetist of great promise for the future.

The flugel horn player in 2000 was Ian Roberts. He was a good musician and always played his part with great passion and flair. However, Ian was a cornet player at heart and he always served the Band better in that role. David Cornelius led the horn section and was a great reader, a consistent performer who possessed an awesome technique, an amazing range and was capable of extreme dynamic contrasts. He was a regularly featured soloist without being fazed. Bob Childs remembers a concert in the Hawth

Dave Cornelius

Theatre in Crawley where Steve Barnsley fell ill during the interval and was unable to return to the stage for the second half to perform his solo. "I went to "Dai" and asked if he'd ever played *On with the Motley,* Dai replied, 'No, but I'll give it a go'. He stood up in front of the capacity audience and gave the best performance I've ever heard to this day. What a star!"

Chris Thomas was ensconced in the Principal Trombone chair in 2000 and has remained with the Band ever since, together with his wife Susan, who plays Principal Baritone. Susan is a superb player with a wonderful sound and Chris is a true concerto performer. No solo is too big for him. He recorded his own solo album with the Band in 2008 and has appeared as guest soloist with many bands including the National Youth Brass Band of Wales and Canada's professional Hannaford Street Silver Band. Bob Childs singles him

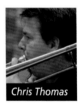

Chris Thomas

out as being one of the outstanding trombonists of his generation, "Christopher Thomas is a super soloist, I often think the strong point of his performance armoury is to be found in the softer slower pieces, but then he'll play the *Blue Bells of Scotland* and *Variations* or Gareth Wood's *Concerto* and I'll be equally impressed. He always displays a truly professional standard of performance and I'm sure if he hadn't dedicated his life to brass bands and over a decade to Cory, he could quite easily be sat in the Principal Trombonist's chair at one of the UK's leading professional orchestras."

Nigel John and his brother Barry were the euphonium section in 2000. Nigel had a silky sound and really filled the instrument. He wasn't a flashy virtuoso soloist, but his band playing was immaculate. With a little help from his brother, Nigel's talents were rewarded when he won the prestigious 'Best Instrumentalist' award for his part in Cory's British 'Open' winning performance on Michael Ball's *Ceremony* in 2000. Nigel stepped down in 2002, David Childs taking the position of Principal Euphonium with the

Nigel John

legendary euphonium virtuoso Lyndon Baglin as second euphonium. However, following Lyndon's retirement, Nigel John returned to the Band to play second euphonium, forming what became to be regarded as a "dream team euphonium section" with David Childs.

Many listeners will remember the emotional duet performance that David and Nigel gave in the Grieg Hall, Bergen, Norway, during Cory's scintillating performance of Philip Wilby's *Revelation* which won for the Band, the own choice section of the European Championships. Austin Davies, the Band's Chairperson remembers sitting at the back of the Band on Eb bass during that performance with tears rolling down his face, "It was simply magical" he recalls.

John Prosser played principal Eb bass with the Cory Band on Peter Graham's *Harrison's Dream* in 2000 and has remained a stalwart playing member ever since. He has been featured as a soloist on many occasions and has recorded several world première solo performances on CD with the Band. John is a dedicated bandsman and Bob Childs remembers asking him to move from Eb bass to BBb bass. "I needed some real experience and depth of sound to accompany Fraser Bish on BBb bass and I had considered asking John to take on this role. I phoned him just before Christmas and asked to meet him. I put my proposition to him and waited and watched for his response. He didn't flinch, he just replied, 'I'll do anything for this Band, when do I start?' What a man, what a bandsman!"

Cornet player Chris Turner joined the Band in 2003, he organises the front bench solo cornet section and is a real utility player, who is equally at home playing Eb soprano cornet, trumpet or flugel. He teaches at the Royal Welsh College of Music and Drama in Cardiff, he transposes at sight and is a great asset to the Band. Bob Childs said, "Chris has been one of my best signings; his embouchure is made of leather, he can play for hours without a rest and his high register is so secure at all dynamics. I often ask Chris to play

Chris Turner

Eb soprano cornet and in truth, I'd consider asking him to play that instrument on a regular basis if I didn't think I'd miss him so much from the front bench of cornets. Above all Chris, his wife Lynne and their baby Carys are firm family friends."

Richard Davies is another high quality soloist who sits in the repiano cornet chair. Like Nigel Guy, he has a lovely tone and was weaned on the slow melody circuit. Whereas Nigel Guy had a 1970s tone similar in character to Philip McCann, Richard is a more modern player, capable of combining a warm lyrical tone with both phenomenal technique and musical intellect. Richard has played Principal Cornet with the Band when Ian Williams was absent and quite often will treat the Band to *My Love is Like a Red Red*

Richard Davies

Rose. Bob Childs remembers the day he joined the Band, "Richard had played with us as a guest player several times before he joined and I'd often jokingly ask him to join, knowing full well he wouldn't leave his local band, Cwmaman. When he eventually phoned me and asked if he could join I couldn't believe my ears. It was like Sir Alex Ferguson of Manchester United receiving a call from Liverpool's Steven Gerard." Richard has played many of the lyrical solos in test-pieces during the past years and his great solo playing has significantly enhanced the Band's performances and contributed to our many successes.

Joanne Childs (nee Deane) joined the Band in 2002 and replaced Ian Roberts on flugel horn. She brought a new dimension to the horn section which could now play extremely softly and really blend tonally with the baritones and euphoniums. Over the years, Joanne has proved to have nerves of steel, never showing even the merest signs of faltering on the big occasion! Having made a joint solo album with Michelle Ibbotson (Eb soprano) in 2008, the disc is called Two Part Invention; Jo is now frequently featured as a soloist in concerts having been appointed the first flugel horn tutor of the National Youth Brass Band of Wales whilst at the same time being the 2009 guest soloist. Joanne has played some fabulous contest performances too, Bob Childs (her father-in-law) said, "In my opinion her most memorable performances have been Michael Ball's *Whitsun Wakes* at the Annual Welsh Regional Area Championships and Derek Bourgeois' *Concerto Grosso* at the

Joanne Childs

European Championships in Groningen. However, her absolute defining moment was when she started *Brass Blöt* at a dynamic that quite frankly I struggled to hear. Each adjudicator commented on her smooth velvet tone and her courage and ability to produce such an atmospheric opening. She was a major contributor to the Band being declared winners of that contest."

Owen Farr is a Welshman who returned to the Principality to play with Cory in 2005 leaving the North of England where he'd been playing with the Williams Fairey band. When he joined Cory and took over the principal horn chair from 'Dai' Cornelius, Bob Childs thought all his Christmases had come at once, as there was a period when 'Dai' played first horn to support Owen as the Band's solo horn. Owen is regularly featured as a soloist with the Band and slotted comfortably into his role as soon as he arrived. He has

Owen Farr

recorded a solo album with Cory, and like Chris Turner, teaches at the Royal Welsh College of Music and Drama in Cardiff. Owen has commissioned many solos for himself and as a guest soloist has given world premiere performances with bands at home and abroad. Bob Childs commented, "Owen is a world class tenor horn player and a talented educator. One of the most gratifying experiences I ever witnessed was the faces of the young musicians of the National Youth Brass Band of Wales when Owen premiered the Gareth Wood *Concerto*. He is an inspirational player with an astonishing technique." Other solos that Owen has made his own are: *Finale* from Mendelssohn's *Violin Concerto* and Phillip Sparke's *Capricorno*.

Euphonium virtuoso David Childs has an extensive CV and is constantly in demand as a guest soloist, travelling regularly throughout Europe and more recently to America and the Antipodes. Nevertheless, he always prioritises the Cory Band dates in his diary. David is a wonderful musician and a fine ambassador for the Cory name; he takes a great interest in the Band's heritage and contributes so much to making and consolidating it's future history. His father is Bob Childs who loves having him in the Band.

David Childs

"I'm extremely proud that David has developed into such a fine player. Cory wouldn't be as successful without his considerable input. He is my sounding board for important musical decisions David has already made three solo albums with Cory, performed several concerti with the Band and as a consequence of his dazzling performances with Cory has been awarded 'Best Instrumentalist' prizes at the:-

     2004 European Brass Band Championships,
     2005 Brass in Concert Championships,
     2006 BBC Band of Wales Championships and the
     2008 Brass In Concert Championships.

He was also awarded the title 'International Euphonium Player of the Year' in 2004, received the prestigious Harry Mortimer Award at the British 'Open' Championships in 2006, was voted 'Player of the Year' in 2004 and 2005 by members of the public through the online brass magazine 4barsRest. He was nominated Cory's 'Player of the Year' in 2008, an award voted for by the Band members themselves. Concert solos associated with David and Cory are: *Brilliante, Harlequin, Carnival of Venice, 'Neath Dublin Skies* and *The Hot Canary.*

Steve Sykes

Since 2000 when John Prosser played Principal Eb bass, Cory Band have had two further section leaders. Gavin Saynor played with the Band for a short period and contributed to a great performance of *Concerto Grosso* at the European Championships in Groningen. He also played a popular and very humorous version of *The Sun Has Got His Hat On.* Simon Howell and Oliver Browne currently share the Eb bass duties, but when discussing Eb bass players, one cannot forget the occasional appearances of the doyen of tuba players the inimitable Steven Sykes who played with the Band during their British 'Open' win in 2007 and the European Championship win in 2008.

Fraser Bish

Fraser Bish is also a stalwart of the Band formerly a member of the highly successful West Glamorgan Youth Band in the 1980's and although not a 'stand up' soloist he contributes much from his position as Principal BBb bass. Many people comment on the big dark sound of the modern Cory Band and Bob Childs openly admits the unique sound of the Band is generated from the lowest voice, "Fraser has a very special way of projecting his sound, so it envelops and darkens everyone else's. He is a wonderful asset to Cory."

Alun Horgan

In recent years Cory Band has re-established the old tradition of featuring percussion soloists. In the past, percussionists mainly played short xylophone solos, however, David Mitchell, David Danford and more recently Gavin Pritchard have managed to relocate the whole percussion set up to the front of the stage in the time it takes for the compere to introduce the item before proceeding to demonstrate highly honed skills to a staggeringly high level on drums, tuned percussion, timpani and other hand held percussion instruments. Alun Horgan is Cory's current principal percussionist and together with Simon Brittlebank, David Danford and Gavin Pritchard played a big part in Cory's first win at the 2008 Brass in Concert Championships held at the Sage, Gateshead.

Chapter 15

If music be the food of love....
Cory – The Banding 'Family'

"The time spent with the Cory band was special - we expected music making of the highest quality and from the first notes played this was evident! However, the warmth and friendliness of the players towards one another and to us as visitors was really appreciated - we were made most welcome and felt part of the Cory "family" It seems to me that in every way, this is a formidable band - a real class act!"

These are the kind and warm words of Stephen Cobb, Bandmaster of the renowned International Staff Band of the Salvation Army after having attended a Cory Band rehearsal with his son Philip. He is by no means the only person to have witnessed and commented on this rare phenomenon. Audiences are always pleasantly surprised to note that the Band although focused and dedicated to producing music of the highest quality also appear to enjoy performing music for each other. Some onlookers prefer to highlight the way the Band interact off stage, where instead of splitting into several small fractured groups, the Band chooses to socialise as a whole unit, often causing some chaos in restaurants and hotels by rearranging tables large enough to accommodate everyone.

This family atmosphere is hardly a coincidence when you consider that in addition to the four members of the Childs' family within the Band there are also three other married couples in the ensemble. As well as the close family links within Cory, many lifelong friendships have developed over years of banding together in Wales, with several of the current Cory personnel having acted as officials for each other's weddings and children's christenings. This all enveloping rich and friendly atmosphere is not exclusive to the Cory Band; there are many bands the world over who can boast similar claims. Indeed many would argue brass banding as a tradition has grown and developed primarily from a father passing on 'the Banding bug' to his sons and more recently his daughters too! Learning from their parents and developing their skills in the same bands as their brothers, sisters and the wider family of cousins, aunts and uncles too. There are very few members in the Band who did not start their banding careers in exactly this way but have revelled in enjoying life in the brass band fraternity. What makes Cory so uniquely special is that this undeniable bond between players exists not in a small village band, but in a band that has become one of the World's most successful Championship section bands since the start of this Millennium.

Family connections that have existed within Cory Band throughout the ages have been briefly mentioned in other chapters and include:
- the John family, Oswald (bass trombone), Norman (Oswald's son and bass trombone player) as well as the euphonium duo brothers, Nigel and Barry;
- The Hearn family, Dick (baritone) father of Jim (horn and treasurer),also Gomer, Charlie and Harold (a true stalwart racking up over 40 years service);
- The Davies brothers - Moss (Principal Cornet), Russ (euphonium), Bill (euphonium and flugel horn) and Edgar (horn) who were all in Dobbings' band;

- The Sheppard brothers - Geoff (horn) and Graham (BBb bass) who played under both Kenney and Stephens:
- The Hendy brothers - Don (cornet), Sid (cornet) and Ernie (baritone) who played under Hargreaves;
- The Bryant brothers - Emlyn (Eb soprano cornet) and Arthur (trombone) and
- The Harris brothers - Steve and Phillip Harris, cornet playing brothers the latter of which is currently in his 29th year of service to the Cory Band.
- Father and son teams have included Walter and Jimmy Hargreaves. The 'Wee' Professor himself - Walter Hargreaves who encouraged his son Jimmy to be featured in several broadcast performances playing cornet solos with

The Sheppard brothers, Geoff and Graham

his Dad conducting. Then there was Jeff Thomas, a former flugel player and for a period of time, Chairperson of the Band, who drafted his son Darren into the ranks. When a test piece required two flugel horns, a move which must have whetted his appetite, as Darren is now a highly respected and much admired member of the existing Cory cornet front row.

- Without a doubt, historically the most famous family, with an entire chapter of this book to themselves are the Trotmans - Aaron senior (BBb bass) father to Aaron junior (cornet), Tom (euphonium), Steve (horn), Haydn (cornet) as well as Tom's son – the versatile John. One member of this family not previously mentioned is Bernice, who, in the 1930's often enjoyed being mistaken for the first female member of Cory when she used to carry her brother John's cornet home for him when he wanted to meet his sweetheart Doreen. John married Doreen who is the late Ron Pryce's sister. Ron, a stalwart supporter of the Band was previously the long term secretary of the Band. Ron and Betty live in 11, Pleasant View, Pentre. John and Doreen live next door, so a closer bond is difficult to imagine. Both families have the life blood of the Cory Band flowing thought their veins!

John and Doreen Trotman

Warm and understanding close friendships have remained a permanent feature of the true camaraderie that has existed between Band members and their wives and partners. Symptomatic of this was the immense contribution made to the Band's future by the now disbanded Ladies' Committee who raised the staggering sum of circa £41k during the difficult years between 1976 and 2000. However, this chapter celebrates the emergence of couples within the Band. This situation of course, has only developed since females became a permanent feature as playing members in the mid 1990s, starting with Vicky Mace who joined the cornet section in 1995 for the British 'Open' Championships and continuing with the first permanent female member, Karen Davies who joined on percussion later that year.

Undoubtedly, the longest serving couple in the Band are Christopher and Susan Thomas, solo trombone and solo baritone respectively. They joined the Band in 2000 already having being married for seven years, "signings" that the new MD, Robert Childs made for the Band. As a couple, brass banding was not new to them, given that they met at the age of 12 when they were both members of the Mid Glamorgan Youth Brass

'Wales on Sunday' feature on Cory Band

Band. They continued to enjoy each others company socially, whilst they were both playing members together in the National Youth Brass Band of Wales as well as both the BTM and Tredegar bands, joining Cory just in time to savour the Band's historic and momentous wins. Chris and Sue have 3 children; Dan aged 14, currently learning the euphonium, Nia aged 11, who has just started tenor horn lessons and Owen aged 5, who is considering following in his Dad's footsteps as a trombonist. Some might argue that Owen's love of brass is not entirely unexpected, given that Sue only missed a few weeks of Band engagements during the later stages of her pregnancy. However, it is clear that for the Thomas family, brass banding is fast becoming a way of life, the entire family frequently travelling en masse with the Band to concerts, competitions and even rehearsals when the baby sitter is otherwise engaged!

Another of Cory's most well known couples are David and Joanne Childs. Unlike Chris and Sue Thomas, David and Joanne have experienced the rigours of playing for different bands. This was when David played for the Brighouse & Rastrick Band and later CWS Glasgow, whilst at that time Joanne was a member of East Yorkshire Motor Services Band before returning to Wales to enjoy a short spell with Tredegar Band. It does not take a logistical expert to note that there were great distances between the locations of their bands of over 300 miles at times. Add this level of demand on their already busy lifestyles, holding down a pair of full time jobs and it seems obvious that the solution was for them to join the same band. The opportunity to accomplish this arose in 2001, when they joined Cory within a few months of each other. Although they had been together since their initial meeting at a National Youth Brass Band of Wales course in 1995, it was not until December 2006 that they became

Joanne and David Childs

another of the Band's married couples. This fortuitous order of events had the added bonus of a ready made world class ensemble full of their friends, to play at their nuptial ceremony in the form and shape of the Cory Band. The presence of the Band to provide music prior to and during the wedding service has now become a tradition when members of the Band are wed.

Christopher Turner carried out the role of best man at David and Joanne's wedding, and it is this friendship that provided the Band with yet another opportunity for a double signing. Chris joined Cory in January 2003, moving back to Wales after an enjoyable period in Yorkshire with the famous Brighouse and Rastrick and Black Dyke bands.

A few months later in August of the same year, Chris' wife Lynne joined the Band on 1st horn. Again, the couple had shared their love of brass playing from an early age and are

Sue and Chris Thomas

Lynne and Chris Turner with baby Carys

yet another product of the National Youth Brass Band of Wales, where they met and fell in love in 1989. In September 2007, Lynne took advantage of a lengthy spell of maternity leave from the horn section for the birth of their daughter, Carys Jane, but has now re-joined the Cory team as Merchandise Officer and Coordinator of the newly formed Cory Supporters' Initiative. This has made a tremendous difference to Chris, who now sees a great deal more of his wife than hitherto, but also now helps him to always bring the appropriate uniform for every band occasion!

Travis and Lucy Griffiths are another couple in the Band who very recently started their own family, with Amelia Hazel being born in December 2008. Unlike the previous couples, Travis and Lucy become Cory members at different times. Travis joined the cornet section in July 2001 when he was unaware of the existence of Lucy. In spite of both of them being taught albeit 12 years apart, by the same fine brass teacher - Mr Laurence Davies, a highly regarded professional trumpet player and previously a Cory Band cornet player himself, it was not until the British 'Open' Championships in 2003 that they first met. Lucy was playing with

Lucy and Travis Griffiths

Cwmaman Band at that time, but it did not take long before they realised that if they were to spend any time together they would both have to play for the same Band, resulting in Lucy joining Cory in October 2004. Three years later they were married on the 19th August 2007, where the tradition of having Cory Band play at the ceremony was not only upheld, but also reported in true celebrity style by several popular newspapers and magazines. It was in one of these articles for the Daily Star that Travis is quoted as saying, "Our wedding day was very special and I

'The Weekly News' feature on Cory Band

don't think it would have felt right unless our Band was there playing for us. There's such a tradition of weddings in the Band now. I think we're all in tune with each other!"

Owen and Helen Farr are the most recent newly-weds to enjoy the warm atmosphere of Cory members providing the music at their wedding. Owen has been principal horn with the Band since May 2004 just after the European Championships were held in Glasgow. Helen was a temporary member for Cory at this competition, as one of the Band's regular horn players was unable to compete that year because of work commitments. Although Helen deputises for the Band from time to time, nowadays she is more regularly seen in the audience cheering Owen on, and also selling CDs during the intervals of the Band's concerts.

It is rather ironic that this chapter was researched and written by the only female in the Band who is not one half of a 'Cory Couple', given the fact that her husband is a professional French Horn player. Notwithstanding the absence of French Horns in the Band, he has been called upon to deputise at several weddings of "Cory Couples." Both Lisa and Oliver (her husband)

Lisa and Oliver Fitzgerald-Lombard

enjoyed the delights of music played by the Cory Band at their wedding. Oliver, perhaps, more so than Lisa, who made a late entry to the Church. **Oddly, the only late entry in her years of service to the Band!**

This rather different perspective does allow Lisa to also present the plight of the long suffering, supportive, non-banding partner, none more so than her mother Lorraine, the wife of Musical Director, Robert Childs. Of course, it is no secret that after meeting Robert on a National Youth Brass Band of Great Britain course in 1972, Lorraine herself used to play regularly with championship section bands, but in order to keep banding as a focus for the family, she has sacrificed her own playing career to keep pace with Cory Band's busy schedule, where she enjoys supporting her husband, daughter, son and daughter-in-law. Her applause is always the loudest and longest, and she can always be relied upon for a very favourable (if a little biased) account of how well the Band has performed!

The infectious, enthusiastic atmosphere generated amongst the members of the Cory Band means that players' partners are always welcomed and treated as one of the Cory family which is invaluable to all concerned. In addition to the aforementioned, 'Cory Couples' all of whom are currently active members of the Cory Band. There are other couples who have also enjoyed periods of active involvement contributing with distinction to the playing standard of the Band.

- Mark and Michelle Bowater (cornet and soprano),
- Alan and Susie Hathaway (percussion and trombone)
- Geraint Chamberlain and his fiancée Laura Davies (baritone & cornet).

Although the aforementioned are no longer playing with the Cory Band, their valuable contributions in the past are readily acknowledged. It is no secret to anyone involved in the brass band movement that banding at all levels, but especially at the prestigious level enjoyed by Cory is an incredibly demanding hobby. However, when partners are able to witness at first hand the rich, musical and social rewards that readily transpire, from a serious involvement in brass bands, it becomes so much easier to understand why so much of themselves is devoted to this wonderful form of music making. This can only lead to a more positive experience for everyone involved. Surely many more would benefit if their bands would emulate the truly unique and amiable atmosphere cultivated at Cory. It's a proven winner!

Chapter 16
Ever Expanding Horizons

Contesting will always be the life-blood of the Cory Band, the adrenalin rush of a contest win still strongly motivates many of the players who dedicate so much of their life to the Band. However, it's also important to strive to widen musical horizons well beyond the contesting arena.

As early as 1910, John Bailey was concerned about concert repertoire, composing and arranging music for the Cory Band. Records show that in the 1930's and 1940's Mr Dobbing and Reg Little were also keen to be innovative: the content of their concerts featuring vocal soloists, harpists and xylophonists in their programmes. Walter Hargreaves' commitment to raising Cory Band's profile in competitions is well documented, but his involvement in the Junior Band, the senior band's very public interface with the Cardiff City Football Club and their involvement in the Rainbow project (see Chapter 4) showed great vision, as a valuable aside from his competitive edge.

From 1970 – 2000, the Cory Band under some great leadership from Major Arthur Kenney and Sq Leader Denzil Stephens managed to carve a substantial contesting legacy as well as realizing wider musical achievements. During this period the Band was financially stretched relying heavily on the unstinting work of the 'Ladies Committee' to raise funds. Financing competitions was a major challenge, so there was little or no money left to develop other musical projects. Nevertheless, they still managed to produce high quality recordings, commissioned a major work from Philip Sparke, toured extensively and were one of the most popular bands broadcast by the BBC. Furthermore, Denzil Stephens single-handedly created a whole new concert repertoire through his skilful arrangements, with *Miller Magic* becoming the Band's unofficial signature tune!

There is little doubt that securing funding from Bernard Jones, Gerald Coleman and the commercial enterprise "Buy As You View Ltd" heralded a new financial era for the Band. An era where musical projects away from the contesting arena could be visualised, planned and executed without the worry of inadequate funding. This, coupled with the instant contesting success of Dr Robert Childs saw the Cory Band develop and polish its musical skills in many other areas of music-making apart from the contest field.

One of the first projects initiated by the new regime was a proactive recording policy. Bob Childs recalls, 'I was able to plan substantial and long term recording projects such as *Brass Band Classics volumes I-IV* as well as unusual recordings like *Heritage, Wildfire, Gaia Symphony* and *The Lighter Side of Elgar Howarth* .' Many of these projects were initially self-funded and only later taken up by major brass band record labels. Bob also nurtured and promoted his team of soloists in the recording studios and is proud of all the solo CDs he has helped to produce featuring Michelle Ibbotson (soprano), Joanne Childs (flugel horn), Owen Farr (tenor horn), Christopher Thomas (trombone) and David Childs (euphonium). Cory are Doyen recording artists and their CDs are distributed by World of Brass. However, in addition to the recordings they produce for Doyen, the Band has also recorded albums for Kirklees Music Publishers, Obrasso Verlag, EMI Records and Zomba Recordings (Sony Classics).

Bob, Cory, Morriston Choir and Wycliffe

Over the years, many of the Band's recordings have won prestigious awards and received universal, critical acclaim. However, 2009 witnessed the Band widening its horizons even further by producing its first DVD. The disc featuring the Band's 125th Anniversary Concert from St David's Hall, Cardiff, and included the incredible playing of American virtuoso trombonist, Wycliffe Gordon. The DVD has quickly risen to the top of the World of Brass DVD charts and is currently their number one best seller.

Other strategies to develop widening musical horizons were to initiate collaborations with other bands, organizations, individuals and to self promote the Band through a Friends Society and a new website. The Band also support charity events whenever possible and have a policy of performing at least two charity engagements each year completely free of charge. Some of the charities the Band have supported in recent years are; Cancer Care Cymru, Teenage Cancer, Valley Boys, local Salvation Army Bands and many other youth organisations.

The Band are an equal-opportunities organisation and do not discriminate against female players. When Bob Childs first joined the Band there were no female members. Now, nominally twenty per cent of the Band are female, just a few years ago this figure had risen to to thirty per cent. Howard Snell at Fodens, and James Watson at Black Dyke were both seen by many as visionaries in welcoming female musicians into their bands. During the past decade, Cory and Bob have done the same. Bob Childs says, 'Its no coincidence that Black Dyke, Fodens and ourselves have consistently filled the top three spots in the World Rankings and I'm particularly pleased that in our 125th year we are part of an elite group leading the way in combining musical success with equal gender opportunity.'

Since 2000, the Cory Band have taken part in many prestigious concerts:-
- 5 - Royal Albert Hall Gala Concerts,
- 6 - British Open Festivals,
- 6 - European Gala Festivals,
- 7 - Royal Northern College of Music Festivals

Also touring extensively in Europe visiting Belgium, France, Germany, Holland, Italy, Luxembourg, Sweden, and Switzerland.

World of Brass and British Bandsman trophy, World No1

Cory in Switzerland

The Band has formed some amazing partnerships with international musicians resulting in concert performances and CD recordings with a wide range of soloists that include:-

- Philippe Schartz (Principal Trumpet, BBC National Orchestra of Wales)
- Philip Cobb (Joint Principal Trumpet, London Symphony Orchestra),
- Derek Watkins and Wycliffe Gordon – both Internationally acclaimed session musicians.

In 2001, the Cory Band was appointed 'Band in Residence' at the Royal Welsh College of Music and Drama. In its official capacity, the Band perform two concerts a year with the College Brass Band and organises two outreach days that involve principal players from the Band interfacing with college students and young players from the local community. During their undergraduate studies, every Royal Welsh College of Music and Drama (RWCMD) student studying a brass band instrument has the opportunity to sit in a Cory rehearsal and when possible, play in a Cory concert. This is a similar system that operates for the College's orchestral students who work with the BBC National Orchestra of Wales and the Orchestra of the Welsh National Opera.

Dr Robert (Bob) Childs is currently the Director of Band Studies at the College and he says, 'The Brass Band Pathway is a unique way of keeping the best brass players in Wales. Until 2001, any Welsh brass band player wishing to go to Music College was forced to move away

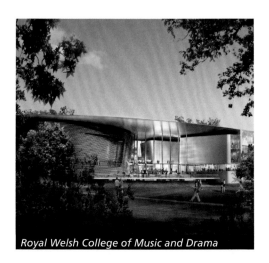
Royal Welsh College of Music and Drama

Chris Thomas at the RWCMD

from Wales to study. I believe that the collaboration between the College and Cory shows great initiative. Since the partnership began we have always had at least three students who are permanent members of the Band. Many bands in South Wales also benefit from a similar partnership with a current poll revealing that the following Bands have RWCMD students in their ranks; Burry Port, BTM, City of Cardiff, Cory, Markham, Mid Rhondda, Parc and Dare, Pontardulais, Tongwynlais, and Tredegar.

The Band also developed a fruitful association with the National Youth Brass Band of Wales. Bob Childs has been the Musical Director of the Band since 2000 and has seen many of the members of the youth band progress to become students of the RWCMD and subsequently members of Cory Band. Commenting on the association between Cory and the NYBBW, Bob said, 'There has always been a strong relationship between the NYBBW and Cory. Bob has been involved in several guises with the NYBBW since its formation in 1982, initially as a senior tutor prior to becoming Musical Director. Some of the early members of the youth band are current members of Cory with Chris Thomas, Sue Thomas and Andrew Williams probably being the most senior ex members of the NYBBW. Currently, Cory has eighteen members who are either ex members or current members of the NYBBW. The strong association with both bands is not only through its membership. Working closely with Keith Griffin, Director of Ty Cerdd Music Centre Wales, Ty Cerdd and the Cory Band have jointly commissioned several major works for Brass Band. Ty Cerdd also invites some of the principal soloists of the Cory Band to be tutors on the NYBBW Summer

Bob with the NYBBW in Canada in 2007

Courses. Current Cory players who have recently been appointed Tutors for the NYBBW are:-

- Christopher Turner (cornet)
- Joanne Childs (flugel horn)
- Owen Farr (tenor horn)
- Christopher Thomas (trombone) and
- David Childs (euphonium).

In addition to the role of tutors most of the players have also appeared as guest soloists with the NYBBW with Ty Cerdd commissioning concerti especially for them.' Works that were collaboratively realized by Cory and Ty Cerdd include:-

- Gareth Wood – *Concerto for Horn*,
- Gareth Wood – *Actaeon*,
- Peter Graham – *On The Shoulders of Giants*,
- Peter Graham – *The Day of the Dragon*,
- Rodney Newton – *Echoes of the East*,
- Rodney Newton – *Concerto for Flugel Horn* and
- Dan Price – *Moonbeams*.

The Cory Band is recognized as one of the leading brass bands in the world today and has for many decades has been the premier band in Wales. In 2002, Cory were honoured to represent Wales in the Queen's Golden Jubilee Celebrations alongside Black Dyke Band (England), CWS Glasgow (Scotland) and First Old Boys Band (Ireland). In 2004, the Band was also chosen to take part in the official opening of the prestigious Wales Millennium Centre, Cardiff. The Band was conducted on that occasion by International Maestro, Owain Arwel Hughes in a very special *Gymanfa Ganu*.

The Band's relationship with Owain Arwel Hughes has developed significantly leading to invitations to the Band to take part in the Welsh Proms Festival on several occasions. These appearances have included the immensely popular 'Last Night of the Proms' concerts where the Band, in addition to impressing capacity classical audiences with individual performances, also played massed items with both the The Liverpool

The official opening of the Wales Millennium Centre

Philharmonic and The Royal Philharmonic Orchestras. Bob Childs remembers attending a 'Last Night of the Welsh Proms' rehearsal when Owain Arwel Hughes conducted Cory Band on Dvorak's Carnival Overture. 'The orchestra was sitting waiting to start their rehearsal when the conductor (Owain) said that he'd like to quickly run through the overture with the Band. From the very first note to the last, the orchestral musicians listened spellbound to the Band's brilliance. They couldn't believe the sheer musicianship and technique of the Band. At the end there was an almighty roar, violinists were tapping stands with their bows and others were shuffling their feet in the customary way to signal their sincere appreciation. It was a great feeling, to be appreciated by leading professional musicians, who had little of no knowledge of the brass band movement. Some of the back desk strings asked the stage crew for extra sound barriers and ear defenders too .... Cory can play very loudly!'

In 2005, the Band welcomed an invitation to perform a joint concert with Dr Stephen Cobb and the renowned International Staff Band of the Salvation Army. The concert took place at the Riverside Theatre, Newport. In the first half each band performed independently but in the second half the Bands combined together. David Childs and Derek Kane performed Peter Graham's *Brilliante* bringing back poignant memories of the Child's Brothers performance of this music. Other programmed items included *Journey into Freedom* (Ball), *The Day of the Dragon* (Graham) and *Procession to Covenant* (Himes).

The Band's inclusive policy of working with musicians from the wider musical environment has enabled players to move outside their brass band comfort zone, giving Cory some wonderfully rewarding and unforgettable musical experiences. They have made several 'Songs of Praise' programmes for the BBC with international artists Aled Jones, Katherine Jenkins and Rebecca Evans. These were truly inspirational. However, if musical director Robert Childs had to choose one luminary that he and the Cory Band have enjoyed working with most of all, it would be the world famous composer Dr Karl Jenkins.

Bob is adamant that "Karl has adopted the Band as his own. The first contact with Karl came through Bob's son David, who had commissioned Karl to write a Euphonium Concerto for him. During one of their sessions together, Karl mentioned that he was thinking about making a brass band and choir CD, David suggested Cory and the rest, as they say, is history."

Karl Jenkins and Cory Band 2007

Karl Jenkins contacted the Cory Band in June 2007 and asked if we would be interested in making a CD of his music with a choir called Cantorion. The choir was originally called 'Only Men Aloud' but EMI Records Ltd suggested that they change their name because they thought 'Only Men Aloud' would restrict record sales. Karl's idea was to fuse two important facets of Welsh culture – brass bands and choirs. The CD was called 'This Land of Ours' and was released in October 2007. It was an instant success, rapidly featuring amongst

The launch of 'This Land of Ours CD' in The Millennium Stadium, Cardiff

the top 10 classical albums at HMV, Virgin and W.H. Smiths record stores. The experience also gave the Band a taste of celebrity status with a video being shot on the side of a Rhondda Valley to be shown on Classic FM TV, as well as making several guest appearances on local television shows and the acclaimed Alan Titchmarsh Show.

The recording sessions took place in Swansea's Brangwyn Hall in August 2007 and the method of the recording was quite unusual. The rhythm had already been recorded so the players all wore one-piece headphones listening to themselves with one ear and the rhythm section through the headset. Once the Band had recorded the music, the choir added their voices and then Karl Jenkins mixed all

This Land of Ours

three elements to his desired balance. The launch of the CD was a grand occasion; taking place in the Millennium Stadium, Cardiff with all the Welsh paparazzi in attendance. This was actually the first time the Band had performed live with the choir. Karl Jenkins was conducting and the performance was broadcast live to several Welsh TV channels.

Karl Jenkins said, 'This is my first recording with a brass band and it has been a privilege to work with the very best in Cory. I was blown away by the quality of their sound and virtuosity. It was a thrill to be able to work with such a fine ensemble. They really are such lovely people as well, which is a real bonus! My eternal thanks to Bob Childs!' As part of the promotion for the CD, Cory, Cantorion and Karl Jenkins performed a live concert at the Brangwyn Hall on 9th December 2007.

Following on from the success of 'This Land of Ours', the Band were delighted when its first CD release of 2008 shot straight to the top of the brass band charts. With 'five out of five' for 'Programme', 'Recording', 'Performance' and 'Presentation', *Enter the Galaxies,* a release featuring premiere recordings of concert works by Dan Price, Paul Lovatt-Cooper, Steven Ponsford, Gareth Wood, Rodney Newton and Peter Graham was awarded 'CD of the Month' in both the July and August editions of the Brass Band World magazine. Reviewer Michael Fowles commented, *"This is no ordinary concert CD. With virtually all the pieces receiving premiere recordings and much of the repertoire being new Cory commissions, this is a 75-minute concert that should be in every brass enthusiasts' collection."*

In recent years, the Cory Band has tried to reach a broader-based audience through its website www.coryband.com Christopher Thomas (trombone) is the driving force behind this initiative and as 'Web-Master' launched the site in 2000. Since then it has developed into an essential part of the Band's publicity and information centre. Concert promoters can download high resolution photos and biographies of the Band and individual members. It is a constant source of current news and displays the Band's concert diary. It also hosts an on-line shop selling Cory Band merchandise. In addition to these services our web-site allows us to promote the Band's many commercial partners (see Chapter 11 page 90). These include; Hercules Music Stands, Eventz – Percussion Hire, Bergeraault Percussion, G.K. Graphic Design, Prima Visa Musikk, Thomas Coaches (Rhondda), Royal Welsh College of Music and Drama.

Another facet of Cory Band's successful and continuing programme of "widening horizons" is their confidence in approaching new music and embracing both new and established composers. During the past decade, the Band has given première performances of music by, Eric Ball, Havergal Brian, Kenneth Downie, Peter Graham, Alun Hoddinott, Elgar Howarth, Karl Jenkins, Paul Lovatt-Cooper, Rodney Newton, Joseph Parry, John Pickard, Dan Price, Goff Richards, Philip Sparke, Philip Wilby, Gareth Wood.

Dr Robert Childs believes that new music is the key that opens doors to BBC broadcasts, overseas tours, recording possibilities and high quality concerts. He insists that having a composer work with the Band on a long term basis affords the composer a much better understanding of player's abilities, their personalities and musical profiles ultimately allowing them to produce music with added dimensions. With this philosophy in mind, the Band created the post of 'Composer in Residence'. The first person appointed to this position was Dr John Pickard, a lecturer in music based at Bristol University. John worked with the Band on all four of his elemental pieces that comprised his massive work *Gaia Symphony* (*Wildfire*, *Tsumani*, *Aurora* and *Men of Stone*). The Cory Band became the first brass band ever to appear at the prestigious Cheltenham International Festival, where they performed the entire symphony. The concert was also broadcast live on BBC Radio 3. The Band has since performed this mammoth work as an entire half of a RNCM Festival of Music concert. They have also made a CD of the work which was the subject of a review by Rodney Newton and published in the British Bandsman magazine:

"The best way to listen to works like John Pickard's epic Gaia Symphony is to actually be there during a live performance. The next best thing is to own a fine digital recording. I have experienced the former (at this year's Cheltenham Festival) and now I am able to enjoy the latter.

Gaia is, of course, something of a 'sonic spectacular' (to borrow a phrase from the early days of stereo) and a showpiece for digital recording. Special effects like the thunder sheet, 'wobble-board' and slapsticks (depicting burning twigs in the Wildfire movement) come off splendidly, being captured with startling fidelity. For those yet to make the acquaintance of John Pickard's Gaia Symphony, the work, considered the longest single work ever written for a brass band (it comes in at 62 minutes on this recording), is in four movements, connected by intermezzi (or 'windows' as the composer calls them) for the percussion section, designed to give, in performance, a chance for the brass players to rest their lips, but also providing a textural contrast for the listener. The colourful work concerns the four elements of water, fire, air and earth and the four movements are entitled Tsunami (evoking the unstoppable force of a tidal wave, all too well demonstrated in the recent past), Wildfire (an account of a double forest fire was the inspiration for this), Aurora - a beautiful movement evoking the Northern Lights (the composer is an astronomer) and Men of Stone (a four-part evocation of various Neolithic circles around the British Isles).

So, what of the recorded performance? As in Cheltenham, the playing is of the highest order, with special laurels going to the soprano playing of Steve Barnsley, the solo cornet playing of Ian Williams, the flugel playing of Joanne Deane, the lovely solo horn of Owen Farr, the impressive Eb bass of John Prosser and David Childs, as ever on superb form in the euphonium solos. There is much consonance in Dr. Pickard's writing and many lyrical moments of which Robert Childs makes much throughout the course of the symphony. The famous burnished 'BAYV sound' is present throughout, despite moments which could have tempted a lesser band to blast.

John Pickard was also involved in the *Heritage* recording having initially uncovered the Havergal Brian work *Battle Song* and encouraged the inclusion of Elgar's *Organ Sonata*. Commenting on the *Heritage* CD John said, 'I realize I'm biased, but I really think that this recording raises the bar in terms of what can be achieved in brass band recording. This is not just a matter of excellence of performance and production, but also of musical intelligence and seriousness of purpose – qualities all too often lacking in the world of brass bands, even in the twenty-first century.'

The Band promoted the CD by providing a workshop at Bristol University where throughout the day John Pickard, Bob Childs and Philip Maund (Editor, The Elgar Society) gave a series of historical lectures. In the evening, the Band played a superb concert, the first half comprising of repertoire from the *Heritage* recording and the second half music from the *Wildfire* CD.

Dr. Pickard's relationship with Band came to an end in 2005, when his *Eden* was selected as the Championship section test piece for the National Championships Finals of Great Britain that year. However, *Gaia Symphony* stands as a monument to one of the most fruitful creative partnerships to grace the brass band movement.

In 2006, the Band appointed Gareth Wood as Composer in Residence and he has written four major works for the Band; *A Tear in the Fabric of Time, Concerto for Horn, Actaeon* and *Brass Triumphant*. All four works have been recorded, but it was *Actaeon* (used as the title track) that received great critical acclaim when it won the Brass Band World CD of the Year Award in 2008. Other nominees for the award were the Black Dyke Band conducted by Sir Colin Davies, Foden's Band conducted by Bramwell Tovey, and Grimethorpe Colliery Band conducted by Elgar Howarth.

Brass Triumphant was written for the Band's 125th Anniversary Celebrations in 2009. The work maps the history of the Band through some difficult times up to the "pinnacle of success" enjoyed at present. The work is in four separate movements with Cory Band playing the beautiful slow movement as part of their winning World Championship programme in Kerkrade in July 2009. Gareth Wood remains the Band's Composer in Residence and is currently engaged in writing several new works for the Band.

Another composer that is associated with the Band is Rodney Newton. Rodney has composed several substantial works for Cory including *The King of Elfland's Daughter* and *Echoes of the East*. He has also written solos for most of the Band's principal players and is always the Band's arranger of choice when vocal or orchestral works need transcribing. Over the years, Rodney has become more than simply a musical associate of the Band. He is a true friend and valued member of the Cory team.

More recently, Dan Price is emerging as a significant part of the Cory backroom team, producing an array of concert pieces and solos for the Band. Dan is a young composer who studied composition with Peter Graham at Salford University. Dan played a major part in the Band's winning Brass In Concert programme in 2008, composing both the slow and sensitive '*Sunrise Over Blue Ridge* and the gripping finale, *An American Tale*. He has also written solos for Joanne Childs, David Childs, Tom Hutchinson and Owen Farr.

Bob Childs readily recalls highlights of the rehearsals leading up to the 2008 Brass In Concert Championships. As well as working on Dan Price's new pieces, the Band were also working on a Big-Band arrangement of Louis Prima's *Sing Sing Sing*. Bob had engaged Barrie Forgie to direct a few rehearsals to help the Band understand the idiom and style of the music. 'Barrie was for many years the leader of the BBC Big Band and he was used to working with professional

jazz musicians. I had rehearsed the Band on *Sing Sing Sing* and I thought we were playing it quite well. However, by time Barrie had finished a two hour rehearsal with the Band, the piece sounded completely different. He also introduced the Band to some intricate choreography which relied heavily on all the players learning the music from memory. It was a great rehearsal and a wonderful experience for the Band. Since then, Barrie has arranged several pieces for us and we also consider him a real friend of the Band.'

A significant problem was highlighted by the choreography required for the Brass in Concert programme and the massive amount of percussion needed. It was patently obvious that the Band's current rehearsal room had become too small and restrictive for present day requirements. This has obviously been the case for sometime, when Cory rehearsed Jan Van der Roost's *Albion*, Philip Wilby's *Revelation* and many other similar large scale pieces. The Band needed to rehearse in a much more spacious and convenient rehearsal facility. If the the Band is to continue to develop and realise even greater musical horizons, then there is an urgent need to relocate the Band to headquarters that will allow for this and for future expansion. Cory Band is very fortunate to have friends who assist financially. Mrs Ann Coleman, widow of Gerald Coleman, has pledged to help the Cory Band fund a new purpose built bandroom.

Gerald Coleman who was the co-owner of Buy As You View Company Ltd had previously played Eb bass with the Mid Rhondda Band for many years. He had also been a member of the Cory Junior Band. The new headquarters of the Band will be called 'The Gerald Coleman Building' and will be a testament and lasting memory of a generous man and musician.

When the new bandroom is built in 2011, it will proudly don the prestigious Blue Heritage Plaque presented to the Band by Rhondda Cynon Taff's Mayor, Mr Robert Smith. The plaque was given to the Band to mark its 125th Anniversary and to recognise the standard of excellence the Band has maintained throughout its history. The new 'state of the art' rehearsal facility will signify yet another new era for the Band and one which will prove to be just as successful as the current headquarters. If recent history is any measure of things to come then the architects need to build an extended display trophy cabinet in the new premises.

May the past work ethic and tradition of achievement remain a foretaste of a continuing, successful, and glorious future for the celebrated Cory Band!

Coda: A Remarkable Tale to Tell!

On 1st May 2010, in Linz, Austria – the joint European Capital of Culture 2009, at the Brucknerhaus Concert hall alongside the River Danube, the Cory Band under the inspirational baton of Dr Robert Childs, made history yet again, by winning their third successive "European Champions" title. It was inconceivable that an achievement of this magnitude should not be included in this book, hence this "Coda" to tell the remarkable tale of this prestigious "hat-trick" of victories.

Although the competition itself takes place over one weekend, in typical Cory tradition the preparations began several months before the event itself. Musical Director Dr Robert Childs is famous for his exhaustive contest preparation, where absolutely "no stone is left unturned;" not surprisingly, the 2010 European Championship contest was no exception. This competition requires each of the invited bands, who must be the Champion band of their respective country, to play not one, but two test pieces. One is chosen by the organisers as a set piece to be performed on the first evening of the event, with the second test piece (performed on the second day) to be selected by each competing band; obviously to display their individual and special strengths in the quality of their music making. Different panels of international adjudicators officiate each part of the competition.

The Cory Band had previously won the title of European Champions on several occasions. In 2008 when the contest was held in Stavanger, Norway, the Band was awarded a record 99 points for their performance of the contemporary set test piece - *Brass Blot* by Hakon Berge. The Band's performance of their own choice work – *Music for Battle Creek* by Philip Sparke was awarded 95 points, placing the Band third in order of merit for this part of the contest. This was the first of their succession of wins. In 2009, the venue was Ostend, Belgium, where the Cory Band won both the set "work" *From Ancient Times by Jon Van der Roost* and their own choice – *On the Shoulders of Giants by Peter Graham*; culminating in an amazing eight point lead over the runners-up.

This was an extra special victory to savour, with the Band's success being partially attributed to the superb quality of the music written by Peter Graham especially for the Band to perform at this event. The title - *On the Shoulders of Giants,* was inspired by the brass playing legends of the past and how they had inspired contemporary brass players to continue to raise standards and levels of performance. Cory's own legends are undoubtedly, the National Championships' "hat-trick" winning Band of the 1980's (known affectionately as Vintage Cory). The current players could not believe that they now had the golden opportunity to stand on the shoulders of these legends and achieve a hat-trick of wins at the European Championships.

Nevertheless, it is timely to reflect that prior to travelling to compete at the 2009 Championships in Ostend, the Band were seriously considering if the continuing escalating costs of these annual visits to this prestigious competition were affordable in future years. Attendance at successive contests was costing the Band circa £20,000 on an annual basis depending upon the location of the host country. Having already pre-qualified

Cory with composer of the winning own-choice piece Philip Sparke

for the invitation to compete at Linz, Austria, in 2010, serious consideration had to be given to the financial implications. However, such concerns were quickly dispelled when the Band realised that there was now an opportunity to achieve the highly prestigious but elusive three in a row wins! So it was on the journey home from Belgium, that the preparation to visit Linz and defend the title of European Champions for the second successive year began in earnest.

History confirms that commissioning a new test piece to perform for the own choice section of the European Championship contest, and giving a world premier performance, can play a significant contribution to a formula for success, as confirmed by the impact of the Peter Graham work used at Ostend. Dr Robert Childs was keen to secure another world class brass band composer, so it was no surprise that Philip Sparke was approached. With a busy schedule ahead of him, Philip was initially concerned about the timescale for completion, but eventually the well worn adage – "ask a busy person" was fruitful and he was commissioned to write a new test piece to be used initially at the European Championship event in Linz. Coincidentally, plans were already in place for the Cory Band to record an entire CD of Philip Sparke's music in 2010, so this new work could be used as the centre piece of this CD.

This exciting news triggered the memories of two members of the Cory Band – Lisa Fitzgerald-Lombard (formerly Childs) and David Childs – both of whom recalled their first experience of attending the European Championships, when as youngsters in 1992, the contest was held in Cardiff and their father (Robert) and uncle (Nicholas) were competing against each other as the Principal Euphonium soloists of the Black Dyke Mills Band and the Britannia Building Society Band respectively. The set test piece on that occasion was Philip Sparke's ever popular but highly challenging – *Year of the Dragon*. Almost two decades later, both Lisa and David were thrilled that they were going to compete at the European Championships performing another Sparke masterpiece, written just for their Band!

With the logistical arrangements for the visit to Linz almost complete, the musical preparation was also in progress. The Cory Band's preparation for the defence of their title was, as always, painstakingly meticulous, but had received an unwelcome setback in March 2010, when competing in the Annual Welsh Regional Championship contest at the Brangwyn Hall, Swansea, playing the set test piece – *English Heritage by George Lloyd*, the Band were awarded the runners up slot with arch rivals – Tredegar – pronounced the winners and becoming eligible as Welsh Champions for the invitation to the European Championships in 2011. The Band's preparation to defend their title of European Champions immediately intensified, spurred on by their keen resolve to restore their injured pride and hard won reputation as well established leaders of the current worldwide rankings.

During the ensuing weeks, MD Dr Robert Childs, lived, breathed and "slept" with both scores – the fixed test piece and the specially commissioned own choice music. Each player responded as anticipated, with the duration of full Band rehearsals being stretched to make best use of time and likewise, the frequency of each sectional rehearsal intensified. Soprano Cornetist – Bert van Thienin who lived in Belgium, was almost solely confined to the Cory Bandroom on his flying visits to Wales! The atmosphere in rehearsals was loaded with a steely, relentless determination to succeed as never before!

The logistical and economical challenges of transporting instruments and the large mutes that were essential for the performances at Linz were overcome by loyal supporters offering to drive a van for the 20 hour journey to Linz, thus enabling the Band to rehearse part way on the journey to London Heathrow airport prior to boarding the early morning flight to Munich and thence by coach to Linz. The fixed test piece for this (2010) contest was *Spiriti* written by the contemporary composer Thomas Doss, who was born and educated in Linz. The music was strongly influenced by Bruckner and Bach, maintaining the traditional impact of the musical history of Linz. The Cory Band quickly developed a healthy regard for this music, which they respectfully described as being the most fiendishly difficult challenge they had encountered in competitive terms.

The rehearsal the night before the European contest is significantly different, because the event does not begin until early evening the next day. This enables a full rehearsal to take place with adequate recovery time for the players during the following day. The Cory Band regarded this rehearsal as special because composer Philip Sparke was present to comment upon the interpretation and performance of his composition – *A Tale as yet Untold*. The Band were delighted to learn he was thoroughly impressed with what he heard in the rehearsal room (and the subsequent contest performance).

The morning of the contest dawned, unveiling stunningly sunny weather. Eventually, the players congregated in the hotel lobby to await news of the draw for order of play for the set test piece. Chairperson – Austin Davies who was at the draw ceremony revealed that the Band had drawn 6th out of the ten band line up, although finding out that Black Dyke were following Cory at number 7 meant that the Band knew a fantastic performance would be required. After a final rehearsal at the Linz AG wind band's headquarters, the Band arrived at the Brucknerhaus Hall and took to the stage. From the first note to the last, the concentration on stage was almost palpable. The performance was undoubtedly one of the best given by the Band, with all of the soloists delivering nothing less than stunning individual contributions. The reaction from the packed audience as the Band played the last note told all that it must have been a very special rendition, as they cheered and treated Cory to a prolonged standing ovation.

Leaving the contest platform the elation of the players was fairly short lived as all realised that the job was only half done and they had to keep their heads for the next stage performance the following day. It was back to the rehearsal room where MD Dr Robert Childs stood in front of the Band and told them how proud he was of the performance. He also paid tribute to the superb soloists and commented that although he did not usually single out

A delighted Bob Childs after a great performance of Spiriti

an individual he felt new Principal Cornet Tom Hutchinson deserved a special congratulations on his first major competition with the Band on the end chair, which received a huge round of applause from the Band.

Fortuitously, the adjudicators were also impressed by the soloists. Torstein Aagaard – Nilsen (Norway) wrote, *"A fantastic reading of the score. Incredible controlled playing from the first note to the last and FLOWERS to the outstanding soloists!"* John Wallace (UK) remarks were similar in praise, *"An irresistible, driving performance that soared effortlessly through all the difficulties. Your soloists were so classy."*

Saturday morning arrived and again the Band met, this time in the breakfast room as the day's competition was to start at 1.00pm, thereby requiring an earlier draw at 8.00am. As players, it is usually considered that the draw for the own choice test piece is not as important as the previous day because every band is playing a different piece. The reality of course is that the Band were very relieved to have a good middle draw again - number 5, and couldn't help feeling sorry for their Celtic cousins from Bon Accord who had drawn 2 the day before and had the dreaded number 1 in this section. A plan for the day was quickly formulated by the MD which allowed anyone who wanted to go to the rehearsal room for an individual warm up (not to mention a British cup of tea, so kindly provided specially for the Band by their rehearsal room hosts) straight after breakfast. The whole Band would go for the pre-contest rehearsal around noon. The day ran smoothly and all too soon the Band found themselves outside the Brucknerhaus Hall once again preparing to "take the stage" for the second time that weekend.

Although the players knew they had played well on the Friday evening, the Band had no idea what the judges Maurice Hamers (Netherlands), Torstein Aagaard-Nilson (Norway) and John Wallace (UK) had decided. This meant that the Band couldn't go and play it safe as there was no telling if the contest was already theirs to throw away or whether they were out of the running entirely. Significantly the performance was even better than the previous evening. The second movement in particular was simply stunning. Philip Sparke's *A Tale as yet Untold* proved very popular with the audience as it is in a similar mould to his much loved *Year of the Dragon*.

The piece and performance also seemed to strike a chord with adjudicators Peter Bassano (UK), Jean-Francois Bobillier (Switzerland) and Edgar Selpenbusch (Austria). Bassano wrote, "This is a fabulous sounding band, a really impressive performance, well done Band and Conductor." Jean – Francois Bobillier's remarks said so elequently, "Fantastique Musique!"

Clearly, Philip Sparke's music had convincingly displayed the Cory Band's technical virtuosity and lyrical musicianship in a performance of immense stature that followed their refined presentation of *Spiriti* the previous evening. Of course, at this stage of the proceedings the result was still awaited!

The mood within the Band was optimistically high, their task was complete – it was now up to the adjudicators. What could have been a long period of tension waiting for the results actually went quite quickly as the Band were actively involved in the post contest Evening Gala Concert. So it was work as usual - yet another rehearsal and performance. Leaving the stage door for the third time in 24 hours, it was time for a refreshing shower and a return to the waiting area outside the main hall of the Brucknerhaus to await the announcement of the results.

As Black Dyke were announced in 4th place, a loud gasp went around the entire audience. The Austrian band – Oberosterreich – were awarded 3rd place to huge cheers from the many home supporters present. Eikanger – Björsvik from Norway were then announced as runners up.

At this point, the Cory players formed themselves into a pseudo-rugby huddle as they awaited their fate – we were either inconspicuous "also rans" or European Champions. The tension was so intense. The announcement revealed what many pundits and a significant majority of the knowledgeable audience had already anticipated – Cory's were crowned European Champions for the third successive year – winning both sections of the contest with a double award of 98 points. As one, the Cory players leapt in the air, cheering, embracing and moving rapidly to the main stage. Yes! The elusive hat-trick had been accomplished and in fine style too!

What makes this hat-trick so significant is the fact that the Cory Band had amassed five winning positions – two pairs and a single in the sequence of six events that comprised three consecutive years as European Champions. The entire Band, together with MD Dr Robert

Childs and composer Philip Sparke, took possession of the stage to express to the full, their unmitigated delight, the Welsh Dragon (flag) providing its unique backcloth to the ecstatic celebrations enjoyed by the Band that continued long into the night.

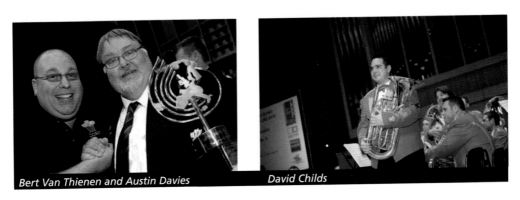

Bert Van Thienen and Austin Davies   David Childs

Composer Philip Sparke expressed his personal tribute to the MD Dr Robert Childs and the Band in the following glowing words:-

"Ever since Cory won their first European Championship title in 1980, when the set piece was my The Land of the Long White Cloud (leading to their commissioning me to write The Year of the Dragon for their centenary), I have had a special relationship with this very special Band. So it was a delight to be asked to write their own choice piece for the 2010 Championships, a project that was a delight from start to finish. "Bob" allowed me to write just what I wanted, without asking for gimmicks or tricks which might give them an advantage and I was delighted that his approach was simply to play the piece as well as possible – a strategy which clearly worked! I am fully aware that it was the quality of their playing and not the piece itself which gave them room to express themselves as a Band, which they did with a Celtic heart that few can match."

In the days that followed the enormity of what the Band had really achieved began to be fully realised. The hard work, determination to succeed and the scrupulous attention to detail implanted by the drive and diligence of MD Dr Robert "Bob" Childs certainly proved to be extremely fruitful.

Significantly, a hat-trick of European Championships had previously been the exclusive domain of English Bands. Not any longer as the record books will continue to confirm!

The contemporary Cory Band have surely provided inspiration for future generations to "Stand on their Shoulders" to maintain the exacting standards that remain synonymous with the name of Cory Band!

Appendix A
The Philanthropic Cory Story by Ida Birch

The benefactor Clifford Cory was born 150 years ago in Cardiff on 10 April 1859 the second son of John Cory and Anna Maria née Beynon and the grandson of Richard Cory known as Captain Cory.

Richard Cory (1799-1882) had moved to Cardiff from Bideford in North Devon in 1838 and his wife Sarah (née Woollacott) and eight children were recorded in the 1841 census at Wharf, Bute Dock. He must have thought that Cardiff offered a promising future having seen it develop over the years during which he had plied his boat from North Devon. Born 14 miles from Bideford in the coastal parish of Hartland, his father Hugh ran the King's Arms. The family's roots, however, are in the nearby parish of West Putford at Cory Barton, an armigerous family descending from a John Cory residing there in the early 1500s whose father was probably Walter. Two Cory brothers, grandsons of John Cory, married Penfound sisters of Penfound Manor, Poundstock, Cornwall. The younger brother Andrew Cory and his wife Jane are 6xgreat-grandparents of Clifford Cory.

As well as developing a provisions business, Richard had another interest, a story related on the occasion when in 1896 John Cory opened The Cory Memorial Temperance Hall in Cardiff built in memory of his father. Richard Cory was the first in Cardiff to sign the pledge and, with others, threw himself into the Temperance movement. The planned meeting at the chapel Richard attended met with opposition from a publican who declared that

Cory Barton, West Pulford, Devon c. 1900

no one should bring such infidel principles into the chapel. Richard replied that if infidelity consisted of lifting the drunkard up out of the gutter and helping him to lead a better life, then he considered it a most desirable kind of infidelity! This episode led to Richard and many others worshipping elsewhere. Premises were found where they could meet for religious and temperance services and they were dubbed Coryites. The opposition of the publicans was vigorous, Richard Cory being the butt of their attacks, his effigy burnt and old tin kettles rattled outside his residence.

The Cory Memorial Temperance Hall, an attractive building much praised when erected, was demolished in the 1980s - replaced by the Capitol Exchange shopping centre. It had cost John Cory £5,000, the equivalent of £285,000 today, a sum John could well afford.

Richard Cory's two eldest sons, John Cory (1828-1910) and Richard Cory (1830-1914), had joined their father and by 1855 'Richard Cory & Sons', were grocers, provision merchants, ship biscuit and bread makers, ship brokers and agents for Wayne & Co. coal merchants. On the retirement of their father in 1859, the brothers John and Richard formed Cory Brothers. They became

John Cory J.P.,D.L., b.1828

Photo courtesy of Cardiff Libraries and InformationService

Richard Cory Esq. J.P. b.1830

Photo courtesy of Cardiff Libraries and InformationService

colliery proprietors and in 1906 it was reported that they owned *Pentre, Gelli, Tynybedw and Tydraw,* in the Rhondda Valley; the *Aberhouse* and steam collieries, Ogmore Valley; the *Rheola Colliery,* Glynneath; the *Tynycwn Collieries,* Glyneath; the *Glyncastle* anthracite collieries and the *Penrhiw Collieries.* There were 5,000 of their wagons on the railway. Cory Brothers were exporting annually *close upon four million tons of coal* in company ships from South Wales, routes expanding with the building of the Suez Canal in 1869. Their success has been attributed to their world wide bunkering (storage) depots including *Aden, Algiers, Bahia, Blanca, Bombay, Bordeaux, Buenos Ayres, Cape Town, Colombo, Constantinople, Corunna, Corcubion, Genoa, Gibraltar, La Plata, La Rochelle, Las Palmas, Madeira, Malta, Marseilles, Monte Video, Nantes, Naples, Oran, Para, Pernambuco, Piraeus, Port Said, Rio Janeiro, Rio Grande, Rochefort, Rosario, Saigon, St. Lucia, St. Thomas, St. Vincent, Seychelles, Santos, Singapore, Smyrna, Suez, Syra, Teneriffe, Tunis, Venice, Vigo, Zanzibar* and *Zea.*

No wonder they were known as the Cardiff Kings of Coal!

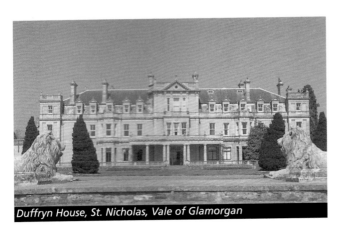

Duffryn House, St. Nicholas, Vale of Glamorgan

John Cory lived at Vaindre Hall, St Mellons before the purchase in 1893 of Dyffryn, in the parish of St Nicholas, Vale of Glamorgan, where the youngest of the four offspring, Reginald, was responsible for designing the gardens with Thomas Mawson. The gardens at Dyffryn House are now used to host occasional concerts and open air performances of operas and plays.

John Cory's actions showed a generous sharing of the wealth acquired through the success of Cory Brothers and other companies with which he was involved. He gave the Maendy Hall in Ton Pentre to the Salvation Army. Much appreciated were Sailors' and Solders' Rests largely financed by

Cory Band outside Dyffryn House, 2000

John in Cardiff, Barry and Milford Haven, to name but a few. The Cardiff Infirmary, the University College and the Police Institute were recipients too. Keen to extend education to his employees, he built libraries. Closing a public house in St Nicholas and building a Coffee Tavern was probably not welcomed by all!

The extent of his generosity was acknowledged when honoured in his life time with the erection of a bronze statue by Sir W Goscombe John in Gorsedd Gardens. The inscription reads:

JOHN CORY.
COAL OWNER,
PHILANTHROPIST.
THIS STATUE IS ERECTED BY HIS
FRIENDS AND FELLOW CITIZENS
AS A TOKEN OF THEIR APPRECIATION
OF HIS WORLD-WIDE SYMPATHIES.
1906

In his will John Cory prefaced the list of bequests " ... *in order that the great work being done and accomplished by the Salvation Army Spezzia Mission and others may not for some time pecuniarily suffer by reason of my death I give to the following persons or Institutions the sums following free of all death duties* ...". He left £20,000 to the Salvation Army, £5,000 to the Spezzia Mission in Italy, £5,000 to the British and Foreign Bible Society, £5,000 to the Ashley Down Orphanage Houses Bristol, £5,000 to the Glamorgan and Monmouthshire Infirmary, Cardiff and a further 21 bequests of £2,000 and seven of £1,000. Thus, he left £89,000 in this manner and

Statue of John Cory, Gorsedd Gardens, Cardiff

on the death of his eldest son Herbert Beynon, his portion was to revert to charitable uses which was estimated at the time to increase the sum to 57 x £250,000, ie £14,265,000 in 2009. He expressed a wish that all his family donate at least one tenth of the income derived from their legacies for and towards religious and charitable purposes. An unusual request, though, *that the Doctor who shall be in attendance on me at my death shall by some surgical operation make certain of my death before I am buried and in consideration of this service I bequeath to him a legacy of twenty six pounds five shillings free of all death duties.*

Offices of Cory Brothers, Cardiff.

Photo courtesy of Media Wales

Corys' Buildings, Cardiff, built 1890

Working alongside his brother John all his life, Richard Cory too has been heaped with praise. He was a generous donor to charities, especially Dr Barnardo's and was closely involved visiting people in the poor areas of Cardiff and patients in hospitals. A tireless supporter of the Baptist Church, Richard took an active role as a preacher and frequently distributed 'tracts'. He served on Cardiff Town Council for 25 years being elected an Alderman in 1883; on the Board of Guardians; and as a Magistrate. Most of Richard's married life was spent at Oscar House on Roath Road where he and his Cornish born wife Emily née Vivian raised a large family but, sadly, they had more than their fair share of losses as several died in childhood. Their son (Richard) Vivian Cory died in the Boer War leaving a wife and daughter. A message Vivian sent to his mother on the way to South Africa, dated 6 Mar 1900, became his will as he expressed his wishes *in case anything happens to me.* The eldest son (Saxton) Campbell Cory committed suicide in 1909. Only seven of their 16 children outlived them.

Richard died in 1914 away from home at Wells Hotel in Llandrindod Wells surrounded by his wife and family. His 1910 will included bequests to charity and in the 4 years before his death he added 12 codicils! In the eleventh he acknowledged the services of his nephew Clifford Cory *not only to myself but also to my late brother John Cory to whom he always showed the utmost loyalty self sacrifice and devotion .... as a token of my esteem and affection and my appreciation of his staunch support of the Protestant Faith and his attitude in regard to Home Rule.*

On Richard's death, Clifford took over as chairman of Cory Brothers Ltd. He had been appointed High Sheriff of Monmouthshire in 1905 and 'The Shipping World' published a

Photo courtesy of Cardiff Libraries and Information Service

John Cory Workmen's Institute opened by Sir Clifford Cory, 1909

© V&A Images Victoria and Albert Museum, London

Sir Clifford Cory

long article including the following:

Mr. Clifford John Cory is the son of this millionaire (John) and philanthropist. He has inherited the personal likeness, and many of his splendid characteristics, and is now considered by the best judges to be among the ablest and most successful men of business to be found in the coal trade of the United Kingdom. As indications of the strenuous business life of Messrs. Cory, it may be stated that they owned the first iron sailing ship, and, again, the first iron steamer registered in Cardiff, and introduced the now famous Glamorganshire coal for the first time to many foreign ports, until now they are, as I have intimated, the largest exporters of coal in the world.

Photo Photo courtesy of Cardiff Libraries and Information Service

Billiard room John Cory Workmen's Institute

Mr. Clifford Cory was born in Cardiff in the year 1859. He was chiefly educated privately, and on the Continent. ...... Following his education, he travelled throughout Europe. Upon returning home, he adopted a business career, and entered the London branch office of the firm, where he spent nine years. He was only nineteen years of age when it was found necessary to send a masterful man to examine into the mismanagement of one of the foreign coal depots of Messrs. Cory. On arriving upon the scene, and appreciating the situation, this lad of nineteen dismissed the manager, exported him home the next day, and set the machinery of the depot in proper working order preparatory for a new manager. This was not an ordinary foreign coaling depot, and the work and responsibility devolving upon Mr. Clifford at this time embraced the quarrying of stone, the construction of buildings, including cottages for the workmen, residences and offices for the firm's staff, the erection of piers and repairing shops, the fitting up of machinery for handling coal, and supplying regular steamers and vessels of the tramp class with "bunkers," water, provisions as well as making provision for the repairs of trading ships and the craft of the firm required for carrying on a very large business. Mr. Clifford showed great initiative and "Cory" courage in extending the business, establishing new foreign stations, and by taking complete charge of the London branch while he was still under the age of twenty-five years.

This source revealed that in his schooldays, Clifford won many trophies for athletics including the best all-round athlete for two years and he *played in the first regular football match that ever came off in South Wales, the teams being captained by his cousin, Mr (Saxton) Campbell Cory, and by Mr. Gordon Lennox, of Pontypridd.*

In 1893 Clifford Cory married Miss Jane Anne Gordon Lethbridge, sister of Lady Carew, at St George's, Hanover Square, London. In addition to the Wedding Breakfast, arrangements had been made for others to join in the celebrations: a banquet for the staff of Cory Brothers Ltd at the Park Hotel; firing of cannons in the districts Ton, Gelli, Pentre and Bodringallt which were represented on the County Council by Clifford plus Punch and Judy shows and tea for the school children; and at the Wesleyan church in Castleton, about 300 people sat down to an excellent spread. London staff were not forgotten – a dinner was arranged for them in the Holborn Restaurant.

A fairy tale wedding? It was not to last – it was soon followed by a legal separation.

Two years later, Clifford Cory purchased Llantarnam Abbey, north of Newport, which stands on the site of a medieval Cistercian Monastery. It was surrounded by 2,000 acres of farmed land. A talented equestrian, Clifford's passion for polo led to 12 acres turned into a polo field. One wonders when he had time to relax!

In her memoirs 'Observations Casual and Intimate' authoress Winifred Graham, the wife of Theodore Cory (son of Richard Cory jnr), revealed life at Llantarnam:

He took us to some delightful Hunt Balls in our younger days, when the lack of certain amenities in his big Abbey astonished me, especially on my first visit there as a bride. The huge fire-places blazing on all sides camouflaged

Llantarnam Abbey, purchased by the Sisters of St Joseph, 1946

the lack of central heating and were even sufficient to warm the lofty entrance hall with its Minstrel Gallery and long church-like stained-glass windows. We were given comfortable adjoining bedrooms where fires also blazed. Then in his home of luxury – came a surprise. My astonishment was great to see an old-fashioned round bath placed on the hearthrug, with large steaming cans of water for my ablutions. The Abbey, with its numerous apartments for visitors, boasted no bathrooms! The large staff seemed to make nothing of carrying cans down the endless corridors and stoking fires from morning till night.

Only a few years before Clifford died at the age of eighty, he decided suddenly to inaugurate bathrooms and central heating. He never did things by halves. Stately marble bathrooms were arranged and owing to the great thickness of the old Abbey walls these alterations cost over £3,000.

When war threatened in 1939, Clifford invited several cousins to his rural home for safety: *Clifford, who never refused us anything, had an extraordinary way of inspiring awe in his dependants and ran the house in spartan fashion. For instance, no visitor was allowed even to put a lump of coal on the fire, the bell had to be rung for the butler to perform this simple office. Early to bed was another fetish in which Clifford expected us to collaborate; so we all trooped upstairs soon after ten o'clock to listen to the wireless in our bedrooms. Occasionally we crept down again, made up the waning fire and unknown to our host broke the rigid rule of retirement.*

After three months, Theodore and Winifred Cory returned home to Hampton, near London, where they immersed themselves in the war effort, especially the Red Cross.

Expansion of Cory Brothers continued as Clifford rose to the challenge when fuel for ships moved to oil. For cars, 'Cory's Motor Spirit' was available at filling stations. In 1923, a site on the Thames was purchased to build an oil storage depot he named Coryton. Coryton was also the name of the residence of Sir (James) Herbert Cory Bt of another prominent Cory family in Cardiff headed by John Cory (1822-1891) who arrived with his wife and family in 1872 from Padstow in Cornwall. His business 'John Cory and Sons' was mainly in shipping. The similarity has given rise to confusion especially with each family having forenames Herbert, Campbell, John and Florence. DNA testing has shown that the two families – originating with Richard Cory's arrival in 1838 and John Cory's in 1872 - are not related, at least not through the Corys!

Clifford became a Baronet (1907), the MP for St Ives, and a Commander of the Order of Leopold. On Clifford's death in 1941, the company's link with the Cory family ended.

Sources:
The Cardiff and South Wales Weekly News
    28 Jan 1893: Marriage of Mr Clifford Cory
    12 Sep 1896: Temperance Movement in Cardiff
The Cardiff and South Wales Daily News
    22 Jun 1906: Cardiff's Great Philanthropist
The Visitation of the County of Devon in the year 1620, Harleian Society
The Shipping Times, Dec 1905
Observations Casual and Intimate by Winifred Graham published by Skeffington and Son Ltd (no date)
Wakeford's Cardiff Directory 1855
The Times
    4 Apr 1910: Wills and Bequests
    18 Jan 1923 Oil bunkering on the Thames
Glamorgan Record Office: Minute Books of Cory Brothers Ltd.
The wills of John Cory dated 01 Jan 1910 and Richard Cory dated 8 Jun 1910
St Nicholas A Historical Survey of a Glamorganshire Parish by Charles F Shepherd
www.screenonline.org.uk Energy (c 1934)
www.nationalarchives.gov.uk/currency

A selection of recordings by Cory Band

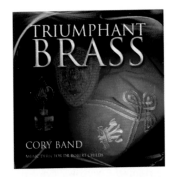

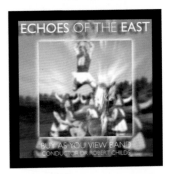

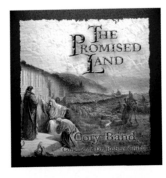

Appendix B
CORY BAND DISCOGRAPHY

God Bless The Prince of Wales
Hen Wlad Fy Nhadau
Cory Workmen's Band
Treorchy Male Choir
Aaron Trotmann & John Davies
Qualiton RD 3164
1957

Listen To The Band No.5
The Famous Cory Workingmen's Band
Conductor: John Harrison
EMI/MFP
MFP Stereo 1313
1969

Trumpets Wild
Cory Band
Conductor: H.A.Kenney
Polydor/99 2485 014 Stereo
Recorded at Llwynypia Boys Club
1971

Granada Festival 1971
Cory Band and others
Conductor: Major H.A.Kenney
EMI Records
Stereo GTVSP 101
Kings Hall Belle Vue Gardens
1971

Cwm Rhondda L.P.
Treorchy Male Voice Choir
The Cory Band
Conductors: Major Kenney
and John Cynan Jones
EMI Records NTS 202
Brangwyn Hall
December **1973**

Entertainments In Brass
The Cory Band
Conductor Major Kenney
Carnival marketed by Polydor
2928 010 MP
1973

Sounds of Brass Series Vol.19
The Cory Band
Conductor: Major H.A.Kenney
Decca Record Company
SB 319 Brangwyn Hall Swansea
November **1974**

National Brass Band Festival Live
The Cory Band and others
Conductor: H Arthur Kenney
PYE Records/Top Brass Series
TB3004 RAH October **1975**

National Champions Salute Siebert
Conductor Arthur Kenny
MSR Midland Sound Recording
MSRS 1397A/B Stereo
1975

The Cory Band's Salute To The New World
Conductor: Bram Gay
Grosvenor Records
GRS.1052 Stereo
1976

The Pride of the Rhondda L.P.
The Cory Band
Conductor Denzil Stephen
and Bram Gay
One –Up EMI Record Ltd
OU 2165
Abbey Road, London **1977**

American Express
The Cory Band
Conductor: Bram Gay
Transatlantic Records Ltd
XTRA1169
1977

Sounds of Brass Series
The Cory Band
Conductor: Denzil Stevens
Decca Record Company Ltd
Llandaff BBC Studio Cardiff
1979

The Cory Band
Conductor Denzil S Stephens
Top Brass Series
TB3023
Congress Theatre Cwmbran
1980

Sound of the Valley L.P.
Stop The Cavalry (side A)
The Longest Day (side B)
Conductor: Denzil Stephens
Stiff Records
BUY133
1981

**Highlights of the
National Championships 1982 L.P.**
The Cory Band and others
Conductor: Major Arthur Kenney
Chandos Records Ltd
ChandosBBRD 1017/8
October **1982**

The Cory Band
Conductor Maj.H.A. Kenney
Polyphonic Reproductions
PRL021D
Brangwyn Hall
December **1983**

Dances and Arias L.P.
The Cory Band
Conductor Maj. H.A. Kenney
Polyphonic Reproductions
PRL025D
Brangwyn Hall
December **1984**

The Cory Band
Conductor Maj.H.A. Kenney
Polyphonic Reproductions
PRL027D
Brangwyn Hall
December **1985**

The Internationale
Billy Bragg
Utillity
1990

Diadem of Gold
Buy As You View Cory Band
Conductor Robert Childs
Doyen
DOYCD120
Cwmbran Council Chambers
2000

Men of Stone
Buy As You View Cory Band
Conductor Robert Childs
Kirklees
KRCD1034
Cwmbran Council Chambers
2001

European Championships 2001
Buy As You View Cory Band
Conductor Robert Childs
Doyen
DOYCD125
Stravinsky Hall, Montreaux, Switzerland
2001

Regionals 2002
Buy As You View Cory Band
Conductor Robert Childs
Doyen
DOYCD128
Cwmbran Council Chambers
2001

Brass Band Classics – Volume I
Buy As You View Cory Band
Conductor Robert Childs
Doyen
DOYCD140
Cwmbran Council Chambers
2001

Salute to Cory
Buy As You View Cory Band
Conductor Robert Childs
Obrasso
CD877
Cwmbran Council Chambers
2001

Heritage
Buy As You View Cory Band
Conductor Robert Childs
Doyen
DOYCD142
Cwmbran Council Chambers
2002

Wildfire
Buy As You View Cory Band
Conductor Robert Childs
Doyen
DOYCD144
St Julian's School Newport
2002

The Glory of Cory
Buy As You View Cory Band
Conductor Robert Childs
Obrasso
CD882
Cwmbran Council Chambers
2002

European Championships 2003
Buy As You View Cory Band
Conductor Robert Childs
Doyen
DOYCD153
Grieg Hall, Bergen, Norway
2003

Brass Band Classics – Volume II
Buy As You View Cory Band
Conductor Dr Robert Childs
Doyen
DOYCD155
Cwmbran Council Chambers
2003

Discovery Brass
Buy As You View Cory Band
Conductor Dr Robert Childs
Obrasso
CD891
Cwmbran Council Chambers
2003

25 Years of the European Brass Band Championships
Buy As You View Cory Band
Conductor Dr Robert Childs
Doyen
DOYCD156
2003

Regionals 2004
Buy As You View Cory Band
Conductor Dr Robert Childs
Doyen
DOYCD157
Cwmbran Council Chambers
2003

Highlights from Champion Brass
Buy As You View Cory Band
Conductor Dr Robert Childs
Kapitol
KPRCD001
Royal Albert Hall, London
2003

Now That's What I Call Brass – Vol 1
Buy As You View Cory Band
Conductor Dr Robert Childs
World of Brass
CD-WOB102
2003

The Magic of Brass: Philipe Schartz
Buy As You View Cory Band
Conductor Dr Robert Childs
Doyen
DOYCD159
Cwmbran Council Chambers
2004

An Italian Night
Buy As You View Cory Band
Conductor Dr Robert Childs
Obrasso
CD898
St Julian's School, Newport
2004

Day of the Dragon
Buy As You View Band
Conductor Dr Robert Childs
Doyen
DOYCD173
Cwmbran Council Chambers
2004

European Championships 2004
Buy As You View Band
Conductor Dr Robert Childs
Doyen
DOYCD176
The Royal Concert Hall, Glasgow
2004

The Wonder of Christmas
Buy As You View Band
Conductor Dr Robert Childs
Amadeus
AMS078
St Teilo's Arts Centre, Cardiff
2004

Brass Band Classics – Volume III
Buy As You View Band
Conductor Dr Robert Childs
Doyen
DOYCD178
St Julian's School & Cwmbran Council Chambers
2004

Regionals 2005
Buy As You View Band
Conductor Dr Robert Childs
Doyen
DOYCD181
Cwmbran Council Chambers
2004

Gaia Symphony: John Pickard
Buy As You View Band
Conductor Dr Robert Childs
Doyen
DOY188
St Julian's School & Cwmbran Council Chambers
2005

Echoes of the East
Buy As You View Band
Conductor Dr Robert Childs
Doyen
DOYCD195
St Teilo's Arts Centre
2005

Welsh Connection: David Childs
Buy As You View Band
Conductor Dr Robert Childs
Doyen
DOYCD200
Cwmbran Council Chambers
2005

Master Brass – Volume Sixteen
Buy As You View Band
Conductor Dr Robert Childs
Polyphonic
QPRL220D
Corn Exchange, Cambridge
2005

Now That's What I Call Brass – Vol 3
Buy As You View Band
Conductor Dr Robert Childs
World of Brass
CD-WOB109
2005

**The Childs – Music was my First Love:
Robert & David Childs**
Buy As You View Band
Conductor Robert, Nicholas & David Childs
Obrasso
CD908
St Teilo's Church, Cardiff
2006

Stars in Brass
Buy As You View Band
Conductor Dr Robert Childs
Obrasso
CD912
St Julian's School, Newport
2006

Brass Band Classics – Volume IV
Buy As You View Band
Conductor Dr Robert Childs
Doyen
DOYCD201
St Julian's School, Newport
2006

Regionals 2006
Buy As You View Band
Conductor Dr Robert Childs
Doyen
DOYCD206
Cwmbran Council Chambers
2006

European Championships 2006
Buy As You View Band
Conductor Dr Robert Childs
Doyen
DOYCD211
Waterfront Hall, Belfast
2006

The Lighter Side of Elgar Howarth
Buy As You View Band
Conductor Dr Robert Childs
Doyen
DOYCD215
St Teilo's Arts Centre, Cardiff
2006

Celtic Charm: David Childs
Cory Band
Conductor Dr Robert Childs
Doyen
DOYCD214
Ysgol Gyfun Rhydywaun, Aberdare
2007

The Promised Land
Cory Band
Conductor Dr Robert Childs
Doyen
DOYCD218
Ysgol Gyfun Rhydywaun, Aberdare
2007

Untold Stories: Owen Farr
Cory Band
Conductor Dr Robert Childs
Doyen
DOYCD225
Ysgol Gyfun Rhydywaun, Aberdare
2007

Brass Band Aid – Into Africa
Cory Band
Conductor Dr Robert Childs
Doyen
DOYCD226
2007

The Noble Trombone: Chris Thomas
Cory Band
Conductor Dr Robert Childs
Doyen
DOYCD228
Ysgol Gyfun Rhydywaun, Aberdare
2007

European Championships 2007
Cory Band
Conductor Dr Robert Childs
Doyen
DOYCD234
Symphony Hall, Birmingham
2007

Another Openin' Another Show
Cory Band
Conductor Dr Robert Childs
Obrasso
CD923
Ysgol Gyfun Rhydywaun, Aberdare
2007

This Land of Ours: Karl Jenkins
Cory Band
Conductor Dr Robert Childs & Karl Jenkins
EMI Records Ltd
5090932
Brangwyn Hall, Swansea
2007

National Brass Band Championships 2007
Cory Band
Conductor Dr Robert Childs
Doyen
DOYCD240
Royal Albert Hall, London
2007

Now That's What I Call Brass – Vol 5
Cory Band
Conductor Dr Robert Childs
World of Brass
CD-WOB130
2007

Actaeon
Cory Band
Conductor Dr Robert Childs
Doyen
DOYCD241
Ysgol Gyfun Rhydywaun, Aberdare
2008

Life Abundant: Philip Cobb
Cory Band
Conductor Dr Robert Childs
Egon
CD-SFZ140
Ysgol Gyfun Rhydywaun, Aberdare
2008

Regionals 2009
Cory Band
Conductor Dr Robert Childs
Doyen
DOYCD246
St Teilo's Church, Cardiff
2008

European Championships 2008
Cory Band
Conductor Dr Robert Childs
Doyen
DOYCD253
Stavanger Hall, Stavanger, Norway
2008

Two Part Invention: Childs/ Ibbotson
Cory Band
Conductor Dr Robert Childs
Obrasso
CD934
Ysgol Gyfun Rhydywaun, Aberdare
2008

Now That's What I Call Brass – Vol 6
Cory Band
Conductor Dr Robert Childs
World of Brass
CD-WOB140
2008

Enter The Galaxies
Cory Band
Conductor Dr Robert Childs
Doyen
DOYCD264
Ysgol Gyfun Rhydywaun, Aberdare
2009

European Championships 2009
Cory Band
Conductor Dr Robert Childs
Doyen
DOYCD
Kursaal, Ostend, Belgium
2009

Highlights from the World Music Contest Brass Band Championships 2009
Cory Band
Conductor Dr Robert Childs
Mirasound
WWM500.158
Rodahal, Kerkrade, Netherlands
2009

CORY BAND DVDS

European Championships 2003
Buy As You View Cory Band
Conductor Dr Robert Childs
World of Brass
WOB101DVD
Grieg Hall, Bergen, Norway
2003

British Open Brass Band Championship 2004
Buy As You View Cory Band
Conductor Dr Robert Childs
World of Brass
WOB108DVD
Symphony Hall, Birmingham
2004

European Contest 2005
Buy As You View Band
Conductor Dr Robert Childs
World of Brass
WOB112DVD
Groningen, Netherlands
2005

Brass in Concert Championship 2005
Buy As You View Band
Conductor Dr Robert Childs
World of Brass
WOB114DVD
The Sage, Gateshead
2005

European Championships 2006
Buy As You View Band
Conductor Dr Robert Childs
World of Brass
WOB118DVD
Waterfront Hall, Belfast
2006

European Championships 2007
Buy As You View Band
Conductor Dr Robert Childs
World of Brass
WOB123DVD
Symphony Hall, Birmingham
2007

European Championships 2008
Cory Band
Conductor Dr Robert Childs
World of Brass
WOB134DVD
Stavanger Concert Hall, Stavanger, Norway
2008

Brass in Concert Championship 2008
Cory Band
Conductor Dr Robert Childs
World of Brass
WOB135DVD
The Sage, Gateshead
2008

European Championships 2009
Cory Band
Conductor Dr Robert Childs
World of Brass
WOB135DVD
Kursaal, Ostend, Belgium
2009

Highlights from the World Music Contest
Brass Band Championships 2009
Cory Band
Conductor Dr Robert Childs
Mirasound
WWM500.161
Rodahal, Kerkrade, Netherlands
2009

Brass and Voices...and all that Jazz
125 Anniversary Concert
Cory Band
Conductor: Robert Childs
Guest soloist: Wycliffe Gordon
Morriston Orpheus Choir
Presenter: Roy Noble OBE
World of Brass WOB 139 DVD
St. Davids Hall, Cardiff
2009

Appendix C
Players Roll of Honour

Cory Band Personnel
National Championships
of Great Britain 1974
Fantasy For Brass Band – Malcolm Arnold

Conductor	Major Arthur Kenney
Soprano	Gwyn Thomas
Principal cornet	Jim Davies
Solo cornets	Stuart Lewis
	Stan Williams
	Richard Dix
	Keith Rees
Repiano cornet	Howard Jones
2nd cornets	Allan Jones
	Graham Lewis
3rd cornets	Ian Jones
	Selwyn Protheroe
Flugel horn	Jeff Thomas
Solo horn	John Bowen
1st horn	Jeff Sheppard
2nd horn	Philip Wicks
1st baritone	Ivor Roberts
2nd baritone	Huw Jones
Solo euphonium	George Davies
2nd euphonium	Roy Roberts
Solo trombone	Don Tanner
2nd trombone	Ivor England
Bass trombone	Norman John
Eb basses	Huw Williams
	John Trotman
BBb basses	Graham Sheppard
	Alan Cleary
Percussion	Clayton McCann
	Keith Williams

Cory Band Personnel
European Championships London 1980
Triumphant Rhapsody – Gilbert Vinter
Land of the Long White Cloud – Philip Sparke

Conductor	Squadron Leader Denzil Stephens
Soprano:	Gwyn Thomas
Principal cornet:	Jim Davies
Solo cornets:	John Neathy
	Richard Dix
	Paul Hedditch
Flugel:	Jeff Thomas
Repiano:	Howard Jones
2nd cornets:	Ian Jones
	Dewi Price
3rd cornets	Ralph Morgan
	Greg Jones
Solo horn	Wayne Cook
1st horn	Robin Davies
2nd horn	Jeff Sheppard
Solo euphonium	Roy Roberts
2nd euphonium	Huw Watkins
1st baritone	Stuart Lewis
2nd baritone	Phil Wicks
Solo trombone	Don Tanner
2nd trombone	Terry Lambert
Bass trombone	Gareth Keys
Eb bass	Brian Davis
Eb bass	Huw Williams
BBb bass	Graham Sheppard
BBb bass	John Trotman
Percussion:	Clayton McCann
	Alan O'Leary

**Cory Band Personnel
National Championships
of Great Britain 1982
*Contest Music – Wilfred Heaton***

Conductor	Major Arthur Kenney
Soprano cornet	Gwyn Thomas
Principal cornet	Jim Davies
Tutti cornets	John Neathy
	Richard Dix
	Ian Waite
	Paul Hedditch
Repiano cornet	Howard Jones
Flugel	Jeff Thomas
2nd cornets	Phil Harris
	Gary Price
	John Lavender
3rd cornets	Steve Harris
	Greg Jones
Solo Horn	Wayne Cook
1st Horn	Robin Davies
2nd Horns	Huw Watkins
	Keith Curtis
1st Baritone	Stuart Lewis
2nd Baritone	Phillip Wicks
Solo euphonium	Roy Roberts
2nd euphonium	Derek Andrews
Solo trombone	Gareth Key
2nd trombone	Don Tanner
Bass trombone	Terry Lambert
E flat bass	John Prosser
	Paul Evans
B flat bass	Graham Sheppard
	Phil Privett
Percussion	Clayton McCann
	Alan O'Leary
	Brian Davies

**Cory Band Personnel
National Championships
of Great Britain 1983
*Ballet for Band – Joseph Horovitz***

Conductor	Major Arthur Kenney
Soprano cornet	Gwyn Thomas
Principal cornet	Jim Davies
Tutti cornets	John Neathy
	Richard Dix
	Ian Waite
	Paul Hedditch
Repiano cornet	Howard Jones
Flugel	Jeff Thomas
2nd cornets	Phil Harris
	Gary Price
	John Lavender
3rd cornets	Steve Harris
	Greg Jones
Solo Horn	Wayne Cook
1st Horn	Robin Davies
2nd Horns	Huw Watkins
	Keith Curtis
1st Baritone	Stuart Lewis
2nd Baritone	Phillip Wicks
Solo euphonium	Roy Roberts
2nd euphonium	Derek Andrews
Solo trombone	Gareth Key
2nd trombone	Don Tanner
Bass trombone	Terry Lambert
E flat bass	John Prosser
	Paul Evans
B flat bass	Graham Sheppard
	Phil Privett
Percussion	Clayton McCann
	Alan O'Leary
	Brian Davies
	John Trotman

Cory Band Personnel
National Championships
of Great Britain 1984
Dances and Arias – Edward Gregson

Conductor	Major Arthur Kenney
Soprano cornet	Gwyn Thomas
Principal cornet	Jim Davies
Tutti cornets	John Neathy
	Richard Dix
	Ian Waite
	Paul Hedditch
Repiano cornet	Howard Jones
Flugel	Jeff Thomas
2nd cornets	Phil Harris
	Gary Price
	John Lavender
3rd cornets	Steve Harris
	Greg Jones
Solo Horn	Wayne Cook
1st Horn	Robin Davies
2nd Horns	Huw Watkins
	Keith Curtis
1st Baritone	Stuart Lewis
2nd Baritone	Phillip Wicks
Solo euphonium	Roy Roberts
2nd euphonium	Derek Andrews
Solo trombone	Gareth Key
2nd trombone	Don Tanner
Bass trombone	Terry Lambert
E flat bass	John Prosser
	Paul Evans
B flat bass	Graham Sheppard
	Phil Privett
Percussion	Clayton McCann
	Alan O'Leary
	Andrew Howells

Buy As You View Cory Band Personnel
British Open 2000
Ceremony-Michael Ball

Conductor	Robert Childs
Soprano cornet	Steve Barnsley
Principal cornet	Ian Williams
Solo cornet	Jeff Fear
Solo cornet	John Southcombe
Solo cornet	John Evans
Repiano cornet	Nigel Guy
2nd cornet	Phil Harris
2nd cornet	Neil Blockley
3rd cornet	Greg Jones
3rd cornet	David Singleton
Flugel Horn	Ian Roberts
Solo Horn	David Cornelius
1st Horn	Keith Curtis
2nd Horn	Robin Davies
SoloEuphonium	Nigel John
	(soloist prize)
Euphonium	Barry John
1st Baritone	Susan Thomas
2nd Baritone	Ron Andrews
1st Trombone	Christopher Thomas
2nd Trombone	Steve Howell
Bass Trombone	Andrew Williams
Eb bass	John Prosser
Eb bass	Austin Davies
BBb bass	Fraser Bish
BBb bass	Mark Richards
Principal	David Mitchell
Percussionist	Martha Davison
Percussionist	Christian Sefton

Committee:	*Austin Davies*
	Greg Jones
	Ian Evans
	John Southcombe
	John Trotman
	Ron Pryce
	Selwyn Protheroe
	John Jones
	Neil Blockley

**Buy As You View Cory Band Personnel
National Championships of Great Britain
2000**
Harrison's Dream - Peter Graham

Conductor	Robert Childs
Principal cornet	Ian Williams
Soprano cornet	Steve Barnsley
Solo cornet	Jeff Fear
Solo cornet	John Southcombe
Solo cornet	Robert Samuels
Repiano cornet	Nigel Guy
2nd cornet	Phil Harris
2nd cornet	Neil Blockley
3rd cornet	Greg Jones
3rd cornet	David Singleton
Flugel Horn	Ian Roberts
Solo Horn	David Cornelius
1st Horn	Keith Curtis
2nd Horn	Robin Davies
SoloEuphonium	Nigel John
Euphonium	Barry John
1st Baritone	Susan Thomas
2nd Baritone	Ron Andrews
1st Trombone	Christopher Thomas
2nd Trombone	Steve Howell
Bass Trombone	Andrew Williams
Eb bass	John Prosser
Eb bass	Austin Davies
BBb bass	Fraser Bish
BBb bass	Mark Richards
Principal	David Mitchell
Percussionist	Martha Davison
Percussionist	Christian Sefton

Committee: *Austin Davies*
Greg Jones
Ian Evans
John Southcombe
John Trotman
Ron Pryce
Selwyn Protheroe
John Jones
Neil Blockley

**Buy As You View Cory Band Personnel
British Open 2002**
Maunsell Forts - John McCabe

Conductor	Dr Robert Childs
Soprano	Steve Barnsley
Principal cornet	Ian Williams
Solo cornet	Ian Roberts
	Ian Bailey
	John Southcombe
Repiano	Nigel Guy
2nd cornet	Phil Harris
	Lisa Childs
3rd cornet	Neil Blockley
	Travis Griffiths
Flugel Horn	Joanne Deane
Solo Horn	Dave Cornelius
1st Horn	Keith Curtis
2nd Horn	Robin Davies
1st Baritone	Susan Thomas
2nd Baritone	Ron Andrews
Solo Euphonium	David Childs
2nd Euphonium	Gareth Ritter
Solo Trombone	Chris Thomas
2nd Trombone	Paul Jenkins
Bass Trombone	Andrew Williams
Eb bass	John Prosser
	Austin Davies
BBb bass	Fraser Bish
	Stewart Baglin
Percussion	David Mitchel
	Jack Egglestone
	Adam Davies
	Jason Bevan

Committee: *Austin Davies*
Greg Jones
John Southcombe
John Trotman
Ron Pryce
Selwyn Protheroe
Neil Blockley

Cory Band Personnel
British Open 2007
Visions of Gerontius **Kenneth Downie**

Conductor	Dr Robert Childs
Soprano	Michelle Ibbotson
Principal cornet	Ian Williams
Solo cornet	Christopher Turner
	Darren Thomas
	Seamus Gallagher
Repiano	Richard Davies
2nd cornet	Lisa Childs
	Phillip Harris
3rd cornet	Neil Blockley
	Travis Griffiths
Flugel Horn	Joanne Childs
Solo Horn	Owen Farr
1st Horn	Lynne Turner
2nd Horn	Lucy Griffiths
1st Baritone	Susan Thomas
2nd Baritone	Gareth Ritter
Euphoniums	David Childs
	Matthew Jenkins
Solo Trombone	Christopher Thomas
2nd Trombone	Paul Jenkins
Bass Trombone	Andrew Williams
Eb bass	Steve Sykes
	Oliver Browne
BBb bass	Fraser Bish
	John Prosser
Percussion	Alun Horgan
	Dave Danford
	Simon Brittlebank
	Alun Hathaway
Committee:	*Austin Davies*
	John Southcombe
	John Trotman
	Ron Pryce
	Selwyn Protheroe
	Neil Blockley
	Chris Thomas

Cory Band Personnel
European Championships Stavanger
Norway 2008
Brass Blot – **Håkon Berge**
Music for Battle Creek – **Philip Sparke**

Conductor	Dr Robert Childs
Soprano	Michelle Ibbotson
Principal cornet	Ian Williams
Solo cornet	Christopher Turner
	Philip Cobb
	Darren Thomas
	Seamus Gallagher
Repiano	Richard Davies
2nd cornet	Lisa Childs
	Phillip Harris
3rd cornet	Neil Blockley
	Travis Griffiths
	Mark Bowater
Flugel Horn	Joanne Childs
Solo Horn	Owen Farr
1st Horn	Michael Franey
2nd Horn	Lucy Griffiths
1st Baritone	Susan Thomas
2nd Baritone	Christopher Straker
Euphoniums	David Childs
	Matthew Jenkins
Solo Trombone	Christopher Thomas
2nd Trombone	Johanna Hirst
Bass Trombone	Andrew Williams
Eb bass	Simon Howell
	Oliver Browne
BBb bass	Fraser Bish
	John Prosser
Percussion	Alun Horgan
	Dave Danford
	Simon Brittlebank
	Gavin Pritchard
Committee:	*Austin Davies*
	John Southcombe
	Neil Blockley
	John Trotman
	Ron Pryce
	Selwyn Protheroe
	Chris Thomas

Cory Band Personnel
European Championships Ostend Belgium
2009
From Ancient Times - Jan Van der Roost
On The Shoulders of Giants - Peter Graham

Conductor	Dr Robert Childs
Soprano	Bert Van Thienen
Principal cornet	Ian Williams
Solo cornet	Christopher Turner
	Darren Thomas
	Seamus Gallagher
Repiano	Richard Davies
2nd cornet	Lisa Fitzgerald-Lombard
	Phillip Harris
3rd cornet	Neil Blockley
	Travis Griffiths
	Nicholas Brill
Flugel Horn	Joanne Childs
Solo Horn	Owen Farr
1st Horn	Michael Franey
2nd Horn	Lucy Griffiths
1st Baritone	Susan Thomas
2nd Baritone	Christopher Straker
Euphoniums	David Childs
	Matthew Jenkins
Solo Trombone	Christopher Thomas
2nd Trombone	Johanna Hirst
	Stephen Sykes
Bass Trombone	Andrew Williams
Eb bass	Simon Howell
	Oliver Browne
BBb bass	Fraser Bish
	John Prosser
Percussion	Alun Horgan
	Mark Halliday
	Simon Brittlebank
	Gavin Pritchard
Committee:	*Austin Davies*
	John Southcombe
	John Trotman
	Ron Pryce
	Glan Lewis
	Neil Blockley
	Chris Thomas

Cory Band Personnel
World Championships Kerkrade Holland
2009
Harrison's Dream – Peter Graham
Into the Light-Wilby, Arfon Forest – Wood,
Brillante – Graham (soloist David Childs)
From Ancient Times- Jan Van der Roost

Conductor	Dr Robert Childs
Soprano	Bert Van Thienen
Principal cornet	Nicholas Walkley
Solo cornet	Christopher Turner
	Darren Thomas
	Seamus Gallagher
	Christopher Avison
Repiano	Richard Davies
2nd cornet	Lisa Fitzgerald-Lombard
	Phillip Harris
3rd cornet	Neil Blockley
	Travis Griffiths
	Nicholas Brill
Flugel Horn	Joanne Childs
Solo Horn	Owen Farr
1st Horn	Christopher Davies
2nd Horn	Lucy Griffiths
1st Baritone	Susan Thomas
2nd Baritone	Christopher Straker
Euphoniums	David Childs
	Matthew Jenkins
Solo Trombone	Christopher Thomas
2nd Trombone	Gareth Robinson
Bass Trombone	Andrew Williams
Eb bass	Simon Howell
	Gethin Rees
BBb bass	Fraser Bish
	John Prosser
Percussion	Alun Horgan
	Gavin Pritchard
	Simon Brittlebank
	Mark Halliday
Committee:	*Austin Davies*
	John Southcombe
	John Trotman
	Ron Pryce
	Neil Blockley
	Chris Thomas

Cory Band Personnel
British Open 2009
Titan's Progress **- Hermann Pallhuber**

Conductor	Dr Robert Childs
Soprano	Bert Van Thienen
Principal cornet	Ian Williams
Solo cornet	Christopher Turner
	Darren Thomas
	Seamus Gallagher
Repiano	Richard Davies
2nd cornet	Lisa Fitzgerald-Lombard
	Phillip Harris
3rd cornet	Neil Blockley
	Travis Griffiths
Flugel Horn	Joanne Childs
Solo Horn	Owen Farr
1st Horn	Christopher Davies
2nd Horn	Lucy Griffiths
1st Baritone	Susan Thomas
2nd Baritone	Christopher Straker
Euphoniums	David Childs
	Matthew Jenkins
Solo Trombone	Christopher Thomas
2nd Trombone	Gareth Robinson
Bass Trombone	Andrew Williams
Eb bass	Simon Howell
	Steve Sykes
BBb bass	Fraser Bish
	John Prosser
Percussion	Alun Horgan
	Dave Danford
	Simon Brittlebank
	Gavin Pritchard
Committee:	*Austin Davies*
	John Southcombe
	John Trotman
	Ron Pryce
	Neil Blockley
	Chris Thomas

Cory Band Personnel
European Championships Linz,
Austria 2010
Spiriti **- Thomas Doss**
A Tale as Yet Untold **- Philip Sparke**

Conductor	Dr Robert Childs
Soprano	Bert Van Thienen
Principal cornet	Tom Hutchinson
Solo cornet	Christopher Turner
	Darren Thomas
	Seamus Gallagher
	Nicholas Walkley
Repiano	Richard Davies
2nd cornet	Lisa Fitzgerald-Lombard
	Phillip Harris
	John Southcombe
3rd cornet	Neil Blockley
	Travis Griffiths
	Nicholas Brill
Flugel Horn	Joanne Childs
Solo Horn	Owen Farr
1st Horn	Ailsa Russell
2nd Horn	Lucy Griffiths
1st Baritone	Susan Thomas
2nd Baritone	Christopher Straker
Euphoniums	David Childs
	Matthew Jenkins
Solo Trombone	Christopher Thomas
2nd Trombone	Gareth Robinson
Bass Trombone	Andrew Williams
Eb bass	Simon Howell
	Robert Graham-White
BBb bass	Fraser Bish
	John Prosser
Percussion	Alun Horgan
	Simon Brittlebank
	Gavin Pritchard
	David Mitchell
	Jeremy Taylor
Committee:	*Austin Davies*
	John Southcombe
	John Trotman
	Glan Lewis
	Neil Blockley
	Chris Thomas

2008 Holland Brass Festival on Friday evening at the church in Schoonhoven

Appendix D
REGISTERED PLAYERS
OF CORY BAND 2000 – 2009

Registered players who played in Cory Band under Bob Childs

Soprano cornets
Bert Van Thienen, Michelle Ibbotson, Dominique Morel, Steve Barnsley.
Cornets
Ian Williams, Tom Hutchinson, Christopher Turner, Darren Thomas, Seamus Gallagher,
Richard Davies, Lisa Fitzgerald-Lombard, Phillip Harris, Neil Blockley, Travis Griffiths,
Nicholas Brill, Christopher Avison, John Southcombe, Philip Cobb, Jeff Fear, John Evans,
Nigel Guy, Greg Jones, Dai Singleton, Ian Roberts, Nicholas Mead, Ian Bailey, Robert
Samuel, Mark Bowater, Nicholas Walkley.
Flugel Horns
Joanne Childs, Ian Roberts.
Tenor Horns
Owen Farr, Christopher Davies, Lucy Griffiths David Cornelius, Keith Curtis, Michael Franey,
Lynn Turner, Robin Davies, Helen Farr, Ailsa Russell.
Baritones
Susan Thomas, Christopher Straker, Gareth Ritter, Shoko Morimoto, Ron Andrews,
Rikki Mc Donnell, Margie Antrobus, Regis Gobet.
Euphoniums
David Childs, Matthew Jenkins, Gareth Ritter, Lyndon Baglin, Nigel John, Barry John.
Tenor Trombones
Christopher Thomas, Gareth Robinson, Johanna Hirst, Paul Jenkins, Steve Sykes,
Steve Howell, Susanne Hathaway.
Bass Trombone
Andrew Williams.
Eb Basses
Simon Howell, Steve Sykes, Robert Graham-White, John Prosser, Austin Davies,
Gethin Rees, Gavin Saynor, Oliver Browne.
BBb Basses
Fraser Bish, John Prosser, Mark Richards, Stewart Baglin.
Percussion
Alun Horgan, Gavin Pritchard, Simon Brittlebank, Dave Danford, David Mitchell,
Jack Egglestone, Tom Clare, Christian Sefton, David Griffith, Jason Bevan, Alan Hathaway,
Adam Davies, Celi Evans, Luke Wyeth.

*Committee: Austin Davies, John Southcombe, Neil Blockley, John Trotman, Ron Pryce,
Selwyn Prothero, Ian Evans, Greg Jones, Chris Thomas.*

Ron Pryce and John Trotman

Cory Band near Treorchy

Appendix E
Principal Players of Cory Band 1884 - 2009

Soprano:
Moss Davies
Emlyn Bryant
Horace Davies
Derick Lewis
Ken Williams
Gwyn Thomas
John Evans
Steve Barnsley
Michelle Ibbotson
Dominique Morel
Bert Van Thienen

Cornet:
Aaron Trotman
Jack Carter
Horace Davies
Gordon Evans
Stan Williams
Colin Stokes
Jim Davies
John Southcombe
Ian Williams
Tom Hutchinson

Flugel Horn:
Harold Hearn
John Trotman
Bill Davies
Jeff Thomas
Ian Roberts
Joanne Childs (nee Deane)

Tenor Horn:
Jim Hearn
Steve Trotman
John Bowen
Wayne Cook
Bernard Williams
Michael Thorne
David Cornelius
Owen Farr

Baritone:
Dick Hearn
Will Armstrong
Vic Maggs
Tommy Roberts
Ivor Roberts
Stuart Lewis
Ron Andrews
Sue Thomas

Euphonium:
John Bailey
W.J. Davies
Tom Trotman
Tom Roberts
George Davies
Roy Williams
Roy Roberts
Bryan Davies
Dean Purnell
Robert Burnett
Lyndon Baglin
Nigel John
David Childs

Tenor Trombone:
George Howells
Arthur Bryant
Ivor Jones
Don Tanner
John Jones
Steve Howell
Christopher Thomas

Bass Trombone
Harry Ingram
Ossie John
Norman John
Terry Lambert
Gareth Key
Paul Reffel
David Short
Julian Kerrel
Andrew Williams

Eb Bass:
Will Pickings
Tom Trotman
John Trotman
Huw Williams
Paul Evans
John Prosser
Gavin Saynor
Steve Sykes
Simon Howell

BBb Bass
Aaron Trotman (senior)
Will Adlam
Mr Summers
Idwell Jenkins
John Trotman
Alan Cleary
Graham Sheppard
Fraser Bish

Percussion:
Trevor Davies
Dick Davies
Tom Hutton
Alan O Leary
Clayton McCann
David Mitchell
Alan Horgan

A proud conductor with the well deserved European Brass Band Championship trophy in 2009

Appendix F
Cory Band Conductors 1884 - 2009

John Treherne	1884-1895
Ernest Ambler	1895-1896
John Bailey	1896-1912
J.B.Dobbing	1912-1939
Redvers (Reg.) Little	1939-1946
Walter B. Hargreaves	1946-1952
L Wainwright	1953-1954
E.Stan. Brown	1954-1956
Aaron Trotman	1957-1959
Thomas (Tom) J. Powell	1959-1962
Gerald Gentry	1963-1963
John Harrison	1963-1970
Major H. Arthur Kenney	1970-1976
Bram Gay	1976-1978
Squadron Ldr. Denzil Stephens	1978-1982
Major H.Arthur Kenney	1982-1988
Brian Howard	1989-1990
Nigel Seaman	1990-1990
Malcolm Brownbill	1990-1990
Squadron Ldr. Denzil Stephens	1991-1992
David Thomas/ H. A Kenney	1992-1993
Michael Antrobus	1993-1995
Graham O Connor	1994-1995
Melvin White	1996-1997
Jeremy Wise/ Ian Holmes	1997-2000
Dr Robert B Childs	2000- to date

Appendix G

Cory Band Contest Results

European Brass Band Championships
Test-piece followed by Own-choice

YEAR	PLACING	CONDUCTOR	MUSIC
1979	2nd	D. Stephens	Symphonic Music – Huber (3rd) Judges of the Secret Court – Berlioz (2nd)
1980	1st	D. Stephens	The Land of the Long White Cloud – Sparke (1st) Triumphant Rhapsody – Vinter (2nd)
1981	6th	D. Stephens	Caliban – Butterworth (5th) Connotations – Gregson(6th)
1982	2nd	Major A. Kenney	Journey Into Freedom – Eric Ball (3rd) Fireworks – Howarth (2nd)
1983	3rd	Major A. Kenney	Ciacona Seria – Badings (7th) Variations on a Ninth – Vinter (2nd)
1984	2nd	Major A. Kenney	Refrains & Cadenzas – Wilson (3rd) Contest Music – Heaton (2nd)
1985	2nd	Major A. Kenney	Royal Parks – Lloyd (4th) Dances & Arias – Gregson (1st)
1986	3rd	Major A. Kenney	The Year of the Dragon – Sparke (3rd) Ballet for Band – Horovitz (4th)
1987	8th	Major A. Kenney	Frontier – Michael Ball (8th) Dances & Arias – Gregson (7th)
1989	3rd	B. Howard	Trittico – Curnow (1st) Diversions on a Bass Theme – Lloyd (4th)
1993	3rd	M. Antrobus	Sounds – Golland (3rd) Harmony Music – Sparke (4th)
1999	5th	J. Wise	Odyssey – Norburry (5th) Of Men & Mountains – Gregson (4th)
2001	2nd	R. Childs	Montreux Wind Dances – Ruetti (1st) Harrison's Dream – Graham (3rd)
2003	2nd	Dr. R. Childs	Aubade – Aagaard-Nilsen (2nd) Revelation – Wilby (1st)
2004	6th	Dr. R. Childs	St Magnus – Downie (6th) Revelation – Wilby (7th)
2005	2nd	Dr. R. Childs	Extreme Make-Over – Johan de Meij (2nd) Concerto Grosso – Bourgeois (3rd)
2006	3rd	Dr. R. Childs	Seascapes With High Cliffs – Wilson (3rd) The Promised Land – Downie (1st)
2007	3rd	Dr. R. Childs	Elgar Variations – Ellerby (1st) Of Men & Mountains – Gregson (5th)
2008	1st	Dr. R. Childs	Brass Blot – Berge (1st) Music for Battle Creek – Sparke (3rd)
2009	1st	Dr. R. Childs	From Ancient Times – Van der Roost (1st) Standing On The Shoulders of Giants – Graham (1st)
2010	1st	Dr. R. Childs	Spiriti – Thomas Doss (1st) A Tale as Yet Untold – Sparke (1st)

Did not compete/qualify: 1978, 1988, 1990-1992, 1994-1998, 2000, 2002.

British Open Brass Band Championships

YEAR	PLACING	CONDUCTOR	TEST PIECE
1922	Unplaced	J. G. Dobbing	Lohengrin - Wagner arr. Johnstone
1942	Unplaced	R. Little	Lorenzo / Pageantry - Keighley - Howells
1943	Unplaced	R. Little	Themes from Symphony No. 5- Beethoven - arr. Wright
1944	Unplaced	R. Little	The Tempest - Johnstone
1945	Unplaced	R. Little	Pride of Race - Wright
1946	Unplaced	W.Hargreaves	Salute to Freedom - Ball
1950	2nd	W. Hargreaves	Resurgam - Ball
1951	4th	W. Hargreaves	The Conquerors - Ball
1952	8th	W. Hargreaves	Scena Sinfonica - Geehl
1955	Unplaced	E. S. Brown	Sinfonietta for Brass Band - Leidzen
1970	Unplaced	A. Meek	Pageantry - Howells
1971	Unplaced	Major Kenney	Festival Music - Ball
1972	3rd	Major Kenney	Sovereign Heritage - Beaver
1973	10th	Major Kenney	The Accursed Huntsman- Franck - arr. Siebert
1974	5th	Major Kenney	James Cook - Circumnavigator - Vinter
1975	4th	Major Kenney	Fireworks - Howarth
1976	4th	B. Gay	An Epic Symphony - Fletcher
1977	8th	B. Gay	Diadem of Gold- Bailey - arr. Wright
1978	Unplaced	D. Stephens	Benvenuto Cellini- H. Berlioz - arr. Wright
1979	Unplaced	D. Stephens	Le Carnival Romain- Berlioz - arr. Wright
1980	Unplaced	D. Stephens	Energy - Simpson
1981	Unplaced	D. Stephens	Variations on a Ninth - Vinter
1982	Unplaced	Major Kenney	Three Figures - Howells
1983	Unplaced	Major Kenney	Connotations - Gregson
1984	Unplaced	Major Kenney	Comedy Overture - Ireland
1985	Unplaced	Major Kenney	Salute to Youth - Vinter
1986	Unplaced	Major Kenney	An Epic Symphony- Fletcher- and Fusions - Blake
1987	Unplaced	Major Kenney	Freedom - Bath
1988	Unplaced	Major Kenney	Contest Music - Heaton
1994	22nd	M. Antrobus	Salamander - McCabe
1995	13th	M. Antrobus	Revelation - Wilby
1996	19th	M. White	The Severn Suite- Elgar - arr. Gay
1997	7th	J. Wise	Whitsun Wakes - Ball
1998	13th	J. Wise	Diversions on a Bass Theme - Lloyd
1999	6th	J. Wise	...Dove Descending - Wilby
2000	1st	R. Childs	Ceremony - Ball
2001	3rd	R. Childs	Les Preludes- Liszt - trans. Gay
2002	1st	Dr. R. Childs	The Maunsell Forts - McCabe
2003	6th	Dr. R. Childs	The Planets Suite - Holst arr. Roberts
2004	2nd	Dr. R. Childs	St. Magnus - Downie
2005	2nd	Dr. R. Childs	A Night to Sing - Tovey
2006	2nd	Dr. R. Childs	Vienna Nights - Wilby
2007	1st	Dr. R. Childs	Visions of Gerontius - Downie
2008	3rd	Dr. R. Childs	Rococo Variations - Gregson
2009	1st	Dr. R. Childs	Titan's Progress - Pallhuber

Did not compete/qualify 1923-1941, 1947-1949,1953-1954,1956-1969,1989-1993.
Cory results preceding 1922 unknown.

National Brass Band Championships of Great Britain

YEAR	DRAW PLACING	CONDUCTOR	TEST PIECE
1924	Unplaced	J. G. Dobbing	On the Cornish Coast-Geehl
1945	Unplaced	R. Little	Overture for An Epic Occasion - Wright
1948	2nd	W. Hargreaves	On the Cornish Coast - Geehl
1949	6th	W. Hargreaves	Overture Comedy - Ireland
1950	Unplaced	W. Hargreaves	Pageantry - Howells
1951	Unplaced	W. Hargreaves	Epic Symphony - Fletcher
1952	6th	W. Hargreaves	The Frogs of Aristophanes - Bantock, arr. Wright
1956	Unplaced	E. S .Brown	Festival Music - Ball
1959	Unplaced	T. J. Powell	Le Roi d'Ys - Lalo, arr. Wright
1960	Unplaced	T. J. Powell	Three Figures - Howells
1961	Unplaced	T. J. Powell	Les Francs Juges - Berlioz arr. Wright
1962	Unplaced	W. Scholes	The Force of Destiny - Verdi arr. Wright
1963	Unplaced	G. Gentry	Belmont Variations - Bliss arr. Wright
1964	Unplaced	G. Brand	Variations on a Ninth - Vinter
1965	Unplaced	J. Harrison	Triumphant Rhapsody - Vinter
1966	Unplaced	J. Harrison	Le Carnaval Romain - Berlioz arr. Wright
1967	6th	J. Harrison	Journey Into Freedom - Ball
1968	8th	J. Harrison	The Mastersingers - Wagner, arr. Wright
1971	3rd	Major Kenney	Le Roi d'Ys - Lalo, arr. Wright
1972	5th	Major Kenney	A Kensington Concerto - Ball
1973	11th	Major Kenney	Freedom - Bath
1974	1st	Major Kenney	Fantasy for Brass Band - Arnold
1975	11th	Major Kenney	Un Vie de Matelot - Farnon
1976	6th	B. Gay	Sinfonietta - The Wayfarer - Ball
1977	17th	B. Gay	Connotations - Gregson
1978	7th	D. Stephens	Checkmate - Bliss arr. Ball
1979	2nd	D. Stephens	Volcano - Simpson
1980	6th	D. Stephens	Carnival Overture - Dvorak arr. Brand
1981	13th	D. Stephens	Blitz - Bourgeois
1982	1st	Major Kenney	Contest Music - Heaton
1983	1st	Major Kenney	Ballet for Band - Horovitz
1984	1st	Major Kenney	Dances and Arias - Gregson
1986	5th	Major Kenney	Diversions for Brass Band - Bourgeois
1988	18th	Major Kenney	Seascapes - Steadman – Allen
1992	9th	Major Kenney	The New Jerusalem - Wilby
1994	14th	M. Antrobus	Theme and Co-operation - Horovitz
1997	6th	J. Wise	On Alderley Edge - Graham
1998	6th	J. Wise	Between the Moon and Mexico - Sparke
2000	1st	R. Childs	Harrison's Dream - Graham
2001	5th	R. Childs	Albion - Van der Roost
2002	2nd	Dr. R. Childs	Masquerade - Wilby
2003	3rd	Dr. R. Childs	Enigma Variations - Elgar arr. Ball
2004	4th	Dr. R. Childs	...all the flowers of the mountain... - Ball
2005	3rd	Dr. R. Childs	Eden - Pickard

2006	4th	Dr. R. Childs	Les Francs Juges - Berlioz arr Wright
2007	3rd	Dr. R. Childs	Music for Battle Creek - Sparke
2008	3rd	Dr. R. Childs	Concertino for Brass Band - Downie
2009	3rd	Dr. R. Childs	The Torchbearers - Graham

Did not compete/qualify: 1925-1938,1946-1947,1953-1955, 1957-1958, 1969-1970, 1985, 1987, 1989-1991, 1993, 19995, 1999.
Cory results preceding 1924 unknown.

Cory Band c. 1982

Welsh Regional Championships

YEAR	PLACING	CONDUCTOR	TEST PIECE
1952	1st	W. Hargreaves	Resurgam - Ball
1957	Unplaced	A. Trotman	Themes From The Ninth Symphony - Beethoven
1958	Unplaced	A. Trotman	The Moor of Venice - Alwyn, arr. Wright
1959	3rd	T. J. Powell	Wuthering Heights - Rayner
1960	1st	T. J. Powell	Themes From Symphony No. 5 - Tschaikowsky, arr. Ball
1961	1st	T. J. Powell	Symphonic Poem, Les Preludes - Liszt
1962	1st	W. Hargreaves	Salute to Youth - Vinter
1963	3rd	W. Hargreaves	Rienzi - Wagner arr. Johns
1964	1st	J. Harrison	Symphony Of Marches - Vinter
1965	1st	J. Harrison	Themes From The First Symphony - Beethoven arr. Ball
1967	1st	H. Nuttall	Festival Music - Ball
1968	3rd	J. Harrison	Themes from 8th Symphony – Beethovern arr. Wright
1969	Unplaced	J. Harrison	Diadem of Gold - Bailey
1971	2nd	Major Kenney	A Joyful Noise - Jacob
1972	1st	Major Kenney	Concert Overture For Brass Band - Tausky
1973	2nd	Major Kenney	The Plantagenets - Gregson
1974	1st	Major Kenney	Variations on a Ninth - Vinter
1976	2nd	B. Gay	Spectrum - Vinter
1977	2nd	B. Gay	Pageantry - Herbert Howells
1978	2nd	B. Gay	The Belmont Variations - Bliss
1979	1st	D. Stephens	Variations for Brass Band - Williams
1980	1st	D. Stephens	Beatrice & Benedict – Berlioz

The Cornet section of Cory Band at Brass in Concert 2008

1981	1st	D. Stephens	Variations on the Shining River - Rubbra arr. Wright
1982	1st	D. Stephens	Essay - Gregson
1987	4th	Major Kenney	Diversions on a Brass Theme - Lloyd
1988	1st	Major Kenney	Ballet for Band - Horovitz
1989	4th	B. Howard	Prisms - Graham
1990	3rd	N. Seaman	The Beacons - Stadman-Allen
1991	8th	D. Stephens	Journey Into Freedom - Ball
1992	2nd	D. Stephens	Frontier - Ball
1993	3rd	A. Kenney	Of Men and Mountains - Gregson
1994	1st	M. Antrobus	Partita - Sparke
1995	3rd	G. O'Conner	Un Vie de Matelot - Farnon
1996	5th	M. White	Sounds - Golland
1997	2nd	J. Wise	A Lowry Sketchbook - Wilby
1998	1st	J. Wise	Montage - Graham
1999	3rd	J. Wise	Blitz - Bourgeois
2000	1st	J. Wise	Variations on an Enigma - Sparke
2001	4th	R. Childs	Jazz - Wilby
2002	1st	R. Childs	Whitsun Wakes - Ball
2003	1st	Dr. R. Childs	Prague - Bingham
2004	1st	Dr. R. Childs	Tristan Encounters - Ellerby
2005	1st	Dr. R. Childs	Rienzi - Wagner arr. Lorriman
2006	1st	Dr. R. Childs	Journey to the Centre of the Earth - Graham
2007	1st	Dr. R. Childs	Isaiah 40 - Redhead
2008	3rd	Dr. R. Childs	Festival Music - Ball
2009	1st	Dr. R. Childs	Salute To Youth - Vinter
2010	2nd	Dr. R. Childs	English Heritage - Lloyd

Did not compete: 1975, 1983-1986.
Cory results preceding 1952 unknown.

Brass in Concert Championships
Own Choice Entertainment Programme

YEAR	PLACING	CONDUCTOR
1979	2nd	D. Stephens
1980	3rd	D. Stephens
1981	5th	D. Stephens
1997	10th	J. Wise
1998	4th	J. Wise
1999	8th	J. Wise
2005	3rd	Dr. R. Childs
2008	1st	Dr. R.Childs
2009	3rd	Dr. R Childs

Did not compete: 1977-1978, 1982-1996,2000-2004, 2006-2007.

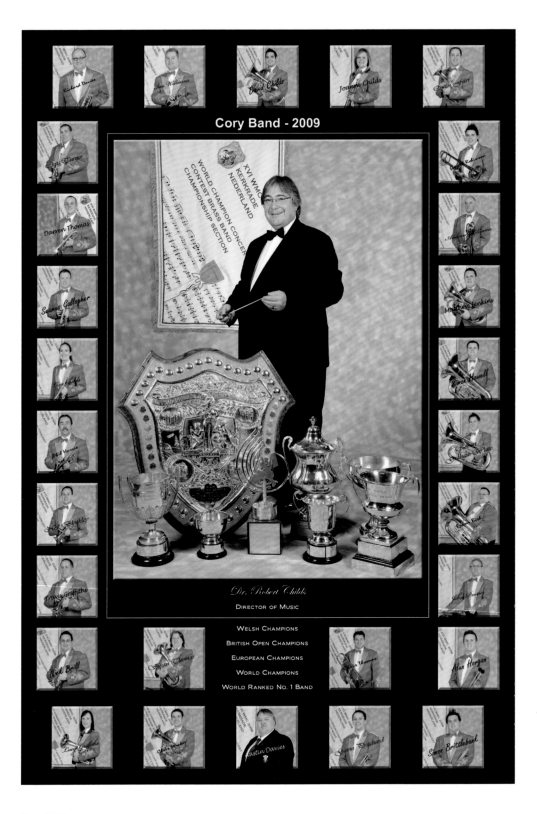

Appendix H
CORY BAND TIMELINE 1884 - 2009

1884	Ton Temperance Band formed, conductor Mr John Treharne
1895	Sir Clifford Cory hears the Band and offers financial assistance.
	Changed name to Cory Workmen's Band and engaged Mr Ernest Ambler as conductor.
1896	Mr John Bailey was appointed conductor
1908	John Bailey wrote the Band's Signature March '*The Singer*'.
1911	Aaron Trotman (senior) joins the Band
1912	J.G. Dobbing appointed conductor.
1923	The Band is believed to have taken part in the first BBC Radio Broadcast.
1925	Changed name to Cory Workmen's Silver Band.
1930	Gained 2nd in lower section at Belle Vue Manchester.
1931	Changed name to Cory Workmens Silver Prize Band.
1937	John Trotman joined the Band on cornet.
1940	Redvers (Reg) Little appointed conductor
1941	Won Welsh Regionals Championships
1943	Won Welsh Regionals Championships
1945	Won Welsh Regionals Championships
1946	Walter B Hargreaves appointed conductor.
1948	Gained 2nd at the Nationals Championships playing *On the Cornish Coast.*
1950	Gained 2nd place at the British Open on *Resurgam*. The highest placing of a Welsh Band in the contest's history.
1950	Received a half a penny a week from all workmen at Gelli Colliery.
1951	Cory took part in Festival of Britain celebrations at the R.A.H. London. took part in the World Premiere of *The Rainbow*.
1955	Started the sale of Tote tickets as a fund-raiser.
1957	Aaron Trotman appointed conductor
1958	The Band was included in the 1958 Guinness Book of Records for being the fastest at producing a recording!
1959	Thomas (Tom) J. Powell appointed conductor
1963	John Harrison appointed conductor
1965	T.J. Powell collapsed and died whilst conducting a BBC Broadcast in Cardiff.
1970	Major H. Arthur Kenney appointed conductor
1971	Won Granada Band of the Year Contest
1974	Won the National Championships on *Fantasy for Brass Band*.

1976	Bram Gay appointed conductor
1976	Ladies Committee formed to help fund raising.
1976	Band toured America.
1978	Squadron Ldr. Denzil Stephens appointed conductor
1980	Won the European Championships on *Land of the Long White Cloud* and *Triumphant Rhapsody*
1982	Major H.Arthur Kenney appointed conductor
1982	Won National Championships on *Contest Music* (hat trick)
1983	Won National Championships on *Ballet for Band* (hat trick)
1984	Won National Championships on *Dances and Arias* (hat trick)
1984	Centenary Celebrations.
1987	Changed name to Christie Tyler Cory Band
1990	Bandroom burnt down
1991	Moved into new bandroom on Partridge Street Ton Pentre
1998	Band changed name to Just Rentals Cory Band
2000	Band changed name to Buy As You View Cory Band
2000	Dr Robert B Childs appointed conductor.
	Won the British Open on *Ceremony*. The first time a Welsh Band won the contest in its 150 year history.
	Won the National Championships on *Harrison's Dream* and achieve the historic 'Double'.
2002	Won the British Open on *Maunsell Forts*
2004	Changed the name to Buy As You View Band.
2004	Performed at the official opening of the Wales Millennium Centre
2005	Performed John Pickard's Gaia Symphony at the International Cheltenham Festival
2006	Topped the British Bandsman World Ranking Table for the first time.
2007	Produced 'This Land of Ours' EMI recording with Karl Jenkins OBE
2007	Completed a double 'hat-trick' of Welsh Regional Championship titles
2007	Changed name to Cory Band
2007	Won the British Open on *Visions of Gerontius*.
2008	Won the European Championships on *Brass Blot* and *Battle Creek*
2008	Won Brass in Concert 25 minute programme.
2009	125th Celebrations
2009	Won the European Championships on *From Ancient Times* and *On the Shoulders of Giants*.
2009	Won the World Championships on *Harrison's Dream* and a 40 minute concert programme.
2009	Won the British Open on *Titan's Progress*.
2010	Won the European Championships on *Spiriti* and *A Tale, as Yet Untold*. Completing a hat-trick of wins.

Appendix H
Bibliography

BOOKS
Bainbridge, C., *Brass Triumphant* (London: Frederick Muller Ltd. 1980).
Boosey and Hawkes, *Sovereign Brass* (London, 1982).
Brand, G. and V., *Brass Bands in the Twentieth Century* (Herts: Egon Publishers 1979).
Brand, G. and V., *The World of Brass Bands* (Herts: Egon Publishers 1986).
Bridges, G., *Pioneers in Brass* (Detroit, Michigan: Sherwood Pub. 1972).
Cook, K., *The Bandsman's Everything Within* (London: Hinrichsen 1950).
Cook,K,. *Oh Listen To The Band,* (London: Hindrichsen 1950)
Cooke, K. and Caisley, L., *Music Through the Brass Band* (London: Hinrichsen   1953)
Greenhalgh, A., *Playing's only part of it* (Oldham: Burnedge Press ltd.1986).
Hailstone, A., *The British Bandsman Centenary Book* (Herts: Egon 1987).
Herbert, T., *Bands: The brass band movement in the nineteenth and twentieth centuries* (Milton Keynes: Open University Press. 1991).
Herbert, T., *The British Brass Band: a musical and social history* (Oxford University Press. 2000).
Herbert, T., and Wallace, J., *Cambridge Companion to Brass Instruments* (Cambridge University Press. 1997).
Hind, H.C., *The Brass Band* (London: Boosey and Hawkes 1934).
Howarth, E. and P., *What a Performance: The Band plays* (London: Robson Books 1988).
Mortimer, H., *Harry Mortimer on Brass* (Dorset: Alpha Books 1981).
Newsome, R., *Brass Roots: A hundred years of brass bands and their music 1836-1936,* (Hants: Ashgate Pub. Ltd. 1998).
Newsome, R., *Beyond the Bandstand* (Chapel-en-le-Frith:Caron Publications 1992).
Newsome, R., *The Brass Band Annual 1990* (London: Boosey and Hawkes 1990).
Russell, D., *Popular Music in England 1840 – 1914* (Manchester University Press: 1987)
Taylor, A., *Labour and Love: An oral history of the brass band movement* (London: Elm Tree Books 1983).
Taylor, A., *Brass Bands* (London: Granada Pub. Ltd. 1979)

MAGAZINES, NEWSPAPERS AND ELECTRONIC MEDIA
British Bandsman, 66-78 Denington Road, Wellingborough, Northants. NN8 2QH
Brass Band World, PO Box 53. Penarth CF64 5XY
The Brass Herald, 2 The Coppice, Impington, Cambridge, CB24 9PP
Sunday Times, 1 Virginia St, London E98 1XY
South Wales Echo, Six Park Street CARDIFF CF10 1XR
Gwent Gazzette, Hereford House, Bethcar Street, Ebbw Vale NP23 6HL
Rhondda Leader, Six Park Street CARDIFF CF10 1XR
Western Mail, Havelock Street, Cardiff CF10 1XR
Mature Times Souvenir, Highwood House, Winters Lane, Redhill, Bristol BS40 5SH
Daily Mountain Eagle Newspaper, Jasper, Alabama U.S.A.
Cory Band Centenary Booklet, Cory Band
www.4Barsrest.com